RIDING
WITH EVIL

RIDING WITH EVIL

TAKING DOWN THE NOTORIOUS
PAGAN MOTORCYCLE GANG

KEN CROKE
WITH DAVE WEDGE

wm

WILLIAM MORROW
An Imprint of HarperCollinsPublishers

HarperCollins books may be purchased for educational, business, or sales promotional use. For information, please email the Special Markets Department at SPsales@harpercollins.com.

FIRST EDITION

Designed by Kyle O'Brien

Library of Congress Cataloging-in-Publication Data has been applied for.

ISBN 978-0-06-309240-2

22 23 24 25 26   LSC   10 9 8 7 6 5 4 3 2 1

This book is dedicated to my four girls: my wife, Angie, and our three daughters, Kaitlyn, Shannon, and Meaghan. Thanks for always believing in me and keeping me grounded in what is important: family. Love you guys!

—Ken Croke

To the law enforcement officers who sacrifice in the name of justice and all the victims whose voices were heard because of those selfless endeavors.

—Dave Wedge

AUTHOR'S NOTE

The events and experiences detailed within this book are all true to the best of my recollection, or as they were told to me by the people who were present. Many of the events are also corroborated through surveillance recordings, law enforcement reports, news articles, or court documents. Some dialogue has been reconstructed from memory to the best of my ability while maintaining the spirit of the conversation, and the sequential order of some incidents has been changed for narrative flow. Some names and identifying details have been changed to protect the privacy of others and ongoing investigations.

It is curious—curious that physical courage should be so common in the world, and moral courage so rare.

—Mark Twain

Beware that, when fighting monsters, you yourself do not become a monster . . . for when you gaze long enough into the abyss, the abyss gazes also into you.

—Friedrich Nietzsche

CHAPTER 1

As I prepared to head to my first official Pagans gathering, in Long Island, Boston Bob came to me with some news.

"Hey, man, Hogman just fucking killed a prospect. Just thought you should know. I heard it from some of the Pagans in the Elizabeth chapter," he told me. "They were blowing lines and something happened. The cops are all over it."

"No shit," I said, feigning apathy. Inside, I was deeply concerned, if not straight up terrified. These guys did not fuck around.

It was 2009, and I was about to enter the biker world. Boston Bob's words drove home the stakes of the operation. My decision to immerse myself in a dark, chaotic outlaw world of drugs, violence, and debauchery came into sharp focus. I wasn't just looking to break up some half-ass biker club that was selling drugs and stealing bike parts for their hogs. I was about to dive into a full-on RICO case targeting one of the "Big Five" outlaw motorcycle gangs, and it already included a murder investigation.

I was pretty sure it wouldn't be the last one.

The unique thing about the case is that it was never supposed to go the way it did. I was never supposed to be the undercover agent on it.

Sometimes life throws you curveballs, they say. And sometimes, in this crazy, random world, a broken water heater might be the thing that changes your life.

Here's how it all started.

In 2008, a call came in to the Boston field office of the Bureau of Alcohol, Tobacco, Firearms and Explosives where I was a supervisor.

"I live on the North Shore," the caller, Jake (not his real name), said. "There's a guy up here in the Devil's Disciples and I think I could make an introduction for you guys."

Jake was a drunk. A really degenerate one at that. He had a rap sheet and knew he could get paid as an informant, which is why he called us. There was always an ulterior motive with those types of guys. You'll see.

We brought Jake into the Boston field office, and because no one in that office had a lot of experience in working outlaw motorcycle gang cases, I was asked to come in. I had gone undercover many times throughout my career, in Los Angeles, Massachusetts, New Hampshire, Arizona, Nevada, Rhode Island, New York, and Colorado. I'd survived shoot-outs with gangbangers and taken down bomb-making white supremacists. I knew the cost of undercover work, including the mental toll, and I knew the commitment it took not only to make a case but to survive with my life and sanity intact.

I had also done a lot of undercover work earlier in California with the Mongols and the Vagos biker clubs. One time, I was busting a biker named Vago Chuck in L.A. We executed a search warrant on his house and were in his bedroom. We had him cuffed. He was standing there in the middle of the room, and he wasn't saying anything. We started tossing the room, when all of a sudden I noticed the fucking wall moving.

I drew my gun, shocked about what was happening. As I looked closer, I noticed a figure. It was a woman—bare-ass naked and covered head to toe in tattoos—and she was chained to the wall. She had so many tattoos, she blended into the wallpaper and I didn't even see her until she moved. They were doing some freaky bondage shit.

But with the cuffs now tight around *his* wrists, all Chuck could do was laugh.

I also got pulled into the infamous Mongols case led by ATF agent Billy Queen, who infiltrated the club in the late 1990s. The agent who supervised the Mongols case involving Queen was John Ciccone. John and I graduated from the academy together, and we were sworn in to ATF on the same day. We were both sent out to L.A. and were roommates for two years. I was brought in to help out on some take-downs and sit in on key interviews in the Queen case.

I learned a lot from that case, and it prepared me well for what lay ahead.

Eric Kotchian, the agent in the Boston office who took the initial call from the informant, was gung ho about the opportunity to get some intel on the Devil's Disciples and the Pagans. He badly wanted to do the case and asked me to do some initial undercover work.

"Hey, I just had this guy come in, and he was talking about Devil's Disciples and patching over to the Pagans," Kotchian told me.

A stocky, easy going agent with a buzzcut, Eric Kotchian joined ATF in 2002 after working for four years as a United States Marshal. We called him "Coach," because of his last name. Eric got along well with everyone due to his laid-back personality.

We talked about the structure of the Disciples and how many members they had in Massachusetts. We also knew they were a support club of the Pagans, which meant they backed them up when needed, were involved in criminal activity with the Pagans, and were allowed at some Pagans events.

"Let's bring him in," I said. "Let's put him on the box."

The "box" is a polygraph. Before I spent any time on this case, I wanted to see if Jake was full of shit. I also wanted to be sure that I wasn't being set up.

Jake wasn't a patched member of an outlaw motorcycle gang—known in law enforcement as an OMG—but he was a biker immersed in outlaw culture, and the information he was giving us made a lot of sense.

There are many ways to be connected to a biker gang. You can be a "hang-around," which is a male known to one or more members who is allowed to party with the club and hang out at their bars and social events. Then there's a "prospect," which is a male seeking to join the club. A prospect is like a pledge in a college fraternity, although the hazing is slightly different, as it often involves threats, beatings, and food and sleep deprivation. They are totally submissive to members and must follow strict rules and fulfill stringent requirements if they are to be accepted. Prospecting in some clubs, especially the Pagans, is hell.

Once a hopeful member successfully completes their prospect time, which in the Pagans is a minimum of six months, and passes the gang's background checks and intense scrutiny, they become a "patched" member. This means they are formally inducted into the gang. They're given a special membership patch, which is a gang logo that's worn on their colors. A biker's colors are like a uniform that consists of a denim jacket adorned with their club's logos and patches, among other insignias. Pagans colors are sacred to the members, never to be touched by a non-member, never allowed to touch the ground or to be disrespected in any way. In the outlaw biker world, club colors are the most important, followed by your brothers in the club, your bike, your dog, and then your "old lady"—they all used that misogynistic term to refer to women—in that order. It can take years to become a patched member.

While Jake was just a hang-around with the Disciples, he knew, and more important, witnessed, enough that I thought it was worth a deeper look. So we brought him in, and he nailed the polygraph. Truthful through and through.

I was forty years old and a supervisor running a ten-agent unit south of Boston. We were based in Bridgewater, Massachusetts, a rural outpost halfway between Boston and Providence that's known more for farming and cul-de-sacs than for gangs and explosives. We were a dedicated bunch, and we put together strong cases, busting up gun and drug rings in rough southeastern Massachusetts cities like Brockton, New Bedford, and Fall River.

We had a nice little operation down there, and I was comfortable. I liked managing my guys, I loved my family—my beautiful wife, Ang, who at the time was an active ATF agent, and our three beautiful girls—and we lived in a quiet little suburban neighborhood in a nice town. It was a good life I had going. I wasn't exactly looking to shake things up. ATF supervisors rarely, if ever, went undercover. That was usually left to the field agents. Today, ATF doesn't allow supervisors to go undercover at all, largely because of my story.

"So what do you think?" Kotchian asked me.

I thought about it for a few minutes. It never crossed my mind that I'd go deep undercover. It was, though, a rare opportunity to get some intelligence, at the very least. The Devil's Disciples Boston chapter was looking to expand and Jake was in their plans. I agreed to check it out for the short term as we decided whether to bring in a long-term undercover agent.

And that's where the case starts. With some drunk who saw some biker shit north of Boston.

Jake and his wife had just had a new baby, and she needed to be vetted. She could blow my cover quickly if she was wishy-washy, ending the case before it began.

"I'll go up to the North Shore and check it out," I told Kotchian. "But I have to meet Jake's wife first. She has to stand up or this won't go anywhere."

We came up with a story that Jake and I grew up together in the Beech Street projects in Roslindale, a blue-collar section of Boston. It was December 2008 and freezing in Boston, the kind of bitter, skin-scraping cold that makes you wonder why the hell anyone lives in the Northeast.

I met Jake's wife in their apartment, and it was clear right away that she was a nice girl. She was smarter than him and definitely had her shit together much more than he did. It made me wonder why she was with him at all. After talking with her a bit, she was on board and understood the stakes. I felt, at least in those first cursory meetings, that she would not blow my cover and would be able to handle questions from the Disciples, if needed.

I'm a big believer in luck and serendipity. Undercover cases are strategic. They're like chess matches, except you can be killed with a wrong move. There are protocols to follow, but you also need lucky breaks, or they can go to hell quickly. This case certainly had its share. The first one happened when Boston Mike's hot-water heater broke and he called Jake for help.

Jake and I went over to Boston Mike's place and walked down the narrow stairs into the basement. It was freezing. It was one of those old New England dirt basements with stone walls and low ceilings. The water line was frozen solid.

I grabbed the blowtorch that was in the basement and started heating up the line to the hot-water heater. I freed up his line and got his water flowing again. He was appreciative and rewarded me with a cold Budweiser. We got to bullshitting about motorcycles and clubs as we stood in the freezing cold basement. Mike was short and stocky, with a scruffy beard and big beer gut. He was in his forties and was covered in tattoos, which was why he was also known as Tattoo Mike.

"We're having a party next weekend," he told Jake. "If you and your bro here want to come, stop on by."

"Yeah, if I can make it I'll stop by," I said.

As soon as the words came out of my mouth, I knew I was off to the races.

I reported back to Kotchian, and the decision was made that I would go to the party. It was still supposed to be a quick, short-term surveillance operation.

Things moved fast. Too fast. Normally, undercover investigations are planned and there's time to get background stories and paperwork in order, known as backstopping. But we didn't have time. Within just a few days, I had to go to the party. Because of that frozen water heater, I had a rare opportunity to get a glimpse into this little corner of the clandestine biker world. It was being served to me on a silver platter.

Because of my past undercover work in South Central Los Angeles, I had an alias with a pretty deep backstory and plenty of backup to support it: Ken Pallis had old addresses, utility bills, rental and employment history, and most importantly, a criminal record and fingerprints on file.

With Ken Pallis's IDs in my wallet and his life story in my head, I made my way to Boston Mike's ramshackle duplex on Boston's North Shore. Jake and I walked into his unit and entered a dark, dingy living room. There was heavy metal playing from a speaker. The kitchen had eighties decor, with Formica countertops, an old ceramic farm sink, linoleum flooring, and fluorescent lighting. I'd best describe the vibe as depressing.

It wasn't really a party. It was more like a small gathering of a few bikers and a couple "old ladies," drinking and doing drugs in a kitchen. Boston Mike and Jake and his wife were there, along with a few other Devil's Disciples, including Bob Hamilton, aka Boston Bob, and another biker named Billy Jacobson.

Mike offered me a beer, and I settled in, listening more than talking. The conversation turned to the club. They talked about a guy who was starting to prospect and discussed a few events the club was planning to take part in. There was no criminal conversation at all. It was all very vague and vanilla and about what I expected.

The beers flowed, and Boston Mike started grilling me a bit about my background. Where are you from? What do you do? That sort of thing.

It was a dance. He was trying to feel me out and find out information about me that he could look into, and I was doing the same. For me, it was also a character evaluation exercise. I needed to learn, quickly and discreetly, without raising suspicion, who was who and what the pecking order was. I needed to figure out, fairly quickly, who was in charge and whom to align myself with to build credibility and gain trust.

"I'm a mechanic," I told them.

I already had a fake job set up at a service station, in case they asked, and had fake pay stubs ready to show if needed. The station owner, who was a trusted friend of mine, was briefed and ready to cover for me if they called.

"And I do some fishing," I said. "I'm from New Bedford, but I come up here all the time."

I already had an undercover apartment in New Bedford. It was a bit of a dump, but I'd put some clothes there and made it look lived in. The fishing piece of my backstory was something I came up with for a few reasons. I told them I poached lobsters, which showed them I was a criminal who liked to make money. I felt it was equally important, in case I got involved with the Disciples, to have an ongoing, built-in excuse to disappear when necessary without raising suspicions. Whatever the situation, if someone was looking for me and I didn't respond, I could always say, "I was out fishing." I couldn't be tracked on the sea.

Having that escape route would prove essential.

As the booze flowed, I noticed people going in and out of a bedroom. They were clearly doing coke, and it didn't take long before there were lines on the kitchen table. I had been in some pretty dangerous drug situations before. I had faked doing coke with Mongols and MS-13 gangbangers in Southern California, so I wasn't afraid of some low-level bikers in an apartment outside Boston.

Simulating using drugs and drinking is always delicate. A lot of agents won't do it because the chances of getting caught are high. But if done right, at the right time, it can be an invaluable tool. In my career, it has served me well several times. Drinking is easy. No one really pays attention to how much someone else drinks, so I was good at nursing beers, dumping them out when no one was looking, or just leaving them somewhere and grabbing another one. Same thing with shots. I've found it's surprisingly easy to say "cheers!" and then sneakily dump a shot out without being seen.

Drug simulation is more difficult and riskier. I always picked my spots very carefully. Mike's party was a perfect opportunity. While they mentioned the possibility of me joining the Devil's Disciples, that's not the main reason I was there, as far as they knew. I didn't go to them looking to get into the gang. I was invited. To them, I was just some guy hanging out. No one there was selling any guns or drugs. And I wasn't there looking to buy or sell weapons or drugs.

I needed to earn street cred and put them at ease that I wasn't a cop or a rat, in case they were suspicious. Cops don't blow lines. Doing coke with them put me on their side of the fence. I'd be one of them.

Mentally, it sucks. Whenever I lined up to do it, I knew that if I screwed up and got caught, I'd be in a dangerous, potentially deadly situation. It was always nerve-racking and it was never easy. The biker underground is a world where nothing is predictable.

Boston Bob, Boston Mike, and Jake were sitting at the kitchen table. Me and Billy Jacobson were standing off to the side, drinking beers. A bottle of Jack Daniel's sat on the table. Boston Mike started cutting up lines on a dinner plate. It's a weird thing because you don't know if they'll offer it to you or not. Some drug guys are generous. Some are cheap fucks who don't want to share their coke. Those guys were my favorite, since they made the decision easy for me. Others share solely to find out who might be a cop.

The guys were boozing hard, and it started getting late. The plate came my way. They were very small lines, which always makes it simpler. My heart rate was going. It was pretty bright in the kitchen, so anyone watching me closely had a good view of what I was doing. Pulling off a simulation was always easier in a dark bar. Not an optimal situation, but I'd been in worse ones, so I decided to make my move. The plate was handed to me.

Whiff . . . my little line was gone. I used some sleight of hand trickery to make it appear I had snorted the line, without actually sniffing it. I wiped my nose, made a fake coke face, and passed the plate along seamlessly. No one noticed a thing. I passed the test.

I went home that night and went into my daughters' rooms and kissed them all as they slept. I crawled into bed next to Ang, but sleep didn't come easy. I was replaying the night's activities in my head and strategizing our next moves. Jake had mentioned that the Pagans were thinking about opening a Boston chapter and were already talking with Boston Bob about how to make it happen.

In bed, staring at the ceiling, I thought about how comfortable my life was in that house. I thought about how much I loved being there, helping our girls with their homework, making dinners with Ang, having family movie nights.

As I closed my eyes, I was pretty sure my life was about to become anything but safe and comfortable.

CHAPTER 2

None of the guys involved in this case are good people.

Some had some redeeming qualities. Some were far worse than others. But none of them were what a normal, law-abiding civilian would call "good." These were the bad guys. In fact, some of them were plain evil.

Boston Bob was born April 30, 1960, in Massachusetts as Robert Hamilton. He looked just like what you would picture when you think of a biker. He was a big guy, standing five feet eleven inches and weighing two hundred and eighty pounds. He had a giant beer gut, thick, dark hair that he pulled back into a ponytail, a black beard, and tattoos up and down his arms.

He was smart enough to know how the biker world worked and how you got into trouble. He knew the land mines that would get you kicked out, busted, or killed. You weren't going to pull the wool over his eyes.

He was a biker through and through. He never talked about sports or politics or anything like that, but he loved to talk about bikes and biker gangs. He grew up in Massachusetts and was once a member of the Outlaws, a violent motorcycle club with forty-eight chapters around the world. He belonged to the chapter in Brockton, a tough city of one hundred thousand people twenty miles south of Boston. Brockton was home to world champion boxers Rocky Marciano and Marvelous Marvin Hagler, which gave the city it's nickname: City of Champions. The Outlaws did nothing to honor that proud moniker.

For them, Brockton was nothing more than a fertile ground for drug dealing, gun trafficking, and mayhem. The city was once the bustling shoe capital of the United States, but after all the mills closed in the sixties and seventies and crack came on the scene in the eighties, the city fell on hard times. The Outlaws were right there to cash in on the despair, selling drugs and guns.

Brockton chapter president, Timothy Silva, was busted in 2008 right around when this case was beginning. He was sentenced to twenty-one years in federal prison for trafficking cocaine. In June 2010, twenty-seven Outlaws from the Brockton chapter and surrounding towns were rounded up in an FBI raid that led to a variety of charges, including attempted murder, kidnapping, assault, robbery, extortion, witness intimidation, narcotics distribution, illegal gambling, and weapons violations. Some of the charges stemmed from a 2009 melee at a Petersburg, Virginia, biker bar during which members of the Outlaws partnered up with Pagans to attack rival Hells Angels.

Boston Bob started his criminal career young. In March 1979, when he was just nineteen, he caught a case for masked armed robbery and drug and weapons possession. He was convicted and sentenced to six years in state prison in Concord, Massachusetts. He was out in less than three and picked back up right where he left off. In 1983, he got five to seven years in state prison for assault with a deadly weapon in Boston.

He bore the scars of a biker and walked with a limp, a prize for getting shot in the leg by a rival while he was in the Outlaws. He nearly lost the leg and had permanent circulation damage that bothered him every day. After the shooting, he left the Outlaws, but he clearly wasn't fit for civilian life. He joined the Devil's Disciples, which is kind of like a minor-league gang compared to the Outlaws.

The night we met at that first party north of Boston, he didn't talk to me much. He was sizing me up, I could tell.

The other guy I met that night, Billy Jacobson, was a Devil's Disciple from Somerville, Massachusetts, a small city next to Boston with a long gangster history. The Winter Hill Gang, which was run by infamous Irish mob boss James J. "Whitey" Bulger, was founded in Somerville and took its name from the city's Winter Hill neighborhood. Billy was no mobster, but he wasn't a pushover either. Intense and serious, he was stocky and looked more like he might have been in the military than a biker, but when he got drunk he chilled out a little and liked to talk.

He talked to me more than Bob did that first night, but I was careful not to seem too eager or forward. I played it cool, hoping to subtly convince them that I was one of them and would be a good fit for their new chapter in Boston.

It worked.

The day after the party at Boston Mike's, Jake called me.

"Hey, they loved you," he said. "They asked all sorts of questions about who you were and how we know each other. 'Is he a good dude?' 'Can he handle himself?'"

"Well, what did you say?" I asked.

"I told them you were cool," he said. "They're planning something in a couple weeks. They want to get together with you again."

They were doing their sizing up. And now I had to do mine. I had to think about whom to align with—Boston Bob or Billy. Bob was openly saying that if the Pagans started a chapter in Massachusetts, that he'd be the president. They wanted me to patch into the Disciples, but they hadn't raised the idea of the Pagans with me. They didn't trust me yet.

"I want to set up time to hang out with these guys individually," I told Jake. "Set it up."

Bob lived in Webster, Massachusetts, a rural town of about seventeen thousand southwest of Boston, near the Rhode Island and Connecticut borders. Jake and I went out and met him at a dive bar. Jake, as usual, got totally smashed. His boozing made me nervous, because, being that drunk, he said stupid things, and I feared his verbal diarrhea would blow my cover. His drunkenness was a huge liability.

Bob was starting to trust me. He talked about how dangerous the

Pagans were and bragged that they were the most violent of all the one percenter clubs.

The Pagans were among the first Outlaw Motorcycle Gangs to embrace the infamous biker term "one percenter." The designation is believed to have come from a 1947 comment by a spokesman for the American Motorcycle Association who sought to separate law-abiding riders from drunken nomads portrayed in an unflattering 1947 *Life* magazine article. Outlaw bikers, including the Pagans, adopted the term as a badge of honor and began wearing diamond-shaped patches with the 1 %ER logo on their colors, a tradition that endures today.

My experience told me Bob was right. The Hells Angels are violent and the most well known, but you also have Hells Angels who are lawyers and dentists. You can be a biker who is not a complete outlaw and be a Hells Angel. That's generally not the case with the Pagans. They were hard-core outlaws—every last one of them. You didn't become a Pagan part time. When you became a Pagan, it was a lifetime commitment. They took your life over.

Formed in 1959 in Maryland, the Pagans claim more than 1,500 members in one hundred chapters up and down the East Coast. They have always been more hard core, more violent, and far more clandestine than the other clubs in the Big Five outlaw motorcycle gangs, which also includes the Hells Angels, the Outlaws, the Bandidos, and the Mongols. The Pagans' biggest claim to fame had always been that they'd never been infiltrated by law enforcement, unlike the Hells Angels and the other clubs.

The Pagans are well known for drug dealing, extortion, extreme violence, weapons trafficking, arson, bombings, and having deep ties to other organized crime factions. Their symbol is the Norse fire god Surtr, sitting on the sun and wielding a sword. Their colors include a denim, sleeveless jacket with the Surtr (pronounced "Sutar") patch on the back in the middle, PAGANS in a white cloud with red trim across the top, and the letters MC—for "motorcycle club"—along the bottom. Unlike other clubs, the Pagans do not put a chapter name as a bottom rocker, because they do not want to make it easy for law enforcement to identify which members belong to which chapter. They also believe that all Pagans belong to the entire "Pagan Nation" and not to individual chapters. The white cloud surrounding the word PAGANS on the back of the colors represents white power, while the red trim represents the blood Pagans have shed defending their beliefs. Along with the MC block patches, those are the only patches allowed on the back of Pagans colors.

The front of Pagans colors is a different story. Members put patches on the front and sides of their colors with symbols like PFFP (Pagan Forever, Forever Pagan), LPDP (Live Pagan, Die Pagan), and 1 %ER.

Gaining the respect and trust of Bob and Billy was crucial if I was ever to get access to that world.

They told me I should prospect for the Disciples. After a few hangouts, they finally opened up about the long-term play, which was for the Disciples to patch over to the Pagans to form a Boston chapter. I learned that Bob and Billy had been spending time with the Long Island chapter of the Pagans out in a rural area east of Manhattan called Rocky Point. The Pagans were considering expanding to Massachusetts, and the Long Island chapter, which at the time was the closest to Massachusetts, was leading the effort. Five members are needed to form a chapter, and it was starting to look like they wanted me as one of the initial five.

"I'm not sure I want to do that," I told them.

I was playing hard to get. I didn't want to seem too eager. I also knew that the Hells Angels controlled Massachusetts, so setting up a new Pagans chapter in Boston would immediately start a war. I kept playing along to see where things would go.

One night, after going out with Bob, I crashed at his house. While my wife, Ang, didn't love me staying out all night, it was part of my plan. I suspected he wouldn't believe that a real cop would crash at his house. It built trust.

With Billy, I met him several times at a South Boston bar called

Murphy's Law, a classic dive. It's the kind of place post-grads go to have cheap drinks and slum it with the locals, but also the kind of place where real gangsters and thugs drink whiskey and plot real crimes. (If you saw the 2007 Casey Affleck movie *Gone Baby Gone*, Murphy's Law was where they shot the final shoot-out scene.) Billy was in the latter group. It was a dark drinking hole befitting our conversations.

One time I took Jake with me to Murphy's Law, and—surprise—he got drunk. His drinking was becoming a problem for the Disciples, the Pagans, and me, and it was becoming clear that neither club would want him. I started going alone to meet Billy. He was talking a big game. He told me the Pagans wanted to open a chapter north of Boston and that they wanted him to be the chapter president.

But Bob gave me some warnings about Billy. He was playing a dangerous game—he was banging one of the Pagans' old ladies. One of the strictest rules they had was that you didn't screw a brother's old lady. Girlfriends and wives were not people to them—they were property—and you didn't touch another member's property.

Billy would find out the punishment for that crime soon enough.

CHAPTER 3

Long Island, January 2009

Hogman, a behemoth of a man with a filthy appearance and an even filthier demeanor, chopped up a pile of coke on the coffee table. The table sat near his bed, a soiled mess of a mattress strewn with rumpled, stained sheets that had not seen the inside of a laundry machine in months. Hogman (real name: Kenny Van Diver) was a Pagan and a disgusting human.

Bennett, a young Pagans prospect, sat drinking a Bud as Hogman stalked the room, each beefy step shaking the nearby bureau and rattling the dirty glasses and empty bottles on top.

Hogman reached his beefy hand down toward his calf and lifted his pants leg to reveal a sheath. He unsnapped it and slid out a double-edged blade. Bennett's wired eyes were fixed on him. Bennett followed Hogman's hand unsheathing the blade. His eyes widened.

Sweating out booze and days of amphetamines, Hogman slowly lumbered his girth toward Bennett, knife out, its blade catching a spark from the sun poking through the half-closed blinds. He dipped the blade down toward the coffee table and dug the tip into the pile of white powder. He lifted out an ample blade-full and brought it up to his nose, snorting it all down with a big whiff.

A party raged just outside the bedroom door. Hogman was drunk and lay down on the bed, fully clothed, with his heavy boots tied up tight, and passed out cold.

Bennett too was wasted. He sat at the table, listening to the pounding rock coming from the cheap speakers, and thought about what lay ahead for him. Bennett was supposed to go with the Long Island chapter to a mandatory Pagans event in Pennsylvania. A "mandatory" is a Pagans gathering that all members and prospects are required to attend. No excuses. Skipping a mandatory was not an option and would be met with dire consequences, including removal. All prospects were required to attend at least two mandatories during their six-month probationary period.

It was six a.m. and the sun was just coming up. Bennett reached into his own pants pocket and pulled out his knife. Like Hogman, he dipped the blade into the coke and lifted out a hefty pile.

Bennett was later found dead in the room. The knife was driven into his eye and into his brain stem. Blood leaked from his face, saturating the cocaine on the table. Police were called to the house and Bennett's bloodied body was removed. Hogman and others at the party were questioned.

Bennett's death became a homicide investigation. We received information that Hogman stomped the back of Bennett's head, driving the knife into the table and the blade through his face, killing him. Hogman, though, claimed Bennett nodded off, accidentally falling on the knife.

Just what happened in that room was something I was determined to find out. It sent shock waves through ATF and was a clear message that the Pagans world was filled with violence, as well as a deadly code of silence.

CHAPTER 4

After I heard the story of Bennett's bloody demise, we had all new risks to evaluate. ATF hadn't even signed off on me going deep undercover and there was a homicide investigation developing. Bennett's body was removed from the house. Hogman claimed he'd found Bennett like that—an apparent accidental suicide. It made no sense, but law enforcement had no hard evidence.

I had concerns about the operation anyway, but the brutality of Bennett's death described to me ratcheted up my anxiety. It also drove me to catch the bastard. The opportunity had literally fallen into my lap. I was being asked to prospect for the Disciples, and it appeared the long play was to prospect for the Pagans. I was hoping I could build trust and glean information to help the investigation into Bennett's death.

Nobody from any law enforcement agency had ever been a Pagans prospect, never mind a full-patch member. I'd passed the first hurdle and was confident I could take advantage of the door opened to me by Boston Bob and Billy. I had a rare shot to use the Disciples to get closer to the Pagans and possibly infiltrate the club, which counted some of the most violent outlaws in the biker underground among its ranks. The plan was to start working with Bob, Billy, and the Disciples and see if the Pagans were serious about starting a Boston chapter.

I had to brief the Special Agent in Charge of the Boston office, Andy Anderson. He had started his career in the Nashville and

Knoxville field offices as a special agent before he was assigned to ATF headquarters in Washington, D.C., where he headed the Critical Incident Management Branch. A devout Catholic and by-the-book administrator, Andy was known as a productive agent and was the public face of the Boston office whenever we had big cases that made news. He was protective of his agents and cautious. He was initially in favor of my being the lead undercover agent on the case, despite my being a supervisor, but Bennett's death put things in a darker light.

"Ken, I don't know about this, man," Andy told me. "I'm not so sure HQ is going to approve you to go try and infiltrate a club that just killed its last prospect.

"This is uncharted territory," he continued. "You're a supervisor, so you aren't even supposed to go undercover. These guys are animals. We can't guarantee your safety . . ."

I mostly agreed with him, but I was also well aware of the rare opportunity in front of us. Andy and I were friends, having worked together for years and shared a few happy hours. He was concerned about the case and also the safety of his friend, which was a tough position for him. I was concerned for my safety too.

"No one on this job has guaranteed safety. Ever," I said. "But this is a chance to get inside with these guys. They're white supremacists, Andy. They're killers. They sell heroin, crack, guns. They are at war with the Hells Angels. They destroy communities. Are we really going to let this opportunity go by? Isn't this what we do, man?"

The Pagans had been terrorizing the East Coast, flooding cities with guns and drugs and running prostitution and gambling rackets, especially in New York, Pennsylvania, and New Jersey. I wasn't about to let them just waltz into Massachusetts and set up shop. I knew Andy made good points, but I also knew that a window had been cracked open for us to climb through. I looked at him sternly, and he saw in my eyes that I was ready to take this assignment.

"Okay, Ken," Andy said. "I'll sign off on it. But you're on a short leash. Any sign of trouble, and you're out. Got it?"

"Sure. First sign of trouble. Out. Got it," I said.

I wasn't sure I believed that. But there was no turning back. I admit that I was wondering if maybe I was in over my head.

Embedding as a full-time undercover—or a "UC" as they're known in ATF—would be a major disruption to the suburban lifestyle Ang and I had built for ourselves. Ang was also an ATF agent, revered in ATF for capturing a serial arsonist in L.A. and working dangerous undercover gigs in New York City, buying guns and drugs from gangsters. She was tough and respected our chosen profession, but she was also well aware of the daily dangers of the job, especially going deep undercover. We had never really discussed one of us going undercover for an extended operation, especially after the kids came along. That part of our life seemed to be in the past. She was concerned about just how deep I would have to go. After all, we had three little girls who needed their dad.

But now the die was cast. I'd gained the trust of Boston Bob, and he was going to introduce me to the Pagans. Andy had reservations and knew it would be an uphill climb with our superiors because of Bennett's death, but he also knew I was perfect for the job. I was prepared, and we both knew it was a very important case for ATF.

"Let's just see where it goes," Andy told me.

"Sounds good. But I'm not doing it to bust a few guys for stolen bike parts or a bunch of bullshit," I said. "If I'm going to do this, I'm going all in. I'm going after the Mother Club."

"Love it," he said. "Let's get 'em."

I took the leap. I started preparing to embed myself in the outlaw biker world in a high-stakes case that I hoped would end with a bunch of bad guys going to prison for a long time. I was going into battle with eyes wide open. I knew the dangers.

I also knew the sacrifices. No more going to the kids' sporting events on weekends, family ski trips, or backyard barbecues for a while. While I knew the timing wasn't great for me or my family, I thought it would be a couple of months at most.

Man, was I wrong.

CHAPTER 5

Just as I was preparing for my first trip to Long Island to officially meet the Pagans, Boston Bob gave me another reason to consider aborting the mission when he told me what happened to Billy Jacobson. Bob's warnings to me about Billy's recklessness were not paranoia. Billy played with fire and he got burned.

Billy and Boston Bob left Boston on a Friday and headed down to Long Island. The plan was for me to come down on Saturday. At around four-thirty a.m. on Saturday morning, I got a text from Bob. I was asleep and planning to leave for Long Island that morning to meet him.

Trip's off. I'll explain later, it read.

I texted Billy. I got no response for hours. Finally, around midday, my phone started buzzing. It was a text from Billy, asking me to give him a call.

"Bro, get out. Don't do this thing. You need to get the fuck out. These people are killers. You're never going to see me again," he said.

"Fuck, man. What happened?" I asked.

He wouldn't elaborate and cut the call short. His last words of "get out" rang in my ear as the phone went dead. I never heard from him again.

I called Special Agent Eric Kotchian, who was the agent in charge of the case, and told him what was going on.

"The trip is off," I said. "It's all fucked up."

"Okay," Kotchian told me. "We'll regroup on Monday. Find out what happened."

I texted Bob: *Dude, what the fuck is going on?*

Bob still didn't trust me. He wouldn't give me details.

It went really bad, he replied. *It's just off and that's all you need to know.*

I looked at my phone and thought about the situation. I texted him back.

Bro, I'm all in here. I'm ready to roll, no matter what happened.

I got no response for hours. Later, he texted me back.

Bro, I'm not even sure I want to do this, he wrote, ominously. *I've gotta think about this.*

Eventually I got Bob to tell me what happened, and it almost stopped the entire case in its tracks.

That Friday, Billy and Bob had headed down to an Irish wake for Bennett at a Pagans dive bar called Mobo, in Miller Place, New York, a small beachside town on rural Route 25A in Long Island. There was a second, post-wake party planned for Saturday night at another Pagans bar called the Wellington in nearby Middle Island, New York, where I was supposed to meet the Long Island chapter and take the first steps toward becoming a Pagans prospect, or at least gather intel on what they had planned for Boston.

Billy and Bob drove down together Friday and went to the memorial and the after party at Mobo. For months, Billy had been banging a tough-talking biker chick named Crystal, who was the old lady of the Trenton, New Jersey, Pagans chapter's sergeant-at-arms, Timothy Fowler, aka Pita.

Pita—which fittingly stood for "Pain in the Ass"—was a former U.S. Marine and a real badass. He had a salt-and-pepper goatee, stood six feet two inches, and weighed two hundred and ninety pounds on a good day. He was extremely violent and had a hair-trigger temper. He was busted in 2006 for kidnapping and conspiracy after he and four other Pagans snatched a member of the rival Bandidos from a bar in New Jersey and held him hostage until he gave up information on another rival. He got a year in jail and three years probation. His rap sheet also included charges of domestic assault in 2001 and 2003 and firearms violations in 1998.

Pita was a real biker—a nasty motherfucker. Billy picked the wrong woman. Boston Bob knew that banging any of the Pagans' old ladies was a really bad idea, but Billy didn't listen.

They walked into Mobo that night, and the party was in full swing. Jack Daniel's and Bud heavies littered the bar and the high-top tables. Among the more than one hundred Pagans at Mobo with Pita that night were Long Island chapter president John "J.R." Ebeling, Ezra "Izzo" Davis, Tracy Lahey, and a Pagan named Hater.

When Billy walked into Mobo, Crystal saw him and looked like she had seen a ghost. She knew Pita would pick up on a vibe, because that's the kind of guy he was, or that someone would make a drunken comment about her fucking Billy. According to Bob, she told Pita that Billy had raped her a few months earlier. I was never able to confirm or refute the alleged rape, but what happened next was confirmed to me by several Pagans.

Pita was furious and corralled J.R., Tracy, and Izzo. They lured Billy into the bathroom. Billy followed, thinking they wanted to talk to him about opening the new Massachusetts chapter. He couldn't have been more wrong.

Billy walked into the bathroom and stepped into a nightmare right out of a Tarantino flick. The four Pagans unleashed a furious beating. They knocked him to the ground and pounded him unconscious, turning his face into a bloody mess. Once they stopped, they all whipped out their dicks and pissed all over him.

"Don't cross swords," one of them joked, as streams of urine poured onto Billy's unconscious face. They howled in laughter.

As the urine caused Billy to regain consciousness, they beat him some more, until darkness overcame Billy again. They stopped, mercifully, summoned Bob to the bathroom, and ordered him to pick up Billy's unconscious body off the slimy tile floor.

Pita was in a blind rage.

"Take his ass back to the motel, and we'll join you there shortly," he said. "When we get there, we're gonna cut off his dick and throw him in the dumpster."

Bob was in shock. Billy was out cold and covered in blood and piss. Bob, terrified for his own life, loaded Billy into his Jeep Cherokee with some assistance from Tracy, started the vehicle, and sped off. But he had no intention of taking him back to the motel, because he knew he'd be involved in a murder rap, at best. At worst, he and Billy would be killed together.

He hit the gas, turned onto Route 25A, and jumped on Interstate 95 North toward Massachusetts. Billy never fully regained consciousness during the ride. He moaned and spit up blood during the trip. Bob didn't stop until he got to Somerville Hospital in Somerville, Massachusetts, where he dumped Billy's limp body at the emergency room door and sped off.

It was the last time I saw Billy Jacobson. To this day, I have no idea what happened to him.

CHAPTER 6

The Long Island guys—especially Pita—were furious that Bob disobeyed them and fled back to Boston. They wanted Billy's blood, and Bob had deprived them of their conquest.

Bob played it smart. He explained that he left because he wanted to avoid a murder rap—for himself and for them. He convinced them that if he had brought Billy back to the motel, and Billy went missing, there would have been video of them bringing Billy into the motel. The cops would have had all their plates and video of every one of them going in and out. It was not a smart play, so Bob took Billy far away to protect them from bringing heat on the club.

He was really just trying to save Billy's life, but they bought his bullshit, which kept the door open for both of us.

The sergeant-at-arms of the Long Island chapter at the time was Jason Blair, aka Roadblock, who was Hogman's half brother. Roadblock was another giant motherfucker—bald, with tattoos up and down his arms, chest, and back, a gray goatee, and piercing, serious eyes. He was six feet and a whopping three hundred and seventy-five pounds. He was a dude you definitely did not want to mess with.

Bob had mentioned my name to Roadblock and told him I was in the running to be a prospect for the Disciples. Bob had talked me up, and they had been looking forward to meeting me at the Wellington. While Billy made sure that didn't happen, the deal wasn't completely off.

The next day, Bob got a text from Roadblock.

Hey, brother, he said. *Our beef isn't with you. We still want you.*

Bingo. I was still in the game.

After Bennett's murder and Billy's disappearance, the fate of the Pagans operation was in jeopardy. ATF wasn't keen on keeping the case going. We knew about a possible homicide and a man who had been beaten to within inches of his life, which put the stakes of the operation into even sharper focus. Just how deep I'd need to go, I wasn't sure at that point.

I told Andy Anderson that Bob was back on board and that he'd invited me to go with him to Long Island for St. Patrick's Day weekend. I briefed Andy on the Bennett and Billy Jacobson situations, as I knew those issues posed a major hurdle toward getting ATF to greenlight the next phase of the operation. We knew the higher-ups would be less than pleased. Not only was ATF doing less and less of that type of deep undercover work, but the brass was certainly not looking to toss an agent into a bloodbath. The Pagans were an attractive target for many reasons, but was it worth the risk, knowing what we knew about Bennett and Jacobson?

There was a murder investigation by the Suffolk County police into Bennett's death. What was my role in that. Was I going undercover to break up the club? Was I looking for evidence in the murder case? Was it too dangerous?

I made the case that I could help in the Bennett investigation, as well as possibly infiltrate one of the most violent outlaw gangs in the biker underground for the first time.

I reconnected with Boston Bob, and we headed to Rocky Point, Long Island, for St. Patrick's Day weekend. The town hosted a parade, there were parties, and a lot of New York and New Jersey Pagans were expected to be in town. There was also a concern that the Hells Angels would show up. I later learned that was the real reason that Bob and I were invited. The Pagans needed more muscle.

To prepare for me to go to Long Island, we built an all-star cover team handpicked by me. It was made up of several agents I had worked with and trusted. Some were from my group in Massachusetts, and many were from Group 6, an ATF group based on the North Shore, just outside of Boston. Picking the team wasn't easy, because I had to make sure that I had agents who understood undercover work, knew biker gangs, and were up for the long days and nights of travel to and from Long Island or wherever else we needed to go. It was going to be a hardship on the guys on the cover team. They too would go without sleep, often eat like crap, and be gone from their families for days or even weeks at a time.

The agents I picked were those whom I knew had my back. I needed guys who wouldn't think twice about running into a hail of bullets to save my ass. I picked a colorful cast of characters.

There was B. J. White, a skinny, athletic former college baseball player from Connecticut who was a good undercover guy. We called him "Shaggy" because he looked just like the character from *Scooby-Doo*.

I brought in Matt O'Shaughnessy, a behemoth of a man who was six feet seven inches and a big frame. He was a gentle giant whom we called "Big Show," but he was also a guy who would definitely be there if the shit hit the fan.

John Mercer was probably the best agent in the Boston field division. He was a legend who made more cases than anyone else in Boston. He pushed the envelope regularly in pursuing cases, and his knowledge and expertise, I knew, would be valuable.

Jeff Kerr, a longtime friend whom I worked out with regularly, was the supervisor. I knew Jeff would not only have my back in the field but also within ATF. Undercover cases inevitably get messy and having someone trusted like him supervising was essential.

I also added Chris Arone, a big dude who can handle himself; Danny Campbell, an Irish college hockey player who grew up in the gritty Charlestown neighborhood of Boston; Bryan Higgins, who was a former Cambridge firefighter before he became an ATF Agent; Joe Steele, a former Bellingham, Massachusetts, cop turned ATF agent; and Danny Meade, a Tufts University graduate who was in my training academy class.

I also brought in George Karelas, a deputy from the Middlesex Sheriff's Office in Massachusetts. He was part of an interagency gang task force that I had worked with for years. He was best friends with Mercer, and I had a great deal of respect for him. A big Greek guy with dark hair, he was dedicated to the job and was a hard worker. I felt comfortable knowing Karelas was on the team.

Eric Kotchian, who started the case out of the Boston office, was the case agent, which meant he ran the day-to-day operations, tracked evidence, wrote reports, interfaced with U.S. Attorney Mike Sullivan and his office, and kept the case on track to build toward prosecution.

Rounding out the team was Tony Thurman, a former All-American cornerback for Boston College who played on the Cotton Bowl winning team led by legendary quarterback Doug Flutie. Tony's nickname from his playing days was "Blade," but he was the chillest guy you would ever meet.

The team tracked my every move, as best they could, staked out dangerous places in advance, and were there to collect evidence and information. They were the guys I would meet with covertly, usually at two o'clock in the morning behind a vacant building, to turn over guns, drugs, recordings, or other vital information. They were my lifeline to the outside world and my eyes and ears, watching out for potential threats. They were a strong team, and they had their work cut out for them.

I set up another trip to Long Island, for the St. Patrick's Day parade in 2009, a few weeks after the assault on Billy. Bob calmed down and decided to stick it out. He told me to meet him at his house west of Boston.

"Hey, man, drive out here and we'll take my car down," he told me.

I was suspicious of Bob after what happened to Billy, but I also knew he made a smart move bringing Billy to the hospital rather than the motel. After consulting with ATF leadership, we decided I'd give it a shot and take the trip down to see if the case was still viable.

I got to Bob's house in Webster, Massachusetts. Bob's old lady and kid weren't home, which was a little weird, because all the other times I went to the house, she was there.

We had a group of ATF agents, assigned to follow me from afar—called a "cover team"—head to New York so they were in place when I got there, which left me on my own at Bob's house.

I parked, walked up to the door of Bob's shithole two-family house that he rented, and knocked.

Bob opened the door.

"Hey, bro," he said, greeting me. I noticed he had brass knuckles with an attached blade in his hand.

"Hey," I said.

Bob wasn't himself. He was on edge, I could tell.

"What's up? How's it going?" I said, trying to ease the tension.

He didn't say anything. He walked to the kitchen, opened the fridge, and took out a couple of Bud tallboys. He opened them both and handed one to me.

"Follow me," he said, heading to the stairs.

We walked upstairs to his bedroom. He walked over to the bureau and took out a packet of white powder.

"Before either of us go anywhere, we're doing a line," he said.

"Sure. All right," I said.

I was trying to play it cool, but in my head I was thinking, *Aw, fuck.* This was not faking a line in a dark bar or during a party; being one-on-one in a bedroom with a criminal, who was likely testing me to see if I was a cop, was far more difficult. It felt impossible. It was a make-or-break moment and I wasn't about to fail before I got to meet the Pagans in Long Island.

Bob had a desk with an old computer on it. He pulled up a chair, poured out some of the powder, and cut up two big lines. I watched as he went through the chopping ritual, thinking about how I was going to pretend to snort mine without him catching me. He had a small straw in one hand and a credit card in the other. He chopped methodically, saying nothing.

He divided up the lines, put down the credit card, and took the straw in his other hand. He leaned his head down toward the powder, put the straw in his nose, and *whiff!!!* His line was gone up his nostril. He shook his head, closed his eyes, grabbed his nose with his free hand, and handed me the straw.

I can't do this. He's right by my face.

I had to think quickly.

"Hey, man. This shit's all lumpy. You got something to cut it up more?" I lied.

He handed me the credit card, and I started chopping it up. I was buying time, hoping he'd look away or turn his back for a second. I moved the line closer and closer to the edge of the desk as I chopped it up, but Bob was watching me like a hawk, right behind me off to one side. I saw him pick up the brass knuckles with the mounted blade.

My mind raced. If I didn't snort it, he'd know I was a cop. I was thinking of coldcocking him, running out to my car, and speeding off. The case would be over, but at least I would be alive. I didn't have my gun on me and I had no cover team. I was on my own with a drugged-up biker with brass knuckles and a knife and most likely a gun on him or close by.

Suddenly, the computer monitor on the desk lit up with a flashing, weird green swirl symbol.

"What the fuck?" Bob said.

He turned, reached behind the monitor, and started playing with the cords.

It was just the distraction I needed at the perfect moment. As soon as he moved, I put the straw in my nose and fake snorted, getting rid of my line using the same technique I'd used at Boston Mike's house. My line was gone. I tossed my head back and grabbed my nose, playing along like I had just blasted coke up my nostril.

He turned around and saw the coke was gone. It worked.

"Nice, brother," he said. "Now we're talking. Let's hit the road."

"Fuck yeah," I said, taking a pull off my Bud. "Let's go see these motherfuckers."

Inside, I was exhaling a furious sigh of relief. My mind was swirling. That could have easily gone tragically wrong. But I got through his test and over another hurdle.

It was time to go meet the Pagans.

CHAPTER 7

Growing up, there were a few things my mother didn't approve of: tattoos, guns, beards, and motorcycles.

I guess I was a huge disappointment.

Motorcycles were something that me and my brother, Mike, were into from a young age, despite my mother's protests. We became experts at hiding them from her and my dad.

Mike and I scraped together money to buy cheap dirt bikes and stashed them in the woods so our parents wouldn't know we had them. We'd say we were going out to play and go rip around on those things, jumping rocks and stumps and speeding through the woods. Our mom would have killed us if she knew.

My first real bike was a Ducati street bike that I got illegally when I was fourteen. I've always loved riding bikes. The thrill of the engine's roar, the thundering vibration, the neck-snapping acceleration, the recklessness and danger—all of it appealed to me. But I always respected the bike and its danger. They were fun to ride, but I was well aware that if I wasn't careful, every full throttle could be my last.

Born in Boston, I was the second of four kids of a CPA and a homemaker. Besides my younger brother, Mike, I had an older sister and a younger sister. My father worked for the Government Accountability Office in Boston, then retired from the federal government and went to work for former Massachusetts State Auditor Joe De-Nucci, a retired world champion boxer.

My mother worked for Kraft Foods for many years but was mostly a stay-at-home mother. We grew up in Roslindale, a blue-collar section of Boston, and moved to suburban Westwood, Massachusetts, when I was six.

I went to Westwood public schools and then to St. Catherine's, a private Catholic school in Norwood, Massachusetts, for junior high. I attended Xaverian Brothers High School, a private Jesuit school, where I played football until I injured my knee.

My parents were big on work ethic, particularly my dad. My first real job was at age fourteen as a dishwasher at Rossi's, a family restaurant in nearby Dedham. After that, I worked as a bag boy at Roche Bros. Supermarkets, where I found my first semblance of a social life. I loved hanging out with the other high school kids who worked there.

After high school, I went to University of Massachusetts Dartmouth, a small public college just outside the waterfront city of New Bedford. We didn't have a ton of money, so I took out loans to pay for college.

Being a CPA, my dad thought—and I agreed—that it would be good for me to pursue an accounting degree. I got good grades in math and business courses, but I didn't love the subject matter, to be honest. I couldn't see spending my life sitting in a cubicle crunching numbers.

My brother, Mike, had a part-time job working at T.J. Maxx as a store security detective. I needed work between semesters, and he got me a job.

I started out doing undercover work to catch shoplifters. To call it undercover work is a slight exaggeration. Basically, I walked around the store posing as a shopper, and if I saw anyone stealing, I grabbed them. I loved it and was immediately good at it. I caught people trying to steal all the time.

I was recruited by Filene's department stores and started working at their flagship store in Downtown Crossing in Boston. It was the late 1980s and that neighborhood was rough, so there was plenty of shoplifting. Job security, I guess. After I graduated from UMass Dartmouth, I went to work for Filene's full time as a security manager.

It wasn't sexy, but I was making $42,000 just out of college and learning how to run investigations. I was living at home and wasn't sure of my future, but it was a steady gig and a respectable career start.

As my investigative skills grew, I started doing internal theft cases for Filene's, looking for inside jobs. I set up hidden cameras, analyzed register trends, and learned about credit fraud. One time I helped uncover a credit-card-fraud ring based in Nigeria.

I became fascinated by the many ways criminals grifted the system and found my calling. I loved the thrill of the chase, but even more, I loved catching people who thought they were smarter than everyone else gaming the system.

Soon, I found out about the federal law enforcement exam and took it, applying to every agency without any real preference: ATF, U.S. Customs, the Drug Enforcement Agency, the FBI, and even the Secret Service. I didn't really know what ATF did.

My dream was to be a federal agent. I didn't want to be a local cop walking the beat and answering calls for domestic assaults, drunks, break-ins, and neighbor disputes. I didn't want to break up bar fights or chase down dudes selling street-level drugs. I have nothing but respect for local cops and the difficult job they do every day, but it wasn't for me.

I wanted to bust up international crime rings, uncover conspiracies and coordinated criminal enterprises. I wanted to use my brain on the investigative side—and use my degree in accounting, as most crimes have a nexus to money. Federal law enforcement seemed like a good fit, because I wanted to work complex investigations.

I scored well on the test and got several interviews and offers from the FBI, Secret Service, ATF, and Customs.

There was an older Filene's detective I worked with named Dick who knew his stuff.

"Dick, I don't know which one to go with," I told him. "I'm leaning toward Secret Service."

Dick looked at me.

"Yeah, kid," he started. "You'll be traveling around a lot, and that seems cool. But that will get old. I'd look at ATF. What they do is really broad, and you'll do all sorts of cool stuff."

I took his advice and accepted a job with ATF in Los Angeles. I remember the night they accepted me. I was a bouncer at the Charlie Horse, a family restaurant and pub in Canton, Massachusetts. I got the news, gave my notice to the manager, and drank in celebration with my friends all night until well after hours.

My ATF start date was July 1, 1990. I had a Pontiac Firebird at the time. I packed it with all my stuff, which wasn't much, and filled the tank. My college buddy Markus volunteered to take the cross-country ride with me. My parents were sad to see me go, particularly my mom. Her fear was that I would stay in L.A. and never return.

My mom was amazing. She hated everything about me being a federal agent—the guns, the danger, my relocation across the country—but she never tried to talk me out of the job and was only supportive. As I hugged her before I left, I promised to be safe and to someday be back. With tears in their eyes, my parents and I said our goodbyes; then I jumped in my car and drove off. About halfway down the street, I noticed Markus was silent. I looked over and he was sobbing like a baby. It was a great icebreaker, and we both began laughing hysterically. Markus is a good buddy and I still bust his balls about the tears to this day.

My starting salary was $16,000 a year. I qualified for food stamps. It was a massive pay cut from Filene's, but I wanted to be a fed, so I made it work. Shortly after arriving in L.A., I found a shithole two-bedroom apartment in West Los Angeles. It was a dump, but it was cheap. After being on the job for a short time I connected with another new agent, John Ciccone, who needed a place to stay. I needed help with the rent, so he moved in.

My dad was big on making me save and told me to put money into my retirement because the government would match up to five percent.

"Dad, if I put in five percent, I can't eat," I told him.

"They sell two cheeseburgers at McDonald's for two dollars. Just put it in," he said.

That was Dad. John and I lived on those two-dollar cheeseburgers for months in one of the worst neighborhoods in L.A. as we started our careers.

If you were going to do the type of work I wanted to do, L.A. was the place to be. It was gangland central. There were Mongols, Vagos, Hells Angels, MS-13, Crips, Bloods, 18th Street, and every other gang known to the Western world. It was truly the wild west.

I lived off Overland Street and worked a lot on the boardwalk at Venice Beach. Back then, gangs overran L.A. The Shoreline Crips owned Venice. It couldn't have been any more different from where I grew up in suburban Massachusetts. Just a few years earlier, I had been at Xaverian Brothers High School, a buttoned-up Catholic school, and now I was hanging out with MS-13 gangbangers in the notorious downtown L.A. neighborhood patrolled by the Los Angeles Police Department's Rampart Division. It was like night and day.

I'm a quick study and picked up the mannerisms and lingo quickly. I fully immersed myself in that gang-ridden underworld of guns and drugs. I learned a lot from my informants. I listened and asked a lot of questions. I hung out with gangbangers every day, and the ability to roleplay became part of my identity.

I loved it. It was my dream job. Even today, as I sit here, I can say that working for ATF was the best job I ever had. I wanted to make an impact. I lived every day dealing with violent crime and helping to stop it. It was a very rewarding career, and there was never a day that I hated my job.

When I first started in L.A., they put me in the arson group. Because I had an accounting degree, the brass figured I'd be good at combing through business records for irregularities to figure out if the owners of burned-out buildings were having financial problems. Turns out, most were.

One of the first major cases I worked on was serial arsonist John Orr, a crazed firefighter who lit a string of fires up and down the coast of California, including one at a Pasadena hardware store that killed a two-year-old boy, his grandmother, a mother of two, and a teenage store employee. He also torched a Warner Bros. studio lot that destroyed the set of the hit TV show *The Waltons*.

I started the case on March 27, 1991, with Glen Lucero, a Los Angeles Fire Department arson investigator, who asked if I wanted to roll out on a commercial fire at a building in Lawndale.

When we got to the scene, we learned about four other similar commercial building fires—one in Redondo Beach and two in Inglewood—that we believed to be connected. One of the incendiary devices used was recovered, and we took a look at the evidence—a piece of yellow notebook paper with three matches secured by a rubber band—that didn't ignite. Eventually, as the investigation progressed, we located a similar device that was used in a fire north of Los Angeles. The device had a fingerprint on it that came back to Orr, a Glendale Fire Department fire captain and member of the Los Angeles County arson task force. I knew Orr and had gone to training sessions with him.

We learned that the same type of device and the same M.O. were used in several fires dating back a decade, including a string near an arson investigators' conference that Orr attended. We also learned that he had written a novel: a dark tale about a twisted arson investigator who sets fires all over California, including in many places where the actual fires occurred. His novel basically laid out a road map and was very damning to his case.

Orr went down as one of the worst serial arsonists in history. Some say he may have set as many as two thousand fires in the eighties and nineties. He was convicted of setting dozens of fires as well as of murder and is serving life in prison.

It was a wild case from start to finish, but the gang cases I was working on were even wilder. I wanted to be out kicking in doors and locking up bad guys. I was single and the only friends I had out there were agents, so, even though the arson squad was my primary responsibility, I volunteered to cover every enforcement and takedown operation and worked gang and gun cases at night. I worked sixteen to eighteen hours a day. I didn't give a shit. I was young and more than willing to run through walls in the name of justice.

Guns and drugs were my daily targets but live gunplay was something I had only heard about in training. That was until one day when I found myself in a shoot-out with gangbangers in a parking garage—something right out of a big-budget Hollywood film.

I was working on a "high intensity drug trafficking case," and we were taking down two Crips we had nailed with multiple kilos of cocaine. I was part of the arrest team that was going to enter the drug dealers' apartment, while another entry team was going in through the underground parking garage. As our teams split up, all of a sudden, shots rang out. There were two shooters: one with a 9mm and another with a TEC-9 submachine gun.

Before I knew it, an agent was shot. Bullets were flying everywhere. The steel door of the garage closed with a thunderous metallic crash, and I was trapped inside along with five other agents. Everyone else was locked out. The shoot-out went on for several minutes, shots ricocheting off cars and cement pillars and gunfire echoing off the cavernous cement walls. One of the Crips was shot twenty-six times. He was hiding behind a car, and a bullet hit his gun and took out his ammo. He was so hopped up on coke, he didn't feel a thing and miraculously survived.

The other guy stood behind a cement column and somehow didn't get shot. When the bullets stopped flying, we got them both into custody. My heart rate was up, to say the least, and I checked my extremities to make sure I hadn't taken a bullet myself. EMTs raced into the garage and tended to the agent who had been shot. Thankfully, he survived, but it was a harsh lesson.

That wasn't practice. It was the real deal.

We had to stick around and be interviewed, and soon there were a bunch of reporters and TV cameras on the scene. I avoided the media and headed back to my apartment. I collapsed onto our ratty couch, cracked a cold beer, and thought about the mayhem that had just unfolded.

I flicked on the TV, and a news story went across the scene: "ATF agent shot." The story had gone national. I immediately called my parents to let them know I was okay.

My parents were concerned, especially my mother.

"Is this really what you want to be doing, Ken?" my mother said. "You have an accounting degree."

"I can't see myself sitting behind a desk every day, Mom," I said. "This is what I want to do, and it's how I can help people."

It wouldn't be the last time I'd have that sort of conversation with my loved ones.

CHAPTER 8

After the coke party at Boston Bob's house, we jumped into his brown Grand Cherokee shitbox and headed toward New York. We took turns driving, and he blew lines of coke off a compact disk cover the whole trip. He offered me some, but I declined. I used the excuse that I was driving and didn't want to get busted. I guess he bought it, and he was just as happy not sharing his coke. Apparently my performance with the lines in his bedroom before we left satisfied him that I wasn't a cop.

We arrived in New York late on a Friday night and drove west on Route 25A into Rocky Point. We stopped by the clubhouse, a small tattoo parlor called the House of Tattoos. It was a discreet storefront on Broadway, the main road that ran through the heart of the sleepy town. The joint was owned by Long Island chapter president John Ebeling, aka J.R.

I met a few hang-arounds there, but most of the club was at a party at Roadblock's house, so we headed that way. I was told I could crash for the night at the house. I had no idea what I was about to get into.

We drove about ten minutes down the road to Roadblock's, a small two-bedroom home in Middle Island that he rented. If you haven't been to that area of Long Island, it's a weird place. It's a couple hours outside of Manhattan, not far from the wealthy beachfront playgrounds of Montauk and the Hamptons, but you might as well be in the Ozarks. The towns are rural, isolated, working-class, and rather run-down. There are old houses that are empty, secluded, and cheap to rent. It's a great place for criminals to hide out and blend in. That's exactly why the Pagans were there.

We walked up the rickety steps into Roadblock's house and were greeted by a bunch of shit-faced and high Pagans. Roadblock was sober and not really excited to meet a new guy. To say he was cold and distant would be an understatement. He was a hardened, very large man with dead blue eyes. His stare was menacing. The little house literally shook with his thunderous steps.

He had several assaults on his record, had served time for attempted murder for gutting a guy with a knife in Long Island in the nineties, and was a volunteer firefighter for the Middle Island Fire Department. It wasn't uncommon for Pagans to be involved in civic groups or have normal jobs. It was one of the ways they blended into the towns where they did their dirt.

The party at his house raged for a few hours. I talked mostly to Bob, as most of the Pagans said very little to me. Some avoided me completely. Roadblock said nothing to me. Every time I looked in his direction, he was staring right back at me with those cold eyes. He was clocking me hard.

At one point, in the early morning hours, the last of the wasted Pagans left Roadblock's house and the only wreckage left was me and Bob. I went into the bathroom to take a leak and the stench of urine permeated my nostrils. I looked at the floor and saw a Hells Angels T-shirt being used as a bath mat in front of the toilet. I wasn't sure if the Pagans had bad aim or purposely pissed on Roadblock's floor solely to desecrate it, but I got the message.

Roadblock told Bob to sleep in the back bedroom and told me to sleep on the floor of the living room. The living room was directly next to the kitchen, with no doors dividing the two rooms. The floor was covered with trash and spilled beer. It was a far cry from the warm, clean bed I shared with Ang every night. I missed home.

I grabbed a dirty blanket and curled up on the floor, surrounded by filth and the scent of stale beer, weed, and cigarettes. Roadblock walked by me thunderously on his way to the kitchen, staring in my direction but saying nothing. The floor creaked and groaned under his enormous weight. He made passes by me repeatedly throughout the night. Each time I heard him walking and breathing, sometimes within a few feet, I woke up from my half sleep. I'm not sure exactly what he was doing, but it was clear he was messing with me.

As I grew more tired, my mind wandered. Would he smash my head in with the axe handle I had seen earlier in the kitchen corner? Would he lay the boots to me while I slept? It was one of the longest nights of my life. I got no sleep.

As dawn came, Roadblock appeared in the kitchen, grabbed a Coke, and ate some sugary cereal. No wonder he was pushing four hundred pounds. Sugar was his lifeblood. He never acknowledged my presence or offered me any food. I got up off the floor, took a piss, and said I was headed out to grab a coffee.

"You want a coffee, bro?" I asked.

"No," he grunted, not looking up from his cereal.

I left the house sore, exhausted, and stinking like death. I texted the cover team, which was staying a town over, and let them know I was still in one piece. I immediately deleted the message after it was sent in case Roadblock or someone else grabbed my phone, which was likely to happen.

That day I spent most of my time at the tattoo shop as the Pagans planned for Sunday's St. Patrick's Day parade through downtown Rocky Point. They were expecting the Hells Angels to attack the clubhouse while the parade was going on, so several Pagans from out of town were headed in to back us up.

ATF was concerned I might get caught in the cross fire of a shoot-out. I was more concerned that Roadblock was going to boot me out—or worse—before I had a chance to get anywhere near the inner workings of the club. It was clear I wasn't welcome or liked very much by him. The tension was high. He watched and tested me every minute that weekend.

That Saturday night, I went out to several Pagan bars with the club. The bars were owned by Pagan supporters who paid "tax" to the club for protection. Members collected envelopes of cash. It was old-school extortion.

There were several brawls that night, all of which were instigated by the Pagans and ended with a group of them giving a beating to whichever poor bastard crossed them. It was disgusting to watch.

With us that night was Hogman, the prime suspect in Bennett's alleged murder and Roadblock's half brother. Hogman was a vile human being with a blood fetish. Three specific disgusting incidents involving blood illuminated the true insanity and depravity of Hogman. One of the first times I met him, we were at a club-sponsored party, and he went into the bathroom to take a leak. After finishing, he came out chewing on a used, blood-covered tampon that he had fished out of the trash.

"I can smell when a chick is on the rag," he proudly boasted, the blood-stained feminine product protruding from his foul mouth.

Another time, some neighbors in Long Island had a cat that gave birth to a litter of kittens. Hogman took it upon himself to lick the blood off the newborn kittens.

But the worst incident—the one that truly haunts me—was when Hogman, some other bikers, and I went to the hospital to visit a "pass around"—a woman who would hang around the club and sleep with various members. The woman was delivering a baby boy fathered by one of the Pagans' nephews.

I was standing in the visiting room near the bathroom door, along with fifteen other Pagans, when I saw Hogman walk into the bathroom. He reached into the catch basin in the toilet and removed a blood clot and popped it into his mouth like a piece of gum. I heard a pop and almost lost my lunch. Thankfully, a nearby Pagan president witnessed the stomach-churning act. He was equally disgusted and threw Hogman out of the room.

I was somewhat relieved to learn that day that some of them had limits. It gave me hope that perhaps there would occasionally be some semblance of normalcy and a respect for humanity. There wouldn't be much, I'd find out, but at least there was some on occasion.

I also learned that Roadblock was the dominant male between him and his brother. Roadblock had more clout in the Long Island chapter, thus his sergeant-at-arms position. He was a clear leader and was violent with a purpose.

Hogman was less abrasive but equally distrusting of me. Maybe it was all the booze and drugs. He took any drug you put in front of him and drank beer like Andre the Giant. He did talk to me and was one of the first to accept me as a hang-around. Meeting Hogman and building a casual relationship that St. Patrick's Day weekend was the opening I needed to start the case.

It was eye opening to see how the Pagans literally ran the town. They slapped guys around, and the bar owners and doormen did nothing. Cops weren't called. The Pagans were the cops in those bars. They were also the judges, juries, and executioners.

After drinking the town dry, we went back to Roadblock's house, where I was sent back to the living room floor to sleep. Just like the previous night, Roadblock continued his pacing past me all night. It was haunting. One time, he stopped next to me, leaned over, and stared down at me as I lay on the ground pretending to be asleep. I could feel his stare. His breath smacked my face and I could smell his stench.

Does this guy ever fucking sleep?

I made it through another sleepless night. The next day was the St. Patrick's Day parade—the reason we came. I didn't have any crimes on record yet, but I was growing more certain that there was an opportunity to infiltrate at some level. I knew I could at the very least become a hang-around, and probably more.

Bob and I were told to stand behind the clubhouse with a few other hang-arounds to ensure no Hells Angels snuck up on the club. Tensions were high. The Pagans had been on a rowdy three-day bender, and whether the Angels showed or not, violence was inevitable.

The whole chapter was "slickback," meaning they weren't wearing colors, so as not to attract the attention of the small army of cops patrolling the parade. It was bone-chillingly cold and depressingly rainy—the kind of St. Patrick's Day that called for lots of booze.

Partygoers drank from plastic Solo cups as they walked up and down Main Street, dressed in green and wearing Mardi Gras–style beads. Members of the cover team blended into the crowd, ready to respond if the Hells Angels showed up or if I needed to get the hell out of Dodge.

The fact that the Pagans were in street clothes was bad news for any drunk that decided to mouth off to the wrong guy. All of them were the wrong guy, colors or no colors. If you fought one, you fought them all. Not surprisingly, that's what happened.

One of the Long Island chapter members was Michael Thornton, nicknamed Tumbleweed, a felon with convictions for drugs and maiming. Yes, that's right—maiming. That's an actual federal criminal charge. The legal definition is "mutilating or inflicting injury upon a person which deprives him/her of the use of any limb." I'm not sure of the circumstances of how Tumbleweed caught that case, but I was made aware of the charges during my prep work before I went to Rocky Point.

Tumbleweed was the oldest in the club and looked like Blue from the Will Ferrell movie *Old School*. He'd lost his leg in a motorcycle accident and had a prosthetic limb. His wasn't a fancy titanium or plastic limb, though. It was wooden—just like a storybook pirate's leg.

A group of drunken revelers walked down the sidewalk, and one of them made the mistake of telling a member to get out of the way. Next thing you know, he was being beaten by several Pagans. Me and Bob heard the ruckus and ran around the front to see the melee. Tumbleweed was in the middle of it, wailing away at this poor sap. At one point, his leg came off and he fell down.

You'd think his fake leg coming off would have ended the brawl, but not with those savages. Tumbleweed hopped up on his good leg and wielded his fake leg as a weapon. He swung it wildly, raining down blows with his own fake leg onto the victim. When the beating stopped, the victim's buddies scraped him up off the ground and hustled him out of the area.

That evening, there was another blowout at Roadblock's house and several out-of-town Pagans joined me in crashing on the floor. Most of them smelled like shit and snored like bears, but somehow it was the best night of sleep I had that weekend. Unlike the other nights, Roadblock didn't do his walking guard duty. Perhaps he was done intimidating me for the time being, or maybe he just passed out. Whatever it was, I took small comfort in the mass of smelly humanity. At least I wasn't the only one there, should that axe-handle-wielding mammoth decide to stalk and intimidate.

As I lay there on the floor, passing out in a sea of dirty bikers, I thought about my beautiful little girls snug in their beds and realized just how far away from my family I had traveled.

CHAPTER 9

I first met my wife, Angelina, at the Federal Law Enforcement Training Center (FLETC) in Glynco, Georgia, in 1990, while attending the agency's Criminal Investigator Training Program. We'd both gotten hired by ATF the same day, on opposite sides of the country.

I was twenty-four and having fun being a young agent in training. She was a few years older and struck me as serious. She was a beauty—in shape, with dark, wavy hair and perfect skin. I was interested, but she wanted nothing to do with me. We hung out in different crowds, and I was pretty sure she thought I was just another knuckleheaded cop.

I invited her out to the bars with me and my friends, but she politely turned me down. I wouldn't say she ignored me, but it was clear she was more focused on our training rather than hanging out. After graduating from the academy, I was sent to L.A. and she went back to New York. I thought it would be the last time I saw her, but fate had other plans for us.

Ang and her family lived in the Brooklyn housing projects. A lot of her family members and friends were alcoholics and drug addicts. She had uncles, cousins, and a brother die from drugs. She knew countless people in her family and community who had either been shot, overdosed, or died of AIDS, and just as many who'd wound up in prison. It was a very tough upbringing, and she developed a thick skin. She could handle herself—and still can.

The police were at her family's apartment constantly, pounding on the door, looking for people. There were fights just outside their door and shootings in the hallways of the housing complex and on the streets right outside her windows.

She was surrounded by sadness and devastation. While that sort of upbringing can break a lot of people, for her, it was motivation. It drove her to do something different. She decided to finish high school and become a cop. After high school, she went to John Jay College of Criminal Justice and pursued a career in law enforcement. Ang was the first in her family to graduate high school, never mind college. She did it all while raising her son, Willie, by herself as a single mom.

In the Brooklyn projects, her chosen profession wasn't well received. Some relatives called her a "pig" and taunted her. They told her she would be forced to go against her own people and that she was a traitor. She just wanted to make a difference. She didn't want communities to be overrun with drugs and guns and despair. She knew there was a better way.

Her first job was as an investigator in the New York City Family Court Division. She then went to work for the New York State Liquor Authority before being hired by ATF. After she finished the academy, she was sent undercover in the New York Field Division, where she worked in the Hispanic community, making drug buys in Harlem and Washington Heights. It was dangerous work, but she spoke fluent Spanish, knew the streets, and fit the part, to become a great undercover agent.

Normally, agents return to FLETC one month after graduating the academy for a second training program for a specific ATF mission. Both of our returns were delayed. Mine was delayed because of the parking garage shootout, while Ang was involved in a gun case where she was required to be a witness. ATF policy is to keep first-year agents out of situations where they might have to appear in court to prevent interruptions in their training schedules, but both of us found ourselves in complex cases that derailed our training.

The shoot-out created a web of courtroom proceedings, while Ang's case was a complicated "924E" armed career criminal bust. The case was actually the first of its kind in New York. Enacted in 1991, 924E was the so-called three strikes rule, which mandated a fifteen-year-to-life sentence for a "career criminal" caught with an illegal firearm. She made the bust and had to see the case through to its conclusion.

Not to sound corny, but it was fate. We both should have been back with our original class a month after leaving basic training, but we weren't. The odds of us ending up in the same class again were minuscule.

When we got back to the academy a year after we should have been there, we were surprised to see each other. We got along better than during our initial training and hung out a bit, but Ang was still standoffish.

"This is not going to be a FLETC romance," she told me flatly. "I'm not interested in that. If you want to date afterwards, though, I'd be into that."

A "FLETC romance" referred to academy hookups. It was common, and there were frequent rumors about agents hooking up. She wanted no part of the rumor mill. I understood, even if I disagreed.

We ended training just before Christmas 1991. A week later, I asked her out and told her I'd fly out to New York. I was going back to Massachusetts for Christmas anyway and figured I'd stop in New York, see Ang, and then head home for the holidays.

My mom wasn't happy, because I hadn't been home in seven months, and she knew a side trip to New York would take time away from my visit home for the holidays. She also knew Ang was different, and that my visit might lead to something serious. I was generally causal when it came to relationships and never gave up family time for a girl.

Ang and I went to a restaurant in Queens called Fishtails, and then I spent the night. We've been together ever since. We did the long-distance-relationship thing for a while, taking turns flying across the country to spend weekends together.

Things moved fast. I proposed in 1992, and we decided to get married that November. ATF, though, once again intervened in our personal plans. The agency's policy is that if you get married, they'll approve a transfer and cover expenses to move your spouse to where you're assigned. They do not authorize transfers if you're engaged or dating—only if you're officially married.

I told a supervisor of our plans, and he informed me that waiting until November was a bad idea, because that was after the start of the next fiscal year, so it would be harder to push through a request for a transfer. It would be easier if we got married in the summer, the supervisor said.

So we came up with a plan. We decided we'd get married quietly so she could be transferred and have a full ceremony in November with family and friends. A friend told us about a justice of the peace in Lake Tahoe, so we rented a convertible and drove up the Pacific Coast Highway to Tahoe on July Fourth weekend. It was hot and we had the top down. The PCH is one of America's most beautiful roadways—the Pacific Ocean glistening off to your side as you wend through some of the most picturesque, mountainous landscape you can imagine. But the California sun wasn't kind to my white Irish skin. I got the sunburn of my life.

We stopped in a little town and bought a gift for the justice of the peace: a colorful variety of cactus plants in a cool glazed ceramic pot. When we arrived at his office in Tahoe, we knocked, but there was no answer. We called the number we were given—no answer.

"Figures," Ang joked. "You're probably happy."

But I wasn't. I was pissed and disappointed. We took the plant and drove back to L.A. A few weeks later, my supervisor came back and reminded me that we needed to get married before August or we'd have to wait a year.

I flew to New York, and we got married at Brooklyn City Hall, surrounded by a colorful cast of characters, which, ironically, included a group of bikers. In October, Ang moved to L.A. and was assigned to an arson squad.

We kept the November wedding date in Massachusetts and were planning to get married at St. Denis, the church I grew up attending in Westwood, Massachusetts. While attending Pre-Cana, the priest asked us for the wedding license, and we showed him the one from New York. He was aghast and told us we couldn't get a Massachusetts license because we already had one in New York.

We explained the situation and asked him to keep it between us.

"Please," I said, "do not tell my mother. It'll crush her."

The day of the wedding, Ang was getting ready at my parents' house while I went out with my groomsmen to pick up our tuxedos and have a pre-wedding cocktail to ease the tension. My mother confronted Ang at the house.

"Are you and Kenny already married?" she asked.

Ang was horrified, but quickly answered no and changed the subject. Mom bought it, but Ang was worried and felt terrible about lying to her. Apparently the priest slipped and accidentally hinted to my mom that we had already gotten married, but he realized his mistake and tried to covered his tracks.

Ang walked down the aisle of St. Denis looking gorgeous. I could see stress on her face, though. When she got to the altar and turned to me, she wore a pained look. She whispered, "I think your mom knows."

"No way," I said, incredulous.

The priest, who was already addressing the congregation, shot us a stern look, annoyed we were talking.

My mother never said anything about it, and we never let on. My mom and dad never found out the truth, but they did know we had a beautiful ceremony at St. Denis and have had a happy marriage ever since. That's really all that's ever mattered to me.

Nine days after the wedding, we conceived our first daughter, Kaitlyn.

We moved into a new place in L.A. and put the cactus in a cardboard box in storage. It sat there for two months. When we eventually removed it from the box, we expected it to be dead, but to our surprise, it was alive and well. We kept it with us in L.A. for the next five years and watched it grow and transform. We put it in storage again after we moved to Washington, D.C. It survived the cross-country move and once again was fine when we removed it from storage.

We moved several more times, and the plant traveled with us to each new home. It became like part of our family.

CHAPTER 10

The morning after the St. Patrick's Day bash in Rocky Point, I woke up on Roadblock's floor, groggy and smelling and feeling like garbage. I couldn't have been farther from the comforts of home and Ang and the girls.

I grabbed my jacket and headed for the door, gingerly stepping over the sea of scum. I should have been cooking pancakes for my little girls and my wife. Instead, I was brushing cigarette butts and nacho crumbs off my filthy denim, picking myself up off a floor in a biker flophouse in Long Island, and trying to figure out my next move.

Bob and I got into his car and my brain was racing. I thought about the case as we drove back to Massachusetts. The Suffolk County Sheriff's Department had an open homicide investigation into Bennett's death, but the Pagans were stonewalling. Hogman wasn't talking. Neither were Roadblock or J.R. The whole chapter stonewalled every cop that asked about Bennett. They simply had no evidence, and they all knew it.

Hogman's story of Bennett passing out on the knife made no sense, but we had no leads. We couldn't prove it unless someone talked. The bikers lived by the mantra that the best way to keep a secret between two people was to make sure one of them was dead.

Bennett's parents were devastated and wanted answers. They knew their son was no angel, but he didn't deserve that. I didn't want Hogman to get away with it.

When I got back to Massachusetts, it was decided I would keep the game going as a hang-around, to see where the case went. By that time, I was texting and calling regularly with Hogman, Roadblock, J.R., and Bob. I traveled back down to Long Island a few times, partied a bit, watched them beat people up on occasion, and started to understand what they were all about.

One thing I learned early was what racists they were. The Pagans were a white supremacist group. They strictly prohibited Blacks from becoming members. They joined the Aryan Nation when in prison, and an unsettling number of members wore white power slogans and Nazi insignias on their colors, including swastikas and SS lightning bolt-style symbols.

I cannot stomach racism of any kind, and it was tough to bite my tongue, especially as the husband of a Puerto Rican woman and the father of three half–Puerto Rican girls. I wanted to punch the bikers when they spewed their racially fueled vitriol and white power propaganda. Part of my job, though, was to go along with it. It made me sick.

Taking down racists fueled me as much as catching Bennett's killer did. The case was becoming all-consuming. Stopping the Pagans from strong-arming and shaking down small businesses motivated me. Their relentless disrespect of women motivated me. Not to mention all the drugs, guns, bombs, and assaults.

I started strategizing with ATF. It was becoming clear that I was going to go undercover long-term. The Pagans were starting to trust me. J.R., Roadblock, and Hogman knew I could handle myself and wanted me down there as muscle. They also knew I'd be perfect to help start a new chapter in Boston.

A big moment in the case came when J.R. invited me down for the first communion of his son in the spring of 2009. The whole chapter was attending, and if I was going to be a prospect, it was another chance for them to feel me out. I figured I could pump up my backstory a bit during the trip, so I packed some lobsters in ice and carried them down with me.

I brought them to J.R.'s house and placed one on the table. They didn't know a lot about lobsters, but coming from New England, I knew quite a bit. There's an old trick where you can rub a lobster between their eyes to the top of their head. After a minute or so, they begin to relax and you can stand them on their head, positioning their claws out in front of them in a headstand position. I lined up several on the table doing headstands. It blew their minds and cemented my backstory as a lobster poacher who worked the docks.

One day that weekend, J.R. and I were on the front lawn of his house drinking beers.

"So, what do you think of doing this thing?" he asked me. "We need people like you in the chapter. We're looking to start a chapter up in Mass. You'd have to start down here first, but you and Bob could eventually start the chapter up in Mass."

I played it cool.

"I don't know, man," I said. "I'm not sure."

"Well, I talked to the Mother Club, and you and Bob are in as prospects if you want," he told me. "I want you down here. Think about it. Let me know by the end of the weekend."

"Okay," I said.

The next afternoon was J.R.'s son's first communion. The after party was a parade of dirty, hungover bikers, stinking up the backyard to welcome one of their sons into God's family. After the get-together back at J.R.'s house, we talked again.

"I'm in," I told him. "Let's do it."

"That's great, man. I'll set it all up," he said.

His son was now officially a Catholic, and I was taking the first step toward becoming a Pagan.

As a prospect, I committed my life to the Pagans. They could call me morning, noon, or night, and I was expected to come running. I was a slave to the gang. I had to prospect for at least six months.

I started going down to Long Island regularly. Each time I went, members talked to me a bit more. Their comfort level with my backstory increased, but many remained suspicious. That's why my backstopping efforts were so important. Fortunately, my alter ego, Ken

Pallis, had a long, involved history and his identity was ready for whatever scrutiny they threw at me.

Backstopping is a dying art. I was good at it. I had a fake Massachusetts license that I obtained through ATF, but there was always a chance they had a mole at the Massachusetts Registry of Motor Vehicles and could find out my real identity. So I exchanged it at the New York DMV for a New York license. That ID was untraceable if anyone tried.

The Pagans took countersurveillance to new levels. It was nerve-racking and became a constant test of wit. While they weren't Mensa candidates, many of them were smart and some were especially genius when it came to crime.

All outlaw motorcycle gangs are clandestine and difficult to penetrate, but the Pagans were the gold standard. Their entire brand was based around never having been infiltrated by cops, and it was well known that they did painfully exhaustive background checks on potential new prospects. They did comprehensive surveillance. They surprised prospects at home or at work. They popped into the local bar to check out prospects' stories. They questioned prospects' friends and family. They questioned my every move and weeks later questioned me again about the same thing. If my answers weren't consistent, they called me on it. It was mental warfare, at all times.

I needed a credit history that went back a long way. Yes, they checked my credit. Fortunately, Ken Pallis had one going back to the nineties, when I created him while working undercover in L.A. When you think about someone's life, and how to create a fake one, there are a lot of considerations. You need pictures to hang around your house, junk mail, bills, proof of employment. It doesn't end. It all seems very simple, but imagine all the forms, like insurance, gym memberships, library cards, that you have acquired throughout your life. I needed to find a way to replicate that in just a few days. It wasn't easy, and it took time. Especially the junk mail part. I had to sign up for mailing lists, go to stores and open accounts, and sign up as a rewards member. All the things that a normal person doesn't really want to do are essential to pull off a fake identity.

They asked about my parents. I told them my dad was ex-military and was from New Hampshire but we'd moved around the country. I said he died, so I had to produce a real death certificate for Ken Pallis's nonexistent dad. I needed a social security card and a birth certificate that showed where I was born.

My mother, I told them, was a crack whore in California and I didn't know what happened to her. That was perhaps the easiest explanation and the one story I told them that was challenged the least. In their world, friends and family regularly disappeared forever for one reason or another, so it raised little suspicion. It was, sadly, a common story.

I had help from ATF to get all the details in order, but we had to do it quickly. The first months of the case were when the Pagans dug hard into my backstory. One slipup, one inconsistency, one false move, and the case would have been over before it began—or worse. I had created a criminal persona: Ken Pallis was a convict who had a felony rap sheet for kicking the shit out of a cop. It was a poor choice of convictions, I later learned.

I spent a lot of time dropping my Boston accent, since I was supposed to be from California. But it would pop out every once in a while. That's why I came up with Ken Pallis's New Hampshire connection, so I could explain the Boston accent if anyone called me on it. You can be assured, they did. Many times.

I picked the name Ken Pallis because I had a childhood friend with the last name Pallis. It was Undercover 101 to pick an easy last name to remember and keep my first name. For the same reason, I chose a relative's birthday for Ken Pallis's birthdate.

The Pagans checked on it all. Ezra "Izzo" Davis was one of their best intel collectors. He wasn't the biggest guy and was on the younger side when I met him, but he was tough, smart, and intimidating.

"If you do anything fucked up in this club, I'm going to be the one that will kill you," he once told me.

With shaggy blond hair and glasses, Izzo was five feet ten inches tall, weighed about two hundred and twenty pounds, and looked more like a pudgy tech guy than a biker, unless you saw the tattoos of jesters and pit bulls up and down his arms, chest, and neck. He had a drug case in New Jersey in 2003 and another one in New York in 2009. He also had a pair of kidnapping cases in New Jersey in 2005 and 2006.

They deployed him dressed in civilian clothes to check out backstories of prospects, including me. They sent him to the garage in Massachusetts where I told them I worked. He came to my apartment in New Bedford and went through my junk drawer. He snooped through my mail.

ATF procurement rules don't allow you to buy merchandise, so I rented couches, tables, lamps, and other furnishings through Rent-A-Center to furnish the place. I scattered clothes about and left takeout containers and half-drunk beers on the coffee table to make the undercover apartment look lived in.

Vehicles were always a pain in the ass. In short-term operations you can use a criminally seized vehicle. The Pagans, though, would surely trace the Vehicle Identification Number of my truck, so I had to make sure I had the paperwork in order. It would have been trouble if it came back to a seized vehicle or a police department. They had cops to run background checks for them. They had people in city and town halls to check out tax and voting records. They were adept at searching online databases. No stone was left unturned.

I had my backstory buttoned up, passed initial reviews, and was ready to become a prospect. It was a moment arrived at by no cop, no state trooper, and no federal agent before me. They gave me a "Prospect Info Sheet" to fill out, which was basically a college application for bikers. It was extremely detailed. In addition to the normal personal information—name, social security number, last five years of addresses, date of birth, mothers' maiden name, employer information, driver's license number, and so on—they required me to provide an extensive list of additional background information. If you've ever refinanced a home, it was that detailed.

I had to give them the VIN of my vehicle; make, model, year, plate, and VIN of my bike; a list of my criminal convictions, broken down by misdemeanor and felony, an "explanation of charges," the sentences, a list of prisons where I had served time, and probation or parole status; the name and address of my old lady, as well as details on how long we had been together and her employment information; a list of properties owned; and a description of my motorcycle riding experience.

The document also asked if I had any family in law enforcement, whether I had ever been in another biker club, and, finally, demanded of me: *Why do you want to be in the Pagans Motorcycle Club?*

At the bottom of the document, there was a legal disclaimer that read: *I give the Pagans Motorcycle Club permission to conduct a background investigation using my personal information provided above.*

I signed away my life. Well, Ken Pallis's life, at least.

CHAPTER 11

The most egregious college fraternity hazing is nursery school compared to what the Pagans put prospects through.

As I prepared to prospect, one of my top priorities was studying the Pagans. I was required to know the history of the club, memorize the rules, and know every detail of the organization, from the meaning of each patch to the riding formations to the protocols on planning trips and getting gas. Wrong answers to questions from members had serious, often violent consequences.

The Pagans, by definition, is a motorcycle club and a nonprofit organization. In reality, it's a criminal gang. Clubs host bake sales and meat raffles. Pagan members sold crystal meth and guns, gang-raped women, brutalized rivals, and extorted businesses.

The rules were strict and comprehensive. They were well organized. Nothing happened involving any club member that wasn't known by the president, vice president, sergeant-at-arms, or others. It was a strict brotherhood.

How much of a family do they consider themselves? Their method of greeting each other is a kiss on the lips. I was told it was a sign of respect and unwavering loyalty. Avoiding kissing another member on the mouth got you cracked in the head with an axe handle or possibly worse. A prospect who refused would be kicked out immediately.

The Pagans are broken down into individual chapters mostly based in small- and medium-sized cities and rural areas. Local chapters range from five members to as many as fifty or more. The Long

Island chapter, when I was beginning to prospect, had ten members. All chapters report to the Mother Club, a well-organized and tight-knit group of longtime Pagans who oversee the whole gang, including approving promotions and new members and setting the rules and agenda for the gang. Each Mother Club member had several chapters that fell under their direct purview, divided geographically. Each member pays dues to their chapter, and the chapter kicks up payments monthly to the Mother Club. A portion of those payments are used by the Mother Club to support Pagans in prison and their families. Putting money in the canteen account of an incarcerated member was another way they showed they were a brotherhood, but it also helped ensure loyalty. It's common practice for organized crime figures to support the families of incarcerated gangsters and send money to them in prison for that very reason: to buy loyalty and, more important, silence.

The Mother Club acted like the gang's board of directors. The national president, vice president, and sergeant-at-arms wielded the same power as the heads of a Mafia crime family. Nothing of consequence is supposed to happen in the gang or in any chapter without the knowledge and approval of the Mother Club. Of course, lots often did, and just like in the Mafia, there were severe consequences for going rogue, breaking rules, or cutting the Mother Club out of deals.

The Mother Club has thirteen members, most of whom are violent felons. They each wear a special patch on their colors with the number 13 in white, outlined in black, signifying their status as a member of the Mother Club.

The national president when I began prospecting in 2009 was David "Bart" Barbeito, a Maryland Pagan with a long felony record. He was charged with kidnapping another biker in West Virginia and indicted on racketeering along with dozens of other Pagans. To this day, I still have T-shirts that were handed out at a Pagan event that read, FREE BART.

After Bart went to federal prison, he was succeeded by Dennis "Rooster" Katona, a career criminal who served four years in federal prison for racketeering in connection with a wild 2002 melee with the Hells Angels at the Hellraisers Ball in Plainview, New York. The bloodbath left one Pagan dead, seven others stabbed, and landed seventy-three Pagans in jail. It was a legendary clash that was often talked about by club members. Those who took part in the brawl and, more important, those who served time in connection with it took on legendary status.

The Hellraisers Ball rumble was also studied closely by gang cops and feds, including me, as it revealed the inner workings of the Pagans like no incident before. Members of the Mother Club took part in the planning and execution of the storming of the Hellraisers Ball, a tattoo convention held by the Hells Angels.

When I got involved in this case and agreed to go deep undercover, my goal was to go after Mother Club members. I wasn't interested in just busting a few thugs with guns or cocaine, or breaking up chapters selling stolen bike parts. I wanted to put a dent in the Pagans and do my part to stop their reign of brutality.

The agency committed to building a RICO (Racketeer Influenced and Corrupt Organization) case and planned to target members of the Mother Club, as well as the presidents, vice presidents, and sergeants-at-arms of all the chapters in New York, New Jersey, and beyond. Based on what we knew of the club's activities already, we were confident we could build strong gun and drug trafficking cases, as well as VICAR (Violent Crimes in Aid of Racketeering) charges. VICAR charges are violent felonies such as assaults or beatings that are carried out to further a criminal enterprise.

In order to prove a RICO case, you first have to prove the entity that's being targeted is an actual organization. The Pagans make that simple, because they all wear colors, have titles and ranks, and they're formally sworn in. Next, you have to prove they committed VICAR acts in furtherance of the organization. Establishing a gang like the Pagans as a criminal enterprise allows investigators to cast a wider net to hold leaders of the organization accountable, even when they may not be directly involved in crimes.

I was committed to doing all I could to make a strong RICO case, but it went well beyond that for me. It wasn't just about locking up a bunch of bikers and securing long prison sentences. If I was going to put aside my life for a significant period of time, I was going to do all I could to intervene whenever possible and disrupt violence and horrific crimes, whether charges came of it or not.

Gaudy jail sentences and sweeping indictments make for good press releases, but oftentimes in these cases, it's crimes that are thwarted and never get reported—attempted rapes, beatings, and the exploitation of vulnerable and desperate people—that matter. How do you measure that as far as value in a law enforcement operation? For me, it meant a lot.

Most of the dangerous and potentially deadly decisions I had to make every day didn't make it into an arrest report or a court file. A lot of it, no one ever knew about. But I knew about it, and that was enough for me. Preventing violence against people who didn't deserve it was more important to me than getting guys two-hundred-year sentences.

The Pagans have a long, sordid, and bloody history. Formed in 1959 in Maryland by Lou Dobkin, a Navy veteran and motorcycle enthusiast from Prince Georges County, Maryland, the Pagans are less notorious to the general public and receive far less attention than their rival Hells Angels. Dobkin was revered as a god in the Pagan world. Pagans respect their history, and members, as well as prospects, have to know the organization's past. Anyone caught talking negatively about Dobkin or not showing the proper respect was dealt with violently, particularly prospects.

In the 1950s, the military did a study on bikers and biker gangs and found that a number learned to ride and became immersed in motorcycle culture while in the service, many as military police officers assigned to bike units. A lot of early Pagans and Hells Angels members joined their respective clubs after leaving the military and drifting toward an outlaw lifestyle.

While smaller in number, law enforcement widely considers the Pagans as big a concern as the Angels, and in some areas of the country, far more of a concern. The Pagans are generally known to be more hard-core, more violent, and more clandestine than the Angels. They are true outlaws, which led to the FBI once declaring them "the most violent criminal organization in America."

It wouldn't take me long to learn why that reputation existed.

The Pagans' first president was John "Satan" Marron, who defected from the Sons of Satan MC and led the Pagans in the early 1960s. As national president, Marron was paid $100,000 a year, a salary that at the time was the same as that of the president of the United States. The club set the salary at the same level as the president as a "show of class," symbolic of the importance of his role.

Another early Pagan legend was Wayne "Big Chuck" Bradshaw, a U.S. Army veteran and a key figure in the formative years of the club in New Jersey. Bradshaw, a savage two-hundred-and-fifty-pound brawler, was an enforcer in the Northern New Jersey chapter before he infamously quit the club and became an undercover cop. Despite his biker background, he had a decorated twenty-year career in the Middletown, New Jersey, police department, much of which he spent in narcotics. The Mother Club was furious with Bradshaw's decision to take the club's secrets directly to law enforcement, but no one stopped him.

In 1982, a Pagan named Glen Turner brutally shot a New Jersey state trooper in the face, nearly killing him. Turner was sentenced to thirty-five years and was released around the time I got involved in this case. I met Turner at a Pagan event once, and he was introduced to me as the guy who shot a New Jersey trooper.

Learning the Pagans' history, traditions, and culture consumed me, because one mistake or one misstep could have meant excommunication. Many ATF higher-ups counted on it and thought for sure the case would fizzle out before it even got going. There was a good reason why the Pagans had never been infiltrated by law enforcement. They were experts at screening prospects.

Their logo, the Norse fire god Surtr sitting on the sun and wielding a sword, is taken from famed comic book illustrator Jack Kirby. Kirby, who came of age in the post–World War II glory years of comics, went on to draw for Marvel. The illustration used for the Pagan logo appeared in the ninety-seventh issue of the 1960s horror/sci-fi comic series, *Journey Into Mystery.*

Anyone impersonating a Pagan or casually wearing their symbols or colors is dealt with harshly. No one—not hang-arounds or anyone other than a member—could have the Surtr symbol or the word "Pagan" on their clothing. A violation was punishable by severe violence.

I learned that sixteen is the Pagan number, because "P" is the sixteenth letter in the alphabet. Similarly, the Hells Angels use eighty-one as their number, after "H" (the eighth letter) and "A" (the first). The Pagans hated the Angels so much that members would avoid saying or writing the number eighty-one at all costs. In fact, when prospects reached their eighty-first day, they said they had "eighty-plus-one" days or "eighty-two minus one," but they wouldn't say the number eighty-one. Funny sidenote: J.R.'s house was number 81 and he got endless shit for it from the club. I'm surprised he moved there, honestly. Numbers, symbols, and colors are very important to members. They are a secret code and, some might say, provide some order to the chaos in their lives.

In addition to traditional one-percenter patches, Pagan members' colors frequently include patches with slogans and symbols, including:

- FTW for "Fuck the World"
- Nazi swastikas, flags, or SS symbols
- WHACK 'EM, STACK 'EM, a murder reference
- FTF for "Fuck the Feds"
- EATIN' AIN'T CHEATIN', misogynist slang
- ARGO, slang for "Ah, go fuck yourself"
- NUNYA, slang for "None of your business"
- I'D RATHER BE NOTORIOUS THAN FAMOUS, a comparison of Pagans to Hells Angels
- NO 81, an anti–Hells Angels slogan

- 1959–2009, a fiftieth-anniversary Pagans patch
- CDC, for "Cunts Don't Count"
- DILLIGAF, for "Do I look like I give a fuck?"

Some Pagans wore giant safety pins on their colors. The reasons were twofold: some were way too fat to button their colors, so the pin allowed them to close their jackets when riding their motorcycles. But more important, it was a nasty weapon. Pagans were known to unhook them and wield them in a brawl. The pins aren't technically a weapon, so they aren't confiscated by cops.

The Pagans' feud with the Hells Angels is legendary. There is a standing order for all Pagans that if you kill an Angel, you have to steal his colors. By contrast, if your colors are stolen by a Hells Angel, you have to avenge the theft with murder.

In the nineties, the Pagans saw its ranks grow, along with its violence. In New Jersey, in 1994, two Pagans were murdered and three others were seriously wounded in the bloody culmination of a turf battle with the Hells Angels.

The infamous Hellraisers Ball melee in New York touched off a war with the Hells Angels. Two weeks after the deadly 2002 clash, a Pagans tattoo shop in Philadelphia was firebombed. Three years later, the Philly Hells Angels vice president was executed by Pagans as he drove his truck on a highway. The Hells Angels closed their Philadelphia chapter after the slaying.

In 2007, federal agents and state cops raided several Pagan stash houses in New York and seized automatic weapons, homemade bombs, and dozens of guns. All of them had been stockpiled for a potential war with the Hells Angels. The gangs detest each other. Just how much, I'd soon come to learn.

As Andy Anderson and I considered the undercover operation, we reviewed report after report about the Pagans. On paper, they were some bad dudes.

In real life, they were monsters.

CHAPTER 12

Back at ATF, there was growing chatter about our case. Agents in the Boston office and at headquarters in Washington knew I was a supervisor and that the case was becoming more unusual and risky by the moment.

They all knew that we were on the cusp of something big, not the least of which was finally penetrating the Pagans. It was something no other law enforcement agency in America had accomplished, and for good reason.

I needed allies, and thankfully, I had a great one in Boston: United States Attorney Michael Sullivan. Sullivan was the district attorney in Plymouth County, Massachusetts, for several years and I worked with him many times on cases developed by my team in Bridgewater, Massachusetts. We worked closely with the cops in Brockton, and I met with Mike regularly. We had a mutual respect. It was hard not to respect a guy like him. We became close after a big case in Brockton involving Cape Verdean gangs. We nabbed the violent leader of one of the gangs, who was responsible for most of the shootings in the city. Sullivan threw the book at the gang leader, and after he was gone, shootings in Brockton dropped by forty percent. The case showed me he was the real deal and that I could trust him. A rare Republican in Massachusetts, he was a hard-nosed DA and had a reputation of supporting hardworking officers. I liked that.

In the summer of 2001, President George W. Bush tapped Sullivan to be the new U.S. Attorney in Boston, but the confirmation was delayed. Bush had his eye on Sullivan not only because he was a Republican, but also because of his reputation of aggressively prosecuting drug and arms dealers. After the 9/11 attacks—which were launched out of Boston—Sullivan became even more valuable to the Bush administration.

On September 14, 2001, he was confirmed by the U.S. Senate as U.S. Attorney in Boston. In another era, he would have been able to ease into the job and to take his time mapping out a strategy to break up gangs and disrupt drug traffickers. Instead, he was thrown into the global 9/11 terror investigation, the likes of which had never before been seen in the United States.

In 2006, he was named acting director of ATF, and for three years, from 2006 to 2009, he served as both the U.S. Attorney in Boston and the United States' acting ATF director. I had great support from Andy Anderson and others in the Boston office, but it didn't hurt that the U.S. Attorney was a longtime, trusted ally. Especially because, before we could really ramp up the case, I needed authorization to commit crimes.

Specifically, I needed to formally be given approval to participate in felonious activity, drug and gun deals and assaults.

The truth is, if I didn't get permission to assault someone, this thing was dead in the water. There was no way I could fully infiltrate the Pagans if I couldn't throw a punch if necessary or put someone in a choke hold. I needed to be able to use my muscle to impress Roadblock, J.R., and the rest of them, if I was to pull it off. The best way to impress the Pagans, unquestionably, was through violence.

I met with Sullivan, and we went through the case. I explained to him the opportunity before us and what I would need. I explained that we had intel that the Pagans wanted to open a Massachusetts chapter and told him the potential problems that would pose. The

Hells Angels owned Massachusetts, despite the presence of the Devil's Disciples and the Outlaws, and a new Pagans chapter would start a war, I argued.

"What are the risks, Ken?" Sullivan asked me.

"Where do you want me to start?" I cracked.

I laid out the vulnerabilities. Sullivan was well versed on bikers, as I personally had done several cases with him involving the Outlaws when he was the Plymouth district attorney and the U.S. Attorney, and he had worked on many others as well. The Outlaws were, and still are, a constant presence in Southeastern Massachusetts.

"How are you going to get the evidence?" he asked me.

I explained how it had all started and that they were now trying to recruit me. I told him about Boston Bob and Roadblock and J.R. and Hogman, although I left out the stories of Bennett and the disappearance of Billy Jacobson. I was confident and factual and assured him that it was in the best interest of justice for Massachusetts and the United States. I believed that then, and I still do today.

"Okay, Ken. I'll sign off," Sullivan told me. "Please be safe. Do your job. And get the bastards."

He also approved federal funding for the operation under the Organized Crime Drug Enforcement Task Force, a program under the Department of Justice designed to combine interagency resources to fight organized crime.

We drafted memos and they went through the proper legal channels, and I was cleared to commit felonies as long as I did my best to mitigate the violence and prevent people from getting severely hurt. Basically, I could sell drugs, act like I was beating the fuck out of people, and witness crimes without intervening, as long as I believed nobody was going to get seriously injured or killed, and as long as I believed it was to further the case.

In situations where I needed to be involved in assaults, I had to try to protect the victim from severe injury while acting like I was taking part in the assault. It was ethically tricky and forced me to walk a fine line, because as anyone who has ever seen a street fight knows, they are nothing if not unpredictable.

If there was a bar fight, and I stood and watched, the case would die. If they asked me to deliver a kilo of coke, I had to do it, or the case would die. Getting those clearances was essential. They would also come back to haunt me.

CHAPTER 13

Boston Bob and I were officially prospects and were given bottom rockers to wear on our denim jackets that read PROSPECT. We were not allowed to have any other Pagan patches and were still prohibited from wearing the Surtr logo.

I was living three or four nights a week at the undercover house in New Bedford, to keep up appearances, and traveling back and forth to Long Island for meetings and events. When in Long Island, I spent most of my time in Rocky Point at the clubhouse, where J.R. was usually doing tattoos or fucking one of the many women who weren't his wife.

Whenever he was there, someone had to be on guard duty in front of the shop, and when I was down there, it would usually be me. He'd come in around noon and stay until one a.m. a lot of nights, and I'd have to stand guard the whole time. He had multiple women coming and going. He and his wife had no relationship at all. They were civil, but her dad was a cop and the whole family knew he was a scumbag, so she really had nothing to do with him. Very strange relationship.

J.R. wasn't the best-looking guy in the world, but for some reason there was no end to the women who would come in and out of the shop to have sex with him. That old myth about women being attracted to bad boys certainly applied, because there were no other redeeming romantic qualities that I could detect. He was constantly banging women, wherever he could, including one time in my truck. I had no say in the matter. Believe me, I didn't want to get in that truck afterwards.

Ang and the girls were adjusting to seeing me less and less, but none of us knew how long the case would go on. When I wasn't in Long Island, I had to stay in New Bedford as much as possible in case any Pagans popped by to check out my story. It was also a good idea to be a presence there so neighbors would see me coming and going, in case any Pagans asked them about me. Which they did.

My first official Pagans event as a prospect took place on Memorial Day weekend in 2009. Bob and I were told to travel to a very remote area of Long Island for a big Pagans event. A club supporter owned a huge field in a rural town and was letting the club use the property for the weekend. Me and Bob rode our bikes down together and arrived the night before. Part of our job as prospects was to do the grunt work setting up for the event.

As we arrived in Long Island, we made a stop at the clubhouse in Rocky Point. I parked my bike out in front of the tattoo shop and walked inside. On the table in the reception area was an axe handle— the gang's weapon of choice—with the insignia PAGAN etched along the side, and a note with my name on it. I opened it and read: *Bring this axe handle with you to the field. J.R.*

As a prospect, I wasn't allowed to carry anything that had the word "Pagan" written on it, particularly an axe handle or colors. It was a test from J.R., and there was no right response. If I took it, I'd be breaking the rules. If I didn't, I'd be refusing an order from the chapter president. It was the first of many no-win situations I'd be put in over the next two years.

I didn't take it.

Bob and I hopped back on our bikes and headed east on Route 25A to meet the rest of the chapter. We rolled onto the field and parked our bikes. We were met by J.R., who immediately saw I didn't have the weapon.

"Where's the axe handle I told you to bring?" he asked in an intimidating tone.

"I didn't bring it," I responded.

"Why not?" he said.

"I'm not allowed to touch anything with the word 'Pagan' on it," I said.

"Your chapter president told you to do it, so why didn't you do it?" he said. "I gave you an order to bring that thing."

"I know the rules," I reiterated. "I'm a prospect. I'm not supposed to touch those."

He glared at me, sized me up, didn't say anything else, and walked away. I wasn't sure if I'd passed his test or not, but I didn't get a beating, so I must have done something right.

Bob and I stayed in tents that night. We were woken up at four a.m. by Roadblock, who told us to get to work. Roadblock, who was sponsoring us as prospects, may have been a violent and angry guy, but he also happened to be an incredible cook. He had us setting up smokers and moving tables and chairs around. He got to work early preparing a brisket that he smoked the entire day. I had never had brisket before, but as I sit here today, I can remember the flavor. It was succulent, sweet, and simply unbelievable. Still to this day the best I've ever had. The guy could cook, I'll give him that.

Roadblock also took his sponsor duties seriously. He was religious about schooling me and Bob on the rules. Part of it was for our own good, but it was also about self-preservation. He needed our muscle, so he needed us to succeed. Also, if we fucked up, it would reflect on him. Poorly. We took it seriously too, because we both knew the stakes. Bob talked a lot about Bennett and Billy Jacobson, so we both knew full well that people could just disappear. Even us. We would literally sit together and study the rules for hours, testing each other, to make sure we were prepared for whatever came our way.

I remember one time, we were studying in a garage in Long Island and Roadblock was there. Bob's old lady kept coming in and telling us to hurry up.

"Bob, come on. We have to go," she said.

She was clueless. Prospects and hang-arounds aren't allowed to bring women around the club, but she didn't care. Roadblock was getting pissed and warned Bob to get her under control.

"I'm going to kill her or you if she doesn't fucking stop," he said.

Those sorts of threats were tossed around regularly, but I knew not to take them lightly. The Pagans earned their reputations and criminal records, and I wasn't going to test any of them. Fortunately for her, Bob's old lady got the message and didn't bother us again.

When Roadblock told me and Bob about the rules of engagement with Mother Club members, I listened. The Long Island event was the first time I met any of the out-of-town chapters as a prospect. Being around full patch members as a hang-around was one thing, but being around full patch members as a prospect was another.

As a prospect I "belonged to the whole Pagan Nation," under the charter, and any member can "school a prospect," which is another way of saying any patch member could mess with me. It was also the first time I was formally introduced to other chapter presidents and the Mother Club as a prospect. I was presented to officers and Mother Club members like a shiny new toy.

It was my first peek into the inner workings of the Pagans and the first time I got close to Mother Club members. We were told to keep our hands by our sides at all times when we were around Mother Club members.

"You guys are going to meet Mother Club members this weekend," Roadblock told us. "You'll meet White Bear. He has a hair trigger. So don't piss him off."

White Bear, a member of the Mother Club whose real name was Michael Grayson, was a scraggly junkie who looked like he'd crawled out of the gutter after living under a bridge for years. He was just a vile human being. He joined the Pagans when he was thirty-four and was a lifer. He was a very bad dude and a crystal meth dealer. He was convicted twice in the late 1970s of dealing meth and angel dust. In 1985, he and a dozen other Pagans were convicted in a federal racketeering case that focused primarily on his drug trafficking.

He also had open charges from the 2003 kidnapping incident in West Virginia involving Bart, the former Pagans national president. White Bear and a local chapter president named Michael "Tyrone"

Trone intervened in a dispute between the Pagans' national vice president and the president of the Charleston, West Virginia, chapter. They were charged with holding members at gunpoint for hours and threatening them with knives as they were questioned one by one about the beef.

As the sun came up on Long Island that morning, Pagan chapters in Harley brigades roared in from all over the East Coast, rumbling onto the field for a weekend of club business and debauchery. The rolling fields of grass became a biker Woodstock dotted with canopy tents and coolers as members of each chapter set up camp for a wild weekend.

Looking out across a stinky sea of outlaws, I was miles from my cul-de-sac and my beautiful girls. I was in the epicenter of East Coast biker culture and was surrounded by killers, drug dealers, rapists, and leg breakers. I was focused on the task at hand, but I'd be lying if I said I wasn't getting a rush from it all.

White Bear showed up with another Pagan named Egyptian. Egyptian was a unique breed in the club. He served as White Bear's consigliere and advisor, even though he wasn't an official member of the Mother Club. He was a businessman who helped set up LLCs connected to club business, which made him a very important part of the operation.

He and White Bear held court at a canopy reserved for the Mother Club. Each time a new chapter rolled in, the president walked over and paid tribute. I took mental notes all day and tried to put names to faces and names to chapters. My head was swirling, and the oppressive heat and brutal sun beating down on me did little to improve my focus.

I was trying to gather as much visual evidence as possible, assuming that my entrée into this ruthless underground of crime and drugs would be short-lived. Besides being conscious of building a criminal case, I spent every minute watching my words and demeanor, so as to not be outed as a cop. Simultaneously, I had to be wary of my status as a prospect and follow club rules to a tee, all while looking over my shoulder day and night in case someone tried to take a shot at the new prospect.

I was on guard duty for much of the day, watching over the Long Island chapter's camp in the stifling early summer sun. J.R. and Roadblock came over to me.

"Come on, prospect," J.R. said. "You're going over to meet White Bear. It's a respect thing and you have to do it. Don't say anything unless asked."

We walked across the field, Roadblock's girth pounding the turf on one side of me and J.R. escorting me on the other. I watched the Mother Club's tent across the field get closer and closer with each step. I spotted White Bear in the middle of the tent. His pallid, sunken face was partially hidden by an unkempt beard and ratty strands of matted hair that stuck to his forehead and fell in front of his lifeless eyes.

We got to the front of the tent. I stood up tall like a new military recruit meeting a general. He didn't make eye contact and looked right past me.

"White Bear, we'd like you to meet our newest prospect," J.R. announced.

When you're a prospect, you don't have a name, especially around Mother Club members. Sometimes I would be introduced as "Prospect Ken," but mostly I was known simply as "prospect."

White Bear glanced at me, unimpressed.

"Where are you from?" he asked coldly.

"From the Pagan Nation," I said, believing that's what he wanted to hear.

"That's great, prospect," he said. "But where are you really from?"

Is this another test? Sweat poured out of my bandana down my face. There was no right answer. *What the fuck do I tell this guy?*

I paused a moment.

"I'm from Boston," I said. Hoping to impress him with some street cred, I added: "The Beach Street projects in Roslindale."

This fucker was from West Virginia. He wouldn't have known

Roslindale from Compton. But impressing him wasn't the point. They just wanted to see if I could hold my own in a tense situation. They wanted to see if I would shit myself talking to a Mother Club member. I didn't, although I was drenched in sweat.

"How's your prospecting going so far?" he asked.

He continued to look past me and was really directing his comments at Roadblock, knowing that Roadblock was my sponsor. It was all very threatening and intended to weed out the weak, as well as impress upon sponsors that their new recruit better work out—or else.

Roadblock answered: "He has a long way to go."

Nothing else was said. He was done with me. Roadblock and J.R. nodded at him, and we turned around and walked away. I was in and out of there, without any casualties, and was happy it was over quickly. Nothing good comes from hanging out with the Mother Club.

As we walked away from White Bear and back toward our encampment, J.R. and Roadblock said nothing. When we got back, they walked off and left me with Bob to get back to work.

It was another test and I passed.

CHAPTER 14

It was hot as hell, and Roadblock had me and Bob working our asses off. I sweated right through my jeans and denim jacket. At one point, as me and Bob were taking a break, I noticed he had a sawed-off shotgun in his tent. As a prospect I was told I was not allowed to have a firearm, unless given permission by the chapter president. Apparently Bob didn't get the memo. Or the gang was giving him special treatment.

The rest of the Long Island chapter showed up, including Hogman and Tracy, who spent the night selling drugs and partying. Funny, I had read in the Pagans' constitution that prospects—which Hogman was at the time—were not allowed to do drugs and that no one in the club was allowed to sell drugs. It also specifically banned heroin, needles, and crack cocaine. I was at my first event and had already confirmed that those rules were a bunch of bullshit.

As a prospect, I was considered a servant, a slave, or even less. It's like college fraternity hazing, except that you can be beaten into a coma or killed at any moment. Hogman wasn't technically a prospect, and because he was Roadblock's brother, he was a de facto member. His status protected him from the relentless mental and physical torture that Bob and I and other prospects endured.

We busted our tails and stood guard duty, but most of that weekend consisted of me being bossed around, belittled, and disrespected.

"Prospect, go get me a burger."

"Prospect, go get me a beer."

"Prospect, go wash my bike."

"Prospect, give me a cigarette."

"Prospect, I need a spark plug."

I just had to take it all.

More tests came. One afternoon, as I was working near the grill with Izzo, J.R., Bob, and some others, one of them threw a set of Pagan colors at me. It was another no-win situation. As a prospect, I was not allowed to touch colors. I also knew that I was not allowed to let colors hit the ground.

Fuck, I thought to myself as the jacket flew toward me.

I made a snap decision and caught the jacket, thinking that letting it hit the ground would be a worse violation than touching it. Before I realized I had the jacket in my hands, I felt a sharp blow to my head and saw stars for a split second.

Izzo had given me a "bang check," a patented Pagan assault maneuver in which you strike someone on the forehead with the palm of your hand. It's used to warn prospects that they are a step away from a beating and to smarten up. Message received.

That little scenario was the kind of thing they did to mess around with prospects, and I was no different. In some ways, it gave me energy, because I was fitting in. They were testing me and I was passing. There was no right response to the colors being thrown at me, but I took the punch and moved on. Their goal was to find out if I would take punishment for the club. Would I stand up, if challenged? Everything they did was to test my character and loyalty.

Late the first evening, I was walking around picking up empties and trash. I saw Pita walk a New Jersey prospect down to meet the Mother Club. We were too far away to hear what was said, but I sure heard what came next.

This guy must have said something wrong because I heard a ruckus and saw him being dragged behind the canopy, flailing. I heard his bloodcurdling screams as axe handles rained down upon him with violent force.

I could hear him screaming, and then whimpering, as they beat the daylights out of him. Part of me wanted to run over so I could see exactly what was going on and who was involved, since I was there to do a job: build evidence. That was off the table, though. I did my best to ignore it and went about my business.

I wondered if similar violence would come my way. After all, we were in a remote field in the middle of nowhere. There were no cops coming to save me or anyone else. My cover team was miles away, and since I was not wearing a wire, they would have no way of knowing I was in trouble. Even if they had known, they wouldn't be able to get there in time to save my ass if a similar fate befell me.

Bob looked over and saw the stress on my face.

"Bro, just ignore it," he said.

It was good advice. We saw Pita later that day. Pita was the Pagan who had sponsored the New Jersey prospect beaten by the Mother Club members.

"You'll never see that guy again. He was shown the door," he chuckled.

He was right. We didn't see that guy the rest of the weekend, or ever again. Just like Billy Jacobson, I have no idea what ever happened to him.

Later that day, White Bear took a walk from his camp to the area where hundreds of bikes were parked, including mine and Bob's. As he walked by our Harleys, parked with the rest of the Long Island chapter's, something stood out to him: our Massachusetts license plates. All the other bikes had New York, New Jersey, Pennsylvania, and other Pagans chapter state tags. Our Massachusetts tags stood out like turds in a punchbowl.

"Who the fuck has Massachusetts plates?" White Bear asked J.R. and Roadblock.

"Our prospects are from Mass," Roadblock told him. "We're prospecting them to start a chapter up there."

"Bullshit," White Bear said. "These fucking guys need to move to Long Island and be part of the chapter here full time. If we do expand, then maybe they can go back. But they need to move down here. Now."

J.R. broke the news to us.

"The good news is, White Bear didn't kick you out of the club," he said. "But you have to move down here. Nonnegotiable."

I was fine with it, but Bob was pissed.

"Fuck these guys," he told me that night. "Let's hold strong. We're not moving. If they want us, they'll come up to Mass."

The real reason they wanted us down there was to beef up the Long Island chapter. There was a lot of chatter about Hells Angels planning something, and there was a constant threat of an attack. I had nothing to lose, so I told J.R. that I'd move down to Long Island.

Now I just had to tell my wife.

CHAPTER 15

Ang and I had an understanding from day one about work. We both knew the risks and demands of the job. We also knew we had to be supportive of each other, but we couldn't be overly protective. It was a very fine line.

We are cops. So we both knew that in order for the relationship to work, we had to trust the other's judgment and respect their difficult decisions.

That foundation of our relationship was there from day one, but it would be a lie to suggest things didn't change at all after Kaitlyn came along. Neither of us was in denial about the harsh realities of the job, but once our first daughter was born, it became clear that one or both of us had to tone things down a bit.

Ang wasn't putting herself in harm's way regularly while doing arson investigations, but I was still going full tilt. I was doing a lot of investigative work, including a lot of undercover cases. I was also part of the L.A. division's Special Response Team, which meant I was out there kicking in doors and chasing gangbangers.

She worried but always kept her poker face. Until it all came to a head one night in Colorado.

I was working an undercover case in L.A. in 1996, buying crystal methamphetamine from gang members who were importing it from Mexico. Back then, most meth cases involved scumbags making the drug out of over-the-counter Sudafed in trailers. A rash of meth lab explosions forced the federal government to act and restrictions were placed on the sale of Sudafed, one of the drug's active ingredients.

The guys I was dealing with had a source in Mexico who had unlimited access to the precursors used to manufacture meth. The Mexican meth was powerful, and the quality and supply went through the roof.

Posing as a white supremacist tweaker, I was buying pounds of meth from them. We arrested one of the dealers and were working on finding the source in Mexico. We flipped the dealer, and he told us he had a source who could get machine guns from Colorado.

He told me he could get something else: bombs. Big ones.

I agreed to trade them a pound of meth for machine guns and a bomb. We met in a seedy motel in L.A. where I traded the drugs for a few machine guns and a low-grade bomb. They were white supremacists and thought I was as well. They were all cranked up, spewing white power bullshit, and I played along. I wanted to see just what kinds of bombs they could get.

"We have a chemist in Kansas," one of them told me. "He can make whatever kind of bomb you want."

It was about a year after the terrorist Timothy McVeigh packed a truck with a fertilizer-based bomb and detonated it outside an Oklahoma City federal building, killing 168 people. McVeigh was inspired by the white supremacist/anti-government novel *The Turner Diaries* and claimed the bombing was in response to the FBI raids at Waco, Texas, and Ruby Ridge. He also claimed the attack was a legitimate retaliatory act against a tyrannical government.

The group I was dealing with spoke McVeigh's language, and I played right into it.

"I can get you stuff to take down a building if that's what you want," one of them told me.

"Yeah, that's what I want to do," I said. "Like Oklahoma. Put in the order."

What I ordered was HMTD—hexamethylene triperoxide diamine. It's a highly explosive organic compound, and the fact that I was able to order it had my colleagues at ATF more than a bit alarmed, especially in light of what happened in Oklahoma a year earlier.

I called a bomb tech.

"You sure it's HMTD?" he asked.

"Yeah, that's what he said," I replied.

"That shit is not to be screwed around with," he told me.

HMTD is heat- and friction-sensitive and reacts to metal. It can only be neutralized with chloroform. It all added up to something very dangerous for amateurs like me to handle.

We were told to pick up the explosives in Colorado. Myself, our informant, my partner on the case, Jim Pollack, and another agent, John Carr, who would later become my contact agent in the Pagan undercover investigation, made the trip to Castle Rock, Colorado, a former mining town halfway between Denver and Colorado Springs.

We arrived at the drop location—a U-shaped roadway behind a closed strip mall. We pulled in around eight p.m., which was when the deal was supposed to happen. The informant and I hung out by the loading docks waiting, tensely, for our connection. Hours passed and nothing. We got a call from our contact who told us the bombs, twelve of them to be exact, were coming from Kansas City and the chemist that built them was delayed.

Agents on ATF's Special Response Team armed with automatic weapons were hiding all over the place—in dumpsters, on roofs, and in cars. We had an army of bomb techs there too in case things went wrong. Many of the agents were ex-military and knew explosives.

Unlike buying drugs undercover, with explosives it's not enough to just purchase the contraband from someone to make a case stick. When you're buying bombs, you've got to get them to describe how the device works, including what makes it detonate. It's a technical aspect of the law, and it's always a challenge. In that case, because of the volatility of the HMTD, it was imperative to make the conversation quick.

"Do not fuck around with that shit," one of the bomb techs told me. "Get the conversation and get the hell out of there."

More than six hours went by before the connection arrived. There were three of them who arrived in a black Chevy Suburban. I walked over to greet them, and they opened the back, showing me the explosives.

"So these are them, huh?" I said. "I know a little about this stuff, but I'm not the bomb guy. So tell me how they work so I can explain it to my guy? Talk to me like I'm a simpleton."

They bought the ruse and described in detail how they worked, pointing out homemade blasting caps, the pipe, the powder, and the end caps. One thing I did know was that the devices could blow from friction or from contact with metal. I knew that safe transport of HMTD was in plastic and that you needed petroleum jelly on the caps to prevent friction.

As one of them showed me the bomb, he started unscrewing the end cap. I heard the unmistakable squeak of metal on metal.

"Hey, dude, what are you doing?" I yelled, fearing my last words were coming out of my mouth. "I'm not the bomb guy, I told you. Just tell me."

He turned the end cap again . . . *squeak*. I knew that one more turn could be the last, and we'd all be blown sky high. I had no idea what he was thinking.

"What the fuck?" I said.

I had enough and threw up the arrest signal, hoping the bomb wouldn't explode. In seconds, agents popped out of dumpsters and emerged from the shadows, guns drawn. He held the bomb in his hand and stared at me blankly.

Everyone was ordered to the ground and all of us hit the deck. As they were taken into custody, the bomb unit isolated the device and we cleared the area. Even the bomb squad wouldn't go near the device. Later, they went back and detonated it using a bomb disposal unit. The explosion was massive. It's not something you like to think about as an agent—being blown to bits—but when you hear a bomb of that magnitude explode, it's hard not to consider what might have happened had it gone off next to you.

The area was crawling with agents. I was giving interviews to higher-ups, wrapping up details, and getting ready to leave. We had that crew dead to rights buying meth and cocaine and selling me machine guns and bombs, including several transactions on video. The bomb maker, Robert J. Bernhardt, and one of his cohorts, James W. Eads, never saw the light of day after they were arrested. Both got life in federal prison in 1998.

After the close call with the bomb, I thought of Ang and our family. Our second daughter, Shannon, had been born a year earlier, and Ang was pregnant with our third daughter, Meaghan. I realized Ang knew what the case was about. She expected the bust to happen several hours earlier, but she never heard from me.

As I came to the realization, I saw a female agent on the cover team. She was a friend of Ang's, and I heard her talking on the phone.

"No, no, relax, it's not that at all," she was saying, clearly talking to someone who was upset.

I knew she was talking to Ang. Although she thought she was helping by letting Ang know I was safe, upon hearing her voice, Ang had assumed the worst.

I grabbed the phone, and sure enough, Ang was upset.

"I'm fine. I know, I'm sorry. But I'm fine," I assured her. "We'll talk later."

Deals of that nature, whether drugs or weapons, always happen on the dealers' time. They aren't always punctual. When a deal doesn't go on time, it's hard not to fear the worst. Ang was fearing the worst. She thought the agent was calling to tell her I was dead.

It was a breaking point for Ang. She was home with our daughters and hadn't heard from me for several hours after I was supposed to be buying enough explosives to blow up a building. After she realized I wasn't dead, she wanted to kill me.

She told me I was taking too many risks. I was doing undercover work and was on the SRT team, kicking in doors and arresting bad guys who often had guns and bombs.

"Something's got to give, Ken," she said. "Either SRT or undercover. You can't do both. You've got to pick. We've got young kids now."

She was right. So I picked undercover.

CHAPTER 16

After White Bear said we had to move to Long Island, I told J.R. I was in but needed to go home to get some clothes and sort out my work situation. In reality, I was heading home to break the news to Ang and the girls that this was going to be a much longer undercover role than planned.

I walked into our house, my boots caked in thick mud and my face and body covered in road dirt and sweat. I was sunburned and stunk of stale beer, smoke, and sweat. I was exhausted, having barely slept all weekend.

I shuffled in, told the girls I loved them, and headed to the shower. After I washed the stench of the weekend off me, we gathered in our bedroom and I gave them all hugs.

The girls knew something serious was going on. Ang did too, not only as my wife, but also as a fellow ATF agent.

"Listen, I'm not going to be around as much for a while," I told them.

My girls, Kaitlyn, Shannon, and Meaghan, were still young. They were in junior high and high school. They looked at me and Ang with their big, beautiful eyes filled with questions that they knew they couldn't ask. They had grown up in our law enforcement family, so they knew from a young age that they were on a need-to-know basis. We also tried to avoid sugarcoating anything for them, while being aware of and sensitive to their fears and emotions.

"Hey, it may sound a little cruel, but this is the job," I told them.

"This is what we're paid to do, and this is what we have to do. Mom will be here every day, and I'll come home when I can. We'll be okay. We'll be fine."

They were still kids, though, and they were worried about their dad. They were also looking at it selfishly and were upset that I wasn't going to be there for them like they wanted. I could see it in their eyes. I could also see that they had no idea what it really meant, or how long it might go on. If they had any idea, the reaction likely would have been much worse. That's why Ang and I only told them the basics and didn't get into a lot of detail.

Kaitlyn, the oldest, was starting to get rebellious and was acting out a bit. She was hanging around with the wrong crowd. Ang and I were both concerned as it became apparent she was more upset about me being away than we expected. Meaghan was too. Shannon was the opposite and retreated into herself. She was stoic and wouldn't talk a lot about how she was feeling.

While we tried to protect the girls from the harsh realities of the job, we learned that they knew a lot more than we thought they did. We tried to keep our work conversations private, but they heard everything in that house. They also weren't stupid. They talked among themselves when they heard things, and all three of them were quite aware that I was undercover in a biker gang. They didn't know how deep undercover I was and they didn't know all the gory details, but they knew I was into some dark and dangerous territory.

I was deep into the role and looked every bit the part all the time. I had to stay in the role because the Pagans were experts at surveillance. I never knew when or where they might pop up. If they followed me and saw me in dorky dad clothes, all cleaned up, the case would be dead.

So even when I was home, I lived like a dirtbag. I was scraggly and smelly and was as heavy as I'd been in my life. I got looks everywhere I went. There was a period where Kaitlyn refused to go out to the store with me because she didn't like that everyone looked at us.

The girls had to make excuses and explain to their friends that their dad wasn't some thug. They had to explain that I was a cop and had to dress like that for my job. They knew they couldn't tell anyone anything more, no matter how many questions were asked. And there were lots.

It was a lot of pressure on them. That was one of the hardest parts of this case—putting my family through the stress and fear.

My family visits became less frequent and were always unannounced, because I was never sure when I could break away to get home. I also didn't want to call or text ahead of time to let anyone know I was coming, in case my calls or texts were being monitored. It wouldn't have been unusual for one of the Pagans to snatch a phone out of a prospect's hand to see who they were texting. My personal phone was hidden away, but I was always overly careful because I never knew when I'd be ambushed by one of the Pagans.

One time, Kaitlyn's first boyfriend was at the house when I came rumbling home on my Harley. She and the kid were outside shooting hoops and talking. They stopped cold as they heard the roar of my bike from blocks away. The bike shattered the quaint silence of the neighborhood. Every time I rode into our town, people outside stopped and stared.

Our neighborhood was quiet, suburban. It was the kind of place where soccer moms drove SUVs and dads drove nice sedans. It wasn't an overly wealthy town, but the houses were nice, lawns were well manicured, and it was safe. A filthy biker thundering down those leafy streets certainly broke the monotony and caught everyone's attention.

Kaitlyn and the kid watched me ride down the street and pull into our driveway. She was happy to see me and ran over to give me a hug. Her boyfriend looked like he had seen Satan himself. His eyes were like saucers.

She introduced me to him, and he shook my hand, trembling in teenage fear. I felt bad, because I'd never been one of those guys who wanted to intimidate my daughters' boyfriends. I wasn't trying to, but my appearance alone left him no doubt that messing with my daughter would be a very bad choice, no matter how nice I acted. I towered over him in my biker denim, with sunglasses, a do-rag on my head, fingerless leather gloves, dusty black boots, and tattoos protruding out from my cutoff sleeves.

Unfortunately, I don't think the kid ever shook the image of me. He and Kaitlyn broke up shortly after.

Existing in suburbia in the state I was in just wasn't easy. Kaitlyn and Meaghan both played youth hockey at the time and I was coaching them. As the case progressed, I was away more and more, so my coaching duties fell to my assistants, and I would show up when I could. One time I snuck home and surprised the girls on the bench. I stood out like a sore thumb. The other coaches were all clean cut with short hair, close shaves, and clean clothes. I looked like a Motörhead roadie, no matter what I did to try to clean up.

One of the little girls skated over and looked up at me, her ponytails poking out from each side of her Bauer helmet.

"Coach Ken, you missed our game last week," she said.

"Yeah, I know. I'm sorry," I told her.

"We played good," she said. "We heard you were partying with Roadblock."

I almost fell off the bench.

"What?" I asked, incredulous.

"Yeah, we heard you were partying with Roadblock," she said.

I needed to nip that sort of locker room talk in the bud. Not only was it not appropriate for the girls to discuss, but I couldn't let the name "Roadblock" start circulating. All it would do is cause me more headaches, lead to more questions, and make me more stressed out.

The last thing I needed was a bunch of hockey dads googling "Roadblock" and "biker" to try to find out what gang I was infiltrating. Between kids with big ears, meddling busybodies, and the Internet, I had my hands full with keeping a lid on what I was doing.

"Aw, no, don't listen to that," I said. "Meg talks too much. It wasn't a party. It was just work."

She shrugged and looked at me. Apparently satisfied with the explanation, she smiled and skated off.

That was the moment I realized Ang and I had to be far more careful about what we said within earshot of the kids. Clearly, they were listening.

Ang was getting concerned too. She saw the changes in me, not just physically but emotionally. One night I was telling her a story and referenced a Pagan named Joe. She did not remember who he was, so I mentioned he was the Pagan that I told her about that smeared peanut butter on his balls and had his dog lick it off. It shocked her that I said it so matter-of-factly.

With an incredulous look on her face, she said, "Ken, do you realize that how you just described that guy was as if you said he had brown hair and blue eyes?"

We didn't talk like that at home, but it just flowed naturally from me because that sort of inappropriate talk and behavior was an everyday thing with the Pagans.

"This is not good," she said.

She had done undercover work herself for years and knew the dangers of long-term infiltration. So we had to have a longer talk.

As an agent, she understood what I felt about the motorcycle gang and knew what I had to do to get a good case to put them away. She was fully supportive and knew it was the right thing to do.

But as a wife, she knew it was dangerous. I was living with them. I was going into drug dens, buying large amounts of coke and meth, setting up gun buys, and was surrounded by violence 24/7. That was whole other story, and she had mixed feelings.

"Hopefully, Ken, I'm not going to lose you to the other side," she said. "Nothing is worth it, if it's going to change who you are."

She knew all too well that ATF had lost a few agents to the dark side along the way, and she did not want me added to that list.

"How far do you wanna go?" she asked.

"I don't know," I answered.

"Are you going to take ten Pagans down? Or are you going to try and take the whole organization down?" she said.

"I want to take down as many as I can."

She paused and looked at me. Our girls were in the next room. I was pretty sure they were trying to listen.

"I have this pit in my stomach, Ken," she said. "These are bad guys. I'm terrified you're going to trip up one day and they're going to find out who you are, and game over. We need you here."

We both knew that I was beyond the point of no return. Despite the domestic realities, we came to an agreement to keep going. We talked about strategy, not as a husband and wife, but as fellow agents.

"I need you to follow the rules, Ken," she said. "If you're going into a location, you're wired and you have a cover team. If the shit hits the fan, they won't get to you as fast as you want them to, but you need them close."

I argued that wearing a wire was more dangerous. I was searched all the time. Getting caught wearing a transmitter would get me hurt or killed. I was wheeling and dealing every day with no wire. Much of the time, the cover team was too far away, so if the shit ever did hit the fan, by the time they got to me I'd be long dead.

"Let's talk about the Hells Angels," she said. "I'm more afraid of them. You're their enemy. You could take a beating or worse."

"I know," I said.

"And the fucking motorcycles . . ." she added.

She turned her big brown eyes away and closed them.

A few years before the Pagans case began, Ang's son had a close friend who died while riding a motorcycle. It was something that haunted her. She knew I was out there with dozens of bikers, screwing down the highway in formation at one-hundred-plus miles per hour, cutting each other off and swerving in and out of lanes of traffic, just inches away from rumbling eighteen-wheelers and drivers talking on their cell phones.

"I can't take losing you, Ken—not to the Pagans, not to the Hells Angels, and not to the bike," she said.

She turned back to me and looked me dead in the eye.

"You get them and you make cases and you lock them up. Then come home to us in one piece."

CHAPTER 17

I left home and rode my Harley back to Long Island. I knew things were going to move fast, but I had no idea just how fast they'd go, or how intense it would get. Those long rides alone were good for strategizing and planning my next moves. Sometimes, though, I dreaded them, because I knew I was driving back into chaos. Other times, they were relaxing trips during which I could clear my head and just be one with the bike and the open road for a while. Riding with the Pagans was stressful. Riding solo was often freeing.

I usually crashed at J.R.'s house or Roadblock's place, or sometimes I'd rent a shitty motel room. I spent my days running around between the tattoo shop, dive bars, and Pagan members' houses as I prepared to move down there. I was looking around for a decent place where I could set up shop for myself, but I needed somewhere somewhat private. I spent a lot of my free time discreetly writing reports and notes in the journal that would become my bible for this case. I had to keep those writings hidden far away. I was always looking over my shoulder.

By that time, I had gotten used to juggling my two distinct identities and leading two totally separate lives. I had two wallets: my real one and an undercover wallet with all my fake IDs, credit cards, and bank cards in Ken Pallis's name, along with my ATF cash. All my bills in Ken Pallis's name went back to a post office box in New Bedford. I kept my real wallet, with my actual IDs and credit cards, hidden away, along with my ATF badge, gun, and my case notebook. Those items caused me a lot of anxiety, because if they were ever discovered, my cover team would most certainly become a body recovery team.

As much as Roadblock, J.R., and the rest of them tested me, I had to test them right back. While my real personal items and government gun were stashed away safely, I kept my undercover personal items in a bag that I carried on my bike. I set a tiny, fine piece of thread that was almost invisible to the eye over the buckle on the bag so that I would know if someone went riffling through it when I wasn't looking. Every time I put a thread across that bag, I'd later find it broken, which confirmed exactly what I hoped—that they were going through my stuff. They were checking me out over and over. That was a good sign. It meant they were taking me seriously and were doing their homework to make sure I was legit and could be trusted in their inner sanctum.

The downside, of course, would be if I slipped up and put something out of the ordinary in that bag that would tip them off, like a receipt I couldn't explain or a phone number or, worse, something that connected me to Ken Croke.

My lobster poaching backstory gave me some wiggle room to get out of town when I needed to, but part of my backstory also entailed that I had girlfriend back in Massachusetts. I had some pictures taken with her that were on my phone and had printed out a few of us together that I hung in the apartment in New Bedford. As far as J.R., Roadblock, Hogman, and the rest of the club knew, her name was Stephanie and she ran a cleaning business in Massachusetts. In reality, she was an ATF agent who was possibly going to join me undercover on the case.

I had many discussions with Kotchian and other ATF brass about whether I should bring another agent undercover with me. I was already in and on my way, but there was an internal dispute about whether another agent should try to join me. We had a lot of calls and meetings about it. Historically, similar long-term undercover operations involved multiple agents. Jay Dobyns, an ATF agent who infiltrated the Hells Angels, had a female agent as a partner, which ended up posing some problems in the case. Darrin Kozlowski, aka Koz, was an ATF agent who infiltrated the Mongols in California. He used several different female agents who came in and out of the case posing as his girlfriends. In other cases, there were multiple male agents undercover. There were plusses and minuses to each strategy.

The negatives of having a male partner were that it was likely the Pagans wouldn't accept him as they'd accepted me. I worked months to get inside. I couldn't just bring in a new guy. That would be suspect. They weren't stupid. There was a reason why the Pagans had never been infiltrated by law enforcement. I wasn't about to blow the chance by being overly aggressive.

On the other hand, there were a lot of benefits to bringing in a female agent. She would be another set of eyes and ears at events, and because they held women in such low regard, she wouldn't be scrutinized as much. She would be cast aside along with the other members' old ladies, and she could gather intel from them.

She could also contact the cover team much more easily. They checked my phone constantly, but they didn't check the women's phones. If I had a problem, I could let her know and she could alert the cover team. It was another important safety net. They also never grilled the women like they did me and other prospects. Most important, she could carry a gun undetected, unlike me. I was often patted down and searched. They didn't do that to women. That seemed like a net positive to me.

From a pure optics perspective, it made sense to bring in an agent as my old lady, because if I had an old lady, I would always have an excuse for texting or making calls. If I was ever asked "Who are you texting?" as I was regularly, I would always have an answer: "My old lady." It made my backstory more believable and would make my life easier.

There were other benefits to bringing in a female partner. There are hang-around women always nearby. I was constantly bombarded by other members saying some woman wanted to blow me or fuck me. I was the new guy—fresh meat to the Pagan groupies. The fact that I had an old lady gave me an excuse to avoid them. Most of the Pagans cheated on their old ladies, but it gave me a layer of protection to be able to say, "My old lady will cut my dick off if I cheat on her." They'd bust balls, but at least I had an out.

The negatives of having a female partner were many. For one, she would have limited access. She could never be at "church"—the Pagans regular secret meetings—and would never be privy to the important conversations in the clubhouse or other situations where members were plotting and scheming. If there was any criminal activity going on, the old ladies were kept far away. If she wasn't liked by members or other old ladies, that could also pose problems. Skirmishes between old ladies were common and the bikers wouldn't put up with drama. If my old lady were part of any, she'd be told to hit the bricks.

The biggest concern, though, was that the Pagans hate women and some were literally violent rapists. At the very least, a female undercover would be subjected to constant toxic masculinity, harassment, and bullying. There was a very real concern that leaving her in the wrong place with the wrong person could put her in jeopardy of being sexually assaulted. Rapes were common in the Pagan underground and bringing a female agent into that world could put her in the dangerous position of having to fend off a rapist. I hated the thought of it.

Taking all options into consideration and thinking about what would be best for the case, I was leaning toward bringing in a female partner, as long as I could find the right one who was up for the challenge. I talked to Ang about it, and she was all for me bringing in a partner. Being an agent herself, she knew the risks of working undercover alone and was concerned for my safety. We discussed the pros and cons of a male versus a female partner, and she agreed that it would be best to have a female on the case.

There weren't many women in the Boston office doing undercover, so we reached out to the Enhanced Undercover Program (EUP) in Washington to find a female agent. ATF gave me a choice of two agents who volunteered to pose as my old lady in the case. The problem was that both lived out of state—one was in Arizona and one was in Miami. I interviewed them, and they were great. Both had done biker undercover cases. But it would have been too complicated to fly them in and out of Long Island and Boston or wherever the hell I needed to be with the club. I needed my old lady to be in the Boston area so she could be with me whenever I needed her.

There was another option. There was a female agent in my group back in Massachusetts.

Stephanie Bears (not her real name) did undercover work and liked doing it. We worked some cases together in the past, including a murder-for-hire case in New Bedford where I posed as a hitman she brought in to handle a contract killing.

Steph knew I needed a female partner for the case and volunteered.

"I've always wanted to do this," she told me. "If you think I can do it, I'm happy to try."

Steph was originally from New York. She had been an agent for about ten years and mostly worked on gun and drug cases. She was very smart. She had a master's degree from a prestigious college in the Northeast. She worked hard and made a lot of good busts but had a reputation for being difficult to work with, and sometimes clashed with coworkers.

There was concern from supervisors and other agents on the case that she wouldn't be a good fit for the role, but there weren't a lot of options and she was willing to do it. My concern was whether she could handle being submissive—as Pagans old ladies had to be—because that's not in her DNA at all. She was intelligent, independent, and strong-willed. She was a federal agent whom people respected. The role required her to be demeaned and dismissed constantly. It's a role that frankly sucks. For her to succeed, she would have to bury her ego and her feelings very deep and live like a second-class citizen. She would have to accept being belittled and treated as an afterthought by a group of Neanderthals who look at women as being less than dogs.

I decided to give her a test to see if she could not only handle the pressure of a dual identity, but play the role authentically and accept being treated like dirt. I brought her to my undercover apartment in

New Bedford to meet Boston Mike. It was a good way to see how she'd act in a biker setting and would give me a sense of whether she was right for the role.

She fit right in and didn't raise any suspicions with Mike. It was enough to convince me she could do it. More important, she wanted the job. That was crucial, because it was a long-term commitment. We didn't know how long the case would go on, but we did know there would be interstate travel and a significant time commitment, at least in the short-term.

Regardless of what anyone else in ATF thought, it was my call because it was my ass out there with the Pagans. I was the one taking all the risk, and I was the one who would have to live with her as my partner.

I made the call and brought her into the case. ATF worked with her to get her backstory in order and backstop her fake identity. I felt good about the decision, but I also knew that if it didn't work out, I could just take her off the case and tell the Pagans I broke up with her. That was another benefit to having a female partner. You could dump a girlfriend without raising any eyebrows, but bros were for life in their world.

With my partner set, we had to check into what other undercover cases, if any, were under way involving the Pagans. There was another case going on in West Virginia. Law enforcement agencies in the area flipped two Pagan associates and turned them into confidential informants in the Charleston, West Virginia, chapter. They were two years into an investigation targeting Pagans in West Virginia, Virginia, Maryland, New Jersey, and Pennsylvania, as well as the Mother Club and the national president.

They were unable to get an undercover agent introduced into the club, and their charges were mostly not related to violence and guns. Relying on informants for prosecutions is always risky, and their case was no different. A few members went to jail for significant time, but most got slaps on the wrist. In a weird way their case helped my investigation, because the Pagans became more confident the cops did not know what they were doing and couldn't penetrate their wall of silence. The weak charges only emboldened them, because the sentences ranged from time served to just a few months in Club Fed. In my opinion, the only way to hurt the club was to infiltrate and build a strong case from the inside out, based on their violence and drug and gun trafficking.

We agreed we would keep the investigations separate but would share relevant information when appropriate. The truth was, the cases had nothing to do with each other. I didn't need their help and they didn't need mine. It was nonnegotiable for me to keep the cases separate. The fewer people who knew about me infiltrating the club, the better. We kept our investigation very quiet.

In addition, there was another long-term ATF investigation of the Outlaws. One of the ATF Virginia enforcement groups had three undercover agents inside the Outlaws who were also purchasing guns and drugs from Pagans in Richmond, Virginia. We had several calls with the Virginia ATF Group as well and learned that their case didn't extend beyond Virginia, so it wouldn't impact our investigation. We came to a similar agreement that we would share information, when appropriate, but would otherwise skate our lanes. The cases were not connected in any way.

With that due diligence done, I only had to worry about my own prospecting and hopefully advancing toward becoming a fully patched member.

CHAPTER 18

Hanging at the tattoo shop became a major part of my life on Long Island. I spent day after day on guard duty for J.R. and watching the clubhouse to make sure the Hells Angels didn't roll up on us. The majority of the time at the tattoo shop was stressful, but it gave me a front seat to everything that was going on in the gang. It also gave me opportunities to intervene and influence situations. Sometimes it allowed me to step in and help those who had no idea that they needed help.

There was a young kid named Joey who would hang around the tattoo shop for hours on end. He was enamored with the biker lifestyle and idolized J.R. Joey was a smart, personable kid who came from a good family, was educated, and had no business being around bikers. The Pagans treated him as a gopher and mentally and physically abused him on a regular basis.

Oftentimes when we were hungry we walked a couple of blocks to Caruso's, an Italian store and restaurant. The food was good and at least partly responsible for the wide girth of many of the chapter members.

One day J.R. was hungry and wanted to walk to Caruso's for a pinwheel. Since the chapter president is not allowed to walk down the street without protection, both Roadblock and I walked with him. Plus, who were we to pass up Italian food? Caruso's always gave us the "Pagan discount," which made for some cheap eats.

On the way out of the tattoo shop Joey asked us to bring him back a pepperoni pinwheel. J.R. agreed and off we went to Caruso's. For safety reasons we almost always brought our food back to the tattoo shop to eat, and that day was no different. On the walk back, J.R. opened the pepperoni pinwheel and set it on a bench. He undid his jeans, reached into his crotch, and with a yelp ripped out a clump of pubic hair and put it inside Joey's pinwheel. He chuckled that the pain would be worth it after watching Joey eat his pubes. He rewrapped the pinwheel, and we walked back to the tattoo shop.

J.R. handed the calzone to Joey, who immediately began scarfing it down, oblivious. Roadblock and J.R. busted out laughing as Joey chowed the pinwheel. As soon as he finished they let him in on the prank, and he immediately left the shop and went around to the back. I am guessing he puked as he was wiping his mouth when he returned to the shop.

It was typical disgusting and juvenile behavior, but to me, it was a sign of very bad things to come for Joey. I realized as I watched J.R. and Roadblock laughing that Joey was in for real trouble if he stayed around the gang. I had seen it before. If they treated you like a doormat as a hang-around, it would only get worse as a prospect, and in reality, they would never let someone they didn't respect become a full patched member.

The pinwheel incident was a way of measuring up Joey, and he failed miserably. He should have reacted far more aggressively and probably should have taken a swing at one of them if he wanted to command any level of respect. The fact that he did nothing showed them that they could do with Joey whatever they wished. And that's a very bad place to be in a gang. I knew right then and there that Joey was in for a world of hurt if he continued on his doomed quest to be a Pagan.

Joey and I developed a good relationship during his time hanging around the tattoo shop, and I always treated him well. He would ask questions about the biker lifestyle, and I would always subtly downplay it.

One day when he and I were alone in the tattoo shop, he asked if

I would sponsor him as a prospect after I became a patched member. Not only did I refuse, I told him I would do everything in my power to make sure he would never become a Pagan. I told him he was better than that, and that the gang life had no future. He looked incredulous, but on some level I think he understood and he eventually stopped coming around the shop.

Years later I heard from a Suffolk County detective named Doug Brant. Brant is the most knowledgeable biker investigator in all of Long Island. He was one of the local cops assigned to assist me and ATF on the case and personally dedicated two years of his life to helping keep me safe during the investigation. He told me Joey never became a Pagan and stayed away from the gang. He got a good job and was living a normal life on Long Island. When I reflect back on my time in the gang, I often focus on the things I was able to do to impact people's lives in a positive way. I like to think Joey was one person whose life took a turn for the better because of this case.

The tattoo shop was where we bonded, planned runs, trips, and events, and organized criminal activity. A lot of us also got tattoos. In the Pagans, tattoos aren't just body art, they are a rite of passage.

I wasn't a big tattoo guy. Ang and I had discussed maybe getting tattoos together one day, but it wasn't a big priority in my life. Saving for college and paying for youth hockey seemed better uses of my time and money in those days.

As I got deeper into Pagan culture, though, I learned more and more what tattoos meant to them. I was at the tattoo shop with J.R. almost every day. We looked at flash and talked about art, and I watched him tattoo people day in and day out. We talked a lot about ink and the whole culture. Most of the guys in the club had ink, but some didn't. It wasn't a prerequisite, but as a new guy, connecting over tattooing was a way to get closer to J.R. and build credibility in the club. He was the chapter president after all.

Sitting in the shop every day, I saw the work being done. J.R. was talented. His shading was high quality, which is a big part of a good tattoo. I talked from time to time with him and other artists about what I might want to get. A couple artists who worked in the shop drew up some pieces for me, but they all looked like crap. They were cartoonish and not anything I could live with having on my body permanently.

As luck would have it, a young, beautiful, recently graduated art major named Tiffany came into the tattoo shop looking to have J.R. mentor her as a tattoo artist. Although she was a talented artist, she needed to develop the skills required to transfer her art from paper to skin. Having her around the shop was like pouring blood into shark-infested waters. Roadblock tried sweet-talking her, and Hogman was obsessed with her. If it hadn't been so dangerous for her, it would have been comical watching them hit on her. She was a bit naïve and mostly dismissed their creepiness.

One night Tiffany and I were talking at the shop, and I mentioned that I was looking to get a tattoo but couldn't find any designs that I liked. I told her about my vision of a tattoo of a grim reaper in a graveyard. It had a lot of meaning to me, especially during the case. I figured if I put the grim reaper on my arm, in the graveyard, then I'd always know where he was. As long as I knew where the grim reaper was, I was safe. It made sense to me.

She asked if she could take a shot at designing something for me. I said sure, and a few hours later she showed me a sketch of a grim reaper in a graveyard that I really liked. As we looked at the drawing and talked, Hogman was sitting across the room staring at us with his vacant eyes. His look was one of jealousy and hatred. I'm not sure Tiffany noticed, but I sure as hell did, and I was concerned for her.

Later that night, Hogman and I were drinking beers and he was doing coke. Out of nowhere, he laid out a plan to brutally rape Tiffany. I couldn't believe my ears. He went into great detail about how he was going to do it.

"I'm gonna split that bitch in half," he said.

By that point, it was bad enough hearing the guys talk about crimes they had committed in the past, but to hear Hogman talk in such detail about a plan to brutalize an unsuspecting woman set off alarms everywhere for me. I tried talking him out of it, but there was no convincing him. I told him it would bring heat on the club and J.R.'s shop, but he said he could care less. It was like watching a dog with a bone that growled if you got too close.

I had two choices: turn a blind eye and hope he didn't do it or tell Tiffany what was coming her way and convince her to leave the tattoo shop, never to return. In my mind there was no choice, morally or legally. I wasn't sure he was going to carry it out, but I wasn't going to wait to find out. After all, he was a guy who ate blood clots and sucked on used tampons for fun.

The next day, I told Tiffany she was in grave danger and that she needed to get out. I told her not to say anything to anybody or they would kick me out. After all, brotherhood always came first—especially ahead of women. Luckily, she didn't say a word and simply disappeared. When I reflect back on the case, that was one of the most satisfying moments for me. Most agents focus on the number of arrests and seizures. I care about the results, of course, but I also liked to tally up the crimes and human suffering avoided because I pretended to be a Pagan. Helping Tiffany get away from the Pagans and escape what could have been a horrific, life-altering experience was worth it all to me.

Her gift to me was the drawing. I told J.R. to put it on my arm.

He turned it into a tattoo, and over the next few weeks, we did multiple sessions. He drew the outline and some coloring. Then we did another session for shading. Then he blew some white into it. It was a long process that involved several sittings.

I did have some misgivings going through the process, I must admit.

What the fuck am I doing? I thought to myself. *Am I doing this for the case? Or is this something I want anyway?*

When it was done, it was a half sleeve that went from my shoulder to my elbow. I loved it and still do.

"Wow, man," I told him after the final session. "How much do I owe you?"

"You're a brother," J.R. said. "I'm not charging you."

"Fuck that," I said. "This is your work."

"Tell you what," he said. "Your old lady can clean up the shop."

"Deal," I agreed.

I liked it. It gave J.R. and the other guys in the club some more comfort with me. It was another way I showed them loyalty and commitment, because there aren't a lot of undercover cops who would get a giant sleeve tattoo to sell themselves as a biker for a case.

Now I just had to figure out how to explain it to Ang.

CHAPTER 19

I was starting to earn respect as a prospect within the Long Island chapter. To become a prospect, I had to pay $500 to the club. My prospecting period was supposed to last one hundred and eighty days before I could be considered for full membership, but prospects rarely, if ever, did it in a hundred and eighty days. Most times it was longer. Members added days for rule violations or just because they felt like it. It was like boot camp for criminals, and I was in the middle of my training.

Roadblock and J.R. knew I was a great addition. While they didn't explicitly say it, it was becoming clear they wanted me to make it through prospecting. They knew I could take a beating and dole one out if needed. My toughness was never in question. Roadblock was like a drill sergeant and was hard on me, but looking back I understand it was because he wanted me to succeed.

He challenged me, but unlike some Pagans who just got off on being assholes, there was a method to his madness. He was religious about teaching me what to do and what not to do. He made sure I knew every rule and every custom. He was so strict with me, but as much of an asshole as he was, a lot of the things he drummed into my head ended up saving my ass, just not in the way he expected.

He prepared me well for my first mandatory—four days of pure hell in a rural field in the middle of nowhere in Youngstown, Ohio. Boston Bob and I packed our bags for the trip, hopped on our bikes in Boston around nine a.m., and rode together to Long Island in the pouring rain. It was a long, cold, and wet trip. We took a ferry across Long Island Sound and made the ride through the winding, tree-lined, and narrow roads that lead out to Rocky Point.

As we rode around a sharp bend about ten minutes from J.R.'s house, a Mercedes crossed the center line and just missed hitting my back tire by a couple inches. It scared the shit out of me. I accelerated to avoid the collision. I was riding a little bit in front of Bob, and he almost got clipped too.

He swerved to avoid the collision. I turned my head to look back as I wrested control of my Harley, and out of the corner of my eye, I saw Bob and his bike go flying off the road into the woods. That was always one of my biggest fears—crashing my bike on one of those treacherous hell rides. I avoided a wreck, narrowly, but Bob wasn't so lucky. He crashed hard and was hurt.

I skidded and pulled over. The Mercedes just kept driving. I hopped off my bike, ran over, and saw Bob rolling around on the ground in the woods in excruciating pain. His bike was nearby, a pile of twisted steel. He was lucky to be alive. He was screaming in pain and holding his leg—the same one he had been shot in when he was in the Outlaws.

"Hey, man, you all right?" I yelled.

"My leg," he screamed. "It's all fucked up."

I made my way through the brush to him.

"Can you stand up?" I asked.

He tried to get up, but he couldn't put any weight on his leg. I got him his cane, handed it to him, and helped him up.

I surveyed his bike—it was a mess.

"This thing ain't going anywhere," I told him.

I called Roadblock.

"Hey, man, Bob crashed," I said. "Can you come pick us up? Bring the trailer because his bike ain't moving."

Roadblock showed up with the trailer. We loaded Bob into the passenger's seat and put his bike on the trailer. It was still pouring rain as I followed them on my bike the rest of the way to J.R.'s house.

When we got to J.R.'s, we went into the garage. It was cold as hell, and I was soaking wet. My clothes and especially my boots were soaked through. Bob was in pain, but he didn't want to go to the hospital. We sat in the freezing garage for hours, waiting to leave for Ohio.

I took a ride to the local Walmart and bought some new boots. They were cheap and uncomfortable but at least they were dry. We finally left Long Island at midnight for Youngstown, Ohio, a trip that should take about eight hours by car but takes up to twelve when you're traveling in a pack of bikers stopping every two hours for fuel and food. The trip was only going from bad to worse.

We drove west in formation on Interstate 80, through Western New York and into the Pocono Mountains of Pennsylvania. The rain stopped when we got into the mountains, but it was frigid. It was one of the longest nights of my life. There were no streetlights on the winding mountain roads, and our bike headlights gave off barely enough light to see anything. The road was pitch-black at times. I blindly followed the guy in front of me, hoping he didn't wreck. I hadn't slept at all and was completely exhausted.

We had two chase vehicles behind us, one a pickup truck with a trailer loaded with grills, tents, food, beer, coolers, and other supplies for the three-day weekend. The other one carried guns, weapons, drugs, and other contraband.

The chase car was there to give members a break from riding, but not prospects. If you've ever ridden a motorcycle, it's physically exhausting in the best conditions. They're heavy, they vibrate, they're loud, and you can't take your eyes off the road for a second. In the rain, cold, and darkness, it's hell. That's why so many of the Pagans were whacked out on coke and meth half the time—so they could endure agonizingly long rides. Bob rode in one of the chase vehicles the whole trip, since his leg was a mess and he couldn't ride. That crash ended up being the best thing that could have happened to him that weekend.

As we rumbled through the mountains, my legs numb from the vibration of my Harley, my eyelids grew heavy. It was around three o'clock in the morning and I was struggling to keep my eyes open. We've all been there, driving while tired, desperately trying to keep our eyes from shutting. It took all my strength and stamina to control that nine-hundred-pound motorcycle on a freezing mountain road surrounded by Pagans.

I felt myself drifting, and soon I was having a dream. I was dreaming that I was climbing a tree and picking a leaf. I saw myself grabbing the leaf and looking at it. In the dream, I heard a loud horn. I had no idea what was going on. Suddenly, I realized the horn wasn't in my dream at all. It was the chase car, blowing its horn because I was sound asleep, drifting off the road.

I never imagined I could fall asleep on a bike. I learned, though, that it can happen pretty easily. Your balance and your speed will keep you going for a while. The horn snapped me out of my dream and saved me from what surely would have been a bad wreck. I veered onto the shoulder of the road, swerved back onto the pavement, and got back into formation.

When we stopped for gas a while later, Izzo came over to me.

"Hey, you gotta stay awake, man," Izzo said. "You wanna do a line of meth?"

"Nah, bro, I'm good. I'm going to take one of these energy drinks," I said.

I lived off Dunkin' Donuts turbo and 5-hour Energy drinks. There were times I could feel my heart racing because of all the caffeine coursing through my veins. Caffeine isn't meth, but guzzling energy drinks and coffee was the only way I could keep up.

We rode for what seemed like forever through those mountains. At one point, my legs fell asleep. I came to a stop sign and couldn't feel my legs and was afraid I wouldn't be able to move them to keep my bike from tipping over when I stopped.

I thought it would never end and felt like I was going to die out there. No matter how tired I got, it simply wasn't an option to tell them I needed a break. They wouldn't have cared and would have told me to leave and that would have been the end of my prospecting and the case. They wouldn't have lost a minute of sleep over it. That's how they weed out prospects. They drive them to the brink, literally.

I kept riding hour after hour, shaking off the lure of sleep as best as I could. The road was a blur, and the darkness was hypnotic. I felt like I wasn't going to make it, until I spotted a crack of pink on the horizon around five a.m. It was the sun starting to come up, and it was beautiful. Seeing that sunrise was a godsend, the inspiration I needed to keep going. It gave me enough energy to stay awake for the rest of the trip.

We rolled into Youngstown in the middle of the afternoon. We pulled into the property, a sprawling field in a run-down industrial area abutting railroad tracks that was home to the Youngstown chapter's clubhouse, an old red-brick commercial building.

There were already other chapters there setting up. As the day wore on, it was eventually crawling with fifteen hundred Pagans ready to party and take care of club business. Tents popped up around the field. RVs for the Mother Club rolled in.

I parked my bike and hoped I'd get to rest and chill for a while. Not a chance, though. I was immediately put to work setting up tents and grills and lugging around ice, beer, food, tables, and chairs. I helped set up a tent and a small stage for the strippers, who performed at all hours throughout the weekend. Some were prostitutes, and members took turns on them in tents.

I was completely sleep deprived and was ordered around day and night. It was one of the longest weekends of my life. It's where I learned the true hell of what biker prospects go through.

I had to be on my toes 24/7. Any Pagan member could—and did—challenge me at any moment, and if I failed their test, they could bang check me, crack me with an axe handle, or worse, add days to my prospecting period. It was nonstop stress, and I was constantly looking over my shoulder.

There were all kinds of crazy rituals and rules. I had to have pockets sewn into my jacket and was required to carry all sorts of random items—toothpicks, aspirin, lightbulbs, lighters, spark plugs, tampons, cigarettes. If a club member asked me for an item and I didn't have it, I paid a price. If they asked for a spark plug for their bike, I better have one.

I was regularly asked how many days I had under my belt as a prospect. Now, remember, there was no schedule here, so days blended together. I'd go weeks not knowing what day it was, but I had to know that prospecting number right off the top of my head. I was required to carry a book around that had my prospect days marked off so members could verify my time. If I got it wrong, days were added to my time.

There were constant mind games, all designed to cause stress and test my loyalty to the club. One time they gave a live cricket to a prospect and told him to keep it in his pocket.

"Next time I see you, this cricket better be alive," he was told.

Try keeping a cricket alive in your pocket for days at a time. It wasn't easy, but he managed to do it. I always wondered if he would have been smart enough to find another cricket if that one died and claim it was the same cricket. It wasn't like they had DNA results to confirm the identity.

Although some of the hazing was minor and stupid, much of it was deadly serious and dangerous. Witching hours were wild hazing sessions that took place in the middle of the night, unannounced, at events and mandatories. They entailed prospects being bossed around, challenged, questioned, and ordered to take on laborious tasks. Sleep deprivation was a favorite tactic. Sometimes prospects were dragged out of their tents and had the shit kicked out of them. I heard guys screaming while being beaten and hoped I wasn't next. It is hard to describe the anxiety of lying in a tent listening to bikers cheering on the beating of a prospect, all the while knowing that your turn might be coming. All of it took place in a remote field that was home to a sea of bikers raging on booze and drugs. It was sheer lawlessness, and it was shocking they didn't kill more prospects.

They were outlaws in every sense of the word. That first Ohio mandatory was sheer hell. I lost eight pounds, and my feet were bleeding profusely from constant walking in boots that did not fit right. At one point, I pulled off my boot to look at my foot and saw my sock was soaked in blood. I put the boot back on, thinking that if I kept it off, the swelling would worsen and I would not be able to get the boot back on. They didn't allow us to wear sneakers, so losing the boots to give my feet a rest was off the table. Going barefoot was also not an option. I thought about trying to explain to a bunch of outlaw motorcycle gang members that I was walking around barefoot because my feet hurt. I'm pretty sure they would have made my feet hurt a whole lot worse. So the boots stayed.

One of the only breaks from the torment I got was when we went on a run. The entire club, including prospects, fired up their bikes and rode in formation around the town in a raucous show of force. It was a brazen way to leave no doubt for neighbors, cops, and rival clubs that we were in town. It was a stunning and imposing display—a parade of filthy bikers riding through Youngstown, the thunder of revving engines and eardrum-rattling mufflers filling the air.

The only good that came of that weekend: I did learn how to grill. They may have been horrible humans, but, man, they were barbecue experts. I sweated my ass off day after day working the grill and God forbid I screwed it up. I was a good student, and to this day, I can grill with the best of them, so I guess I have the Pagans to thank for that. Many times in recent years Ang has said that the best thing that came out of the case was my grilling skills.

That weekend at the Ohio mandatory, I was put in a tough position when Roadblock handed me a stack of Pagan propaganda pamphlets with the most racist imagery and messages I'd ever seen in my life. I won't go into the disturbing details, but suffice to say, it was right out of the KKK playbook. It was some really vile shit.

Many of the Pagans were white supremacists, but the ones who were the worst were the ones who had served time. The Pagans and Hells Angels hated each other on the streets, but in prison, they all joined the Aryan Nation to survive. A lot of them had Nazi and SS tattoos or iron cross tattoos, which didn't go over well in prison unless you had the protection of the Aryan Nation. Once behind the walls, many of them became further indoctrinated into the white power movement and proselytized to other members when they were back on the streets.

In May 2009, a Pagan named James "Jimbo" Kelly wrote a letter from the Suffolk County Correctional Facility to J.R. that I read. It sounded like a KKK recruitment flyer.

The white supremacist logos many members wore on their colors were subtle, but I soon realized white supremacy was a big part of Pagan culture. They weren't burning crosses, but the racism many spewed was persistent, blatant ,and strong. Many talked openly about the white race being superior. Blacks were the problem with America, not the Pagans or their guns, crystal meth, and racketeering. The problem to them wasn't bikers, it was gangsters in Chicago. America's problem wasn't Hells Angels battling Pagans. It was Crips and Bloods, Black gangs taking over urban neighborhoods, selling dope and shooting cops. They believed their own racist bullshit and doubled down every chance they got.

They would deal with the Mongols, which included a lot of Latinos, and the Barbarians, which had many Black members, but only for what suited them—drug or gun connections. They didn't look upon them as equals and often made that known in the most racist language imaginable.

If we went into a Pagan bar, there were rarely people of color there. If there were, they didn't stay long, because there was usually trouble immediately and the Pagans removed them, often by force. I heard many disgusting conversations in which guys disparaged old ladies who had previously slept with Black or Latino men.

The racism was especially overt at mandatories. Those events were like biker flea markets, and with no outsiders, they were free to flex their white power muscles at will. Chapters sold T-shirts, stickers, and jewelry, and traded or sold patches, including some with racist and Nazi slogans. One day, an older Pagan covered in prison tats gave me some white power patches to put on my colors. One was a Nazi flag and the other a Nazi SS patch. He acted like he was letting me into an even more secret club and doing me a favor. I played along and just said, "Thanks, brother," and put them in my pocket. As much as I needed to fit in, I never put them on my colors. I put them away in a drawer, and no one ever asked about them.

When I first started hanging around the Pagans and started hearing that stuff, it was obviously shocking and uncomfortable. I wasn't raised that way, and it wasn't part of my life. But as time went on, I don't want to say I became desensitized, but I learned to detach and ignore it. I had no choice. There was an adjustment period of getting used to their racist ways, of course, and as I immersed myself in the club, I tried to steer clear of it whenever possible.

As for the pamphlets that weekend, I didn't hand them out, but I did keep them in case we ever had hate crimes we needed to prove.

Racism was a constant undercurrent, and it was exhausting. People often ask me if I got friendly with any of the Pagans, and of course there were some members who were less despicable than others, and some who were tolerable. But witnessing their flagrant racism over and over served as a reminder of why I was there: to make cases to put them in prison.

They made it easy for me.

CHAPTER 20

At the end of the weekend, we hopped on our bikes and started the long exodus east toward New York. I was exhausted from no sleep and was once again struggling to keep my Harley straight. My eyes grew heavy, and the highway lines blurred. At least on the ride back, it didn't rain.

We stopped to fuel up at a gas station. I called Steph and told her to get a message to the cover team to let them know where we were headed. The plan was for me to ride east with all the chapters until we got into New York. I told them I had to go poach lobsters in Massachusetts to make some money. They were supposed to head toward Long Island, and I was going to head back home. The truth was, I just needed to get away from them for a couple days after the hell I went through in Ohio. Steph told me the cover team had already gone ahead without me and would meet me in Connecticut after I left the Pagans in New York.

While I was on the phone with Steph, Roadblock walked up to me and got right in my face. He had never done that before, so I knew something was seriously wrong. I switched into my biker persona and pretended I was talking to my old lady.

"Yeah, I'll call you later. Yeah me too," I said, and hung up.

Roadblock stared me down, inches from my face.

"There's a change of plans," he said gruffly. "You're coming back to Long Island."

"What's up?" I asked.

"Don't fucking worry about it. You'll find out when we get to Long Island," he said, and walked away.

As the conversation unfolded, a group of fifteen Pagans were glaring at us. I had a bad feeling. Everyone fired up their bikes, and we hit the road again and trekked for two hours. We stopped every two hours to fuel up. That happened about five times. Each time we stopped for gas, none of the other Pagans talked to me. I was ignored. They stared at me like I was a mortal enemy. When I walked over, they stopped their conversation and ordered me away.

"Prospect, go away," one said. "Go guard the bikes."

My bad feeling got worse. At our next fuel stop, I pulled out the phone and called Steph back.

"I just got ordered back to Long Island," I told her.

We were both concerned my cover had been blown and I was walking into a trap.

"Get out of there. Just leave," she told me.

"Nah, this is gut check time. I gotta stay," I replied.

We rode on again for another two hours. I rode in the middle of the pack but felt totally alone, without a friend, and my cover team was miles away. At the next stop, just after dusk, one of the Mother Club members called me over. A group of approximately twenty-five Pagans were standing in a clearing near the woods in the darkness, out of sight from the public. I walked toward them and was encircled by Pagans. I could sense the tension.

Fear washed over me. I was sure they'd found out I was an agent. I scanned their scowling faces, wondering which of them might throw the first blow. My body tensed up, preparing for battle, as I looked around for an escape route.

"Hey, there's a fucking problem," one of them said.

My heart raced. I was in the fight alone. My backup was more than a hundred miles away, and I couldn't even shoot my way out of this situation. One of them drew near and stood just inches from my face.

I waited to feel violence, but it didn't come. His demeanor shifted from anger to almost contrition.

"We have bad news. You're out," he said.

I was shocked, but felt a wave of relief. I thought I was facing a life-or-death fight. My cover hadn't been blown, because if it had, they would have told me they knew I was a cop right then. I was confident I wasn't going to be killed, but I needed to figure out what happened and why I was being tossed out.

After the initial shock wore off, I got mad. Pissed in fact. I had just had the worst weekend of my life. I did everything necessary to fit into their sadistic culture. I saw strippers getting gang-banged. I listened to the screams of midnight beatings. I saw drugs consumed like candy. There were guns galore. I took mental notes the whole time to build the case. Ken Croke, the ATF agent, had a notebook full of violations. In that sense, it was a productive weekend.

But Ken Pallis, the Pagan prospect, was sleep deprived, starved, and exhausted from being treated like a dog. I'd complied with their fucked-up rituals and rules. I was tired from being ordered around and made to do chores and errands for the gang. I endured a weekend of indentured servitude for a bunch of coked-out, drunken bikers who kept me and my fellow prospects on edge for days, to test our loyalty and commitment, and sometimes just for their own sick kicks. My blood boiled that after all that I was being kicked out.

I reminded them that they recruited me.

"You guys can go fuck yourselves. I don't give a fuck," I said. "I did what you wanted. I didn't beg to be here. You guys came after me."

I looked at J.R., the chapter president.

"You're not going to vouch for me, J.R.?" I asked.

My question was met with silence. It turned out, the night before there was a dustup among the club's leadership, and the national vice president, Jesse, was removed. Not only was Jesse removed, he was savagely beaten with axe handles. Jesse was trying to stage a coup to take over as national president, but his plan was exposed and fell apart there in Ohio. His planned coup ended in his own blood being shed.

I was collateral damage, because Jesse, a friend of J.R.'s, was the one who vouched to the Mother Club for me and Boston Bob. Once Jesse was out, anyone he vouched for was considered compromised and was also out—including me.

"Fuck you guys," I said, and jumped on my bike. "Fuck all of this."

I sped off, ramping my bike up to over one hundred miles per hour. A few members chased me, but I wanted nothing to do with them—case or no case. I hit the gas. I needed a break. I had to think. I had to sleep.

I turned onto I-95 North and headed back toward Boston. They stopped pursuing me after a few miles.

The cover team was miles ahead of me. I called my supervisor and told them I was done and was heading home. I met the cover team in Connecticut and got into their vehicle. We put my bike in a trailer and I collapsed in the back seat.

"I'm done. We've got some charges. I'm out," I said. "Take me home."

Mentally and physically exhausted, I didn't say another word. I fell asleep all the way back to Boston.

Meanwhile, my phone was blowing up with texts and calls from the Long Island chapter. J.R. and Roadblock kept calling. Hogman texted and called. They wanted to find a way to fix the problem and bring me back to Rocky Point.

My supervisor, Andy, called and urged me to stick it out.

"I'm done with this," I told him.

I had been away from home most of the past several months. I missed my girls. I hadn't slept in days. I had been living with animals in filth, surrounded by drugs, booze, strippers, debauchery, and violence. I needed time to decompress and figure out my next move.

"Can we meet on Tuesday?" Andy asked. "We'll do a debrief."

"Fine, whatever," I said, and fell back asleep.

I went home and saw my family for a couple days. It felt good to be there with my girls, have a hot shower, put on some clean clothes, and not be surrounded by criminals and depravity. Ang and I talked about the investigation and weighed the risks. Besides missing her husband, she was concerned for my safety. Going back amid the Pagans' escalating tensions with the Hells Angels put me at risk. I was a pawn in their deadly game, and it was only a matter of time before it turned violent. We both knew it.

Ang was not only my wife, the mother of my kids, and a fellow agent; she was an experienced and damn good undercover cop. We shifted out of family mode and into coworker mode and went through all the scenarios. I could walk away, I could go back and try to get back in as a prospect, or I could go back in to gather more intel and close out the case. The safest move was to walk away, but I wasn't ready and Ang could tell.

I rested for a few days and tried to feel normal. Ang and I decided I should talk to Andy, so I met him at the ATF office in Boston.

"I'm not saying you have to stay in. But if you could just maintain contact, it would help. Let's see where it goes," Andy told me.

"Andy, I have no interest in doing this anymore," I said. "I'm exhausted."

He understood but was persistent.

"Just get back to them and let's see what they want to do," he said.

His persistence worked. He convinced me to respond to some texts to keep the door open. I did, and sure enough, Roadblock and J.R. asked me to come back to Long Island to work it out. They told me they wanted me there. I knew they needed me and were going to do everything they could to get me back in as a prospect. That's what I was afraid of, to be honest.

"We're going to make this right. We're going to get you back in," J.R. told me.

Part of me was happy and part of me was sick to my stomach.

CHAPTER 21

've said before that dumb luck played a huge part in this case and my survival, but of all the lucky breaks, getting kicked out may have been the biggest—quite possibly saving my life.

After J.R. and Roadblock kicked me out and took away my prospecting patch, they and the rest of the Long Island chapter headed back to Rocky Point and resumed business. On August 25, 2009, there was a summer concert in Rocky Point. The Hells Angels decided to crash it. That night, J.R.'s phone rang.

"Hey, man, the maggots are rolling into town tonight. Be on the lookout," one of J.R.'s local sources told him, referring to the Angels by their Pagan-given pejorative nickname.

"Okay. I'm calling Elizabeth, Bergen, Trenton, Asbury Park, and some of the other Jersey chapters for backup," J.R. said into the phone.

The backup did not arrive in time. Roadblock was on guard duty alone outside the clubhouse. It should have been me on watch that night, but because I had been kicked out, the job fell to Roadblock. Instead of being on patrol, I was back home resting in Massachusetts.

Roadblock was an imposing figure as he stood out front, his beefy frame stalking back and forth, sending a message to those who passed not to mess around. J.R. and two artists were inside the shop, where a sawed-off shotgun was kept in the back room.

As he stood on the sidewalk, Roadblock heard the thunder of bike engines coming closer. A pair of Hells Angels appeared out of the darkness and rode by the clubhouse, stopping down the street. Then two more. Then two more. And then some more. Members of the Angels' support clubs the Mortal Skulls and Demon Knights joined. Soon, there were twenty-five hostile Pagan enemies gathered in the street and on the sidewalk, creeping closer to Roadblock.

J.R. popped his head out the door and saw what was happening. The whole front of the building was glass windows, so he and the two artists could see the crowd of Angels growing out front. None of them came out. Not even J.R. with his shotgun.

Roadblock stood his ground as he was surrounded by Angels, each with a death stare in his eyes. Roadblock kept his hand near the 9mm handgun he had tucked into his waistband. He stood firm, his back to the shop. At one point, a couple of clueless concertgoers headed to the show walked right through the middle of the emerging confrontation. You would have thought they'd notice all the Hells Angels colors and perhaps crossed the street. They're lucky no one started swinging while they were strolling through, oblivious to the violence about to unfold.

Roadblock nervously stayed on his post as the mob of blood-thirsty Angels circled him, about to make him their victim. He surveyed the situation.

The Angels moved in. One of them, a monster of a man towering over Roadblock, came around his backside. Roadblock shifted his girth and spun his head around to look at the guy. Just as he turned, the president of the Hells Angels Long Island chapter, Mario, stepped up right in front of him and threw a haymaker, landing a crushing blow on Roadblock's jaw that buckled his tree-trunk legs and sent him crashing to the ground with a thud.

It was a frenzy. The Angels pounced on him, rat-pack style. They swung ball peen hammers—the Angels' weapon of choice—and rained ugly blows down upon Roadblock's bald head. They stomped his face, chest, and legs. They openly wound up and booted him as hard as they could in the ribs and head. They pulled the 9mm from his waistband, but for some reason decided not to finish him off. The

Angels retreated and scattered, leaving Roadblock bleeding and unconscious on the sidewalk.

A surveillance camera mounted to a utility pole across the street by local police recorded the whole episode. Police and EMTs showed up. The Angels all escaped, and none were arrested.

Watching the tape, you'd think he was dead. He was taken to the local hospital and flown by helicopter to a larger trauma center where he stayed for several days recovering from a slew of injuries, including broken ribs and a fractured skull.

The Pagans were at war with the Angels. It made my decision to go back even more difficult. They didn't give a flying fuck about me. I was just a soldier in their army. I could handle myself and take a beating, they knew. They needed expendable guys like me to step in when violent clashes erupted. I was torn.

That night, I got a text from J.R.

Roadblock got the shit kicked out of him by the maggots, he texted.

I tried calling him back, but he didn't answer. He called me the next day.

"Hey, man," he said. "Can you get down here? Roadblock got fucked up by the Angels last night. We need you, bro."

"Okay, man," I said. "You need me, I'll be down there."

Roadblock texted me pictures of him after the beating. He was a mess. You could actually see the imprint of a boot on his bald head.

"You heard what happened . . . These motherfuckers," he told me. "Not everyone down here is stand-up. I need you to come down, bro."

I decided to give the case another shot. I packed my bag and rode back to Long Island. I wasn't sure if it would get me in again as a prospect, but I knew it would get me respect and a chance to stay in the game.

I called the ATF supervisor and briefed him on what had happened. The information made it all the way up to Andy Anderson, and he and the other higher-ups in the Boston office agreed it was an opportunity to keep the case going. The New York office had concerns about safety because of the Roadblock beating, but they deferred to the Boston Field Division, since it was our case.

ATF brass in Washington, D.C., was getting concerned as well about the level of violence coming out of the case. They already didn't like it because of the murder of Bennett and were concerned, rightfully, that a Pagan in the club I was in was nearly stomped to death by Hells Angels. Headquarters also found out I was the one who was supposed to have been on duty at the tattoo shop that night, which didn't help. Some in the D.C. brass called on Andy Anderson to shut the case down.

Their argument was that it wasn't worth the risk, because I already had enough to bring a lot of charges. But Andy and I knew we needed much more to make this a RICO case and disrupt the Pagans' East Coast operations, so we pushed back. If we'd shut the case down at that point, we would have had some small-time gun and drug cases, but we were far short of the avalanche of video, audio, and other documentation we needed to meet the RICO standard. The door had been reopened, though, and we had another bite at the apple. Andy and I knew we had a chance to go all in and build a case that could truly have an impact. Andy stood his ground and, over the objections of headquarters, gave me approval to go back in.

I knew the Long Island chapter needed me, and I knew they would look to avenge Roadblock. I also knew the Hells Angels weren't going to stop.

"Look, the cover team can't be there for you all the time," he said. "They're miles away most of the time. You saw what just happened to Roadblock. If that happens to you, these guys won't make it there to save your ass."

I hopped on my bike and headed back down. Boston Bob got the call to come back too, but he didn't go. I think he didn't want to get shot again, but I also think he was tired of the biker lifestyle and didn't want to move to Long Island.

I stayed in contact with Bob and kept tabs on him for the purposes of the case, but I never saw him again.

CHAPTER 22

I rode my Harley back into Rocky Point and headed to Roadblock's house. He and his old lady had just moved from a small, two-bedroom house into a converted garage owned by one of his friends from the volunteer fire department. You entered through a side door and into a big open room with a kitchen, a bed in the corner, and a small bathroom.

Roadblock was laid up on the couch. His face was all swollen and covered in cuts and bruises. He was in rough shape. There was a shotgun in the corner of the room, next to the bed. I walked over to the couch.

"Hey, bro," I said. "How you doing?"

"I'm pissed," he answered. "Why didn't J.R. come out? Why was he cowering in the clubhouse while I was getting my ass kicked in the street? Why wasn't he in the hospital bed right next to me?"

He and J.R. were very tight. I never heard either one of them say a negative word about the other. The beating changed their relationship and drove a wedge between them that would only grow.

"I get that I'm sergeant-at-arms, but whoever is there at the clubhouse needs to jump in," he continued. "They didn't come there to beat me. They came to get him. He's the fucking president."

I didn't know what to say. We sat in silence for a few moments. He was groggy from pain medication and was hurting. I tried to play Switzerland. If I sided with Roadblock, and J.R. found out, my chances of getting back into the club were nil. If I sided with J.R.,

Roadblock, who was my original sponsor, would make my life a living hell if I did get back into the club. I tried to act like I cared without taking a side.

"Listen, now that you're back," he said, "you need to watch your back when you're out there on guard duty at the clubhouse."

We both knew the beating he took would escalate the fight with the Hells Angels. We knew they'd be back again. We also knew the Pagans had to retaliate. It was just a matter of time.

I said goodbye and rode my Harley over to the clubhouse. After the attack on Roadblock, the clubhouse was under even heavier security, and J.R. started closing up early. Normally, he'd stay there until one or two a.m., banging chicks, drinking, or giving late-night tattoos to drunks. The beating changed that. J.R. was scared shitless.

When I got there, he was getting ready to close up and told me to meet him at his house. I rode to J.R.'s place and met up with the rest of the gang: Pita, Izzo, Tracy, and Hogman were all there. They welcomed me back and said they appreciated that I came right down. I was still pissed I was removed as a prospect but they knew they needed me now more than ever, so I had some leverage.

J. R. arrived and we were sitting around his house when all of a sudden Roadblock appeared in the doorway. None of us expected to see him because he was supposed to be at home recovering. I noticed he was wearing sneakers. I had never seen him in sneakers before. One time I was wearing sneakers and he laid into me.

"You don't wear sneakers. You wear fucking boots," he told me. "That's what bikers wear."

He was wearing sneakers, though, because he was a mess and they were more comfortable. Seeing him hurting and in such rough condition got the gang all fired up. They wanted revenge.

"Those motherfuckers," Izzo said.

I had my recorder on me and hoped it was recording. I knew they were about to get into some serious club business. Roadblock came in, and they went over to the kitchen table and sat down. I sat in a chair nearby, expecting them to tell me to go outside.

Normally, a prospect wouldn't be allowed to sit in on that type of conversation, never mind a hang-around, which is what I was at that point. They never told me to leave, though. What happened next laid the foundation for the whole case.

Over the next two hours, they talked in explicit detail about a plot to exact retribution against the Hells Angels for the brutal beatdown of Roadblock. They were going to bomb them.

"If we can find a spot where they're together . . . . fuckin' grenade right in the fuckin' chest," Tracy said.

They considered a plan to wait for them on a highway overpass and drop a homemade explosive packed with steel ball bearings into the middle of their pack as they rode in formation.

"Drop it right down in the middle of the pack and take twenty, thirty dudes out," J.R. said.

Izzo raised concern that innocent civilians could get caught in the carnage.

"If there's a car next to them or anything, it's going through the car. They're fucking hardened steel bearings," he said.

"Hardened steel bearings encased in fucking steel makes for a bad explosion," J.R. added, detailing the explosive. "That's what you know I use."

They called bombs "Christmas presents" and talked about delivering them to Angels chapter president Mario, the one who threw the first punch taking down Roadblock, and his brother, who was sergeant-at-arms for one of the Hells Angels support clubs.

"If you're gonna fuckin' hit Mario, you gotta hit his brother too," Roadblock said. "If you hit one, you gotta hit the other, both of them gotta go. You can't leave a brother to avenge the other one . . . you hit two of those fuckin' mopes."

"That's our best bet, to do a little bit of homework, find out where two of them live," Tracy chimed in.

I couldn't believe my ears. All at once, they'd let their guard down and now I was inside their inner circle.

Tracy said they should strap a bomb to Mario's head.

"That would be perfect, be perfect," he said. "I'm telling you, fuckin' duct tape it to his fuckin' head. Yeah, hold still, motherfucker, I'm going to fit you for a hat."

They talked about blowing up Mario's family's gas station near Islip, Long Island.

"Problem is you got cameras and shit over there," Roadblock said.

"That's the key, not coming in the way everybody else comes in," Tracy said. "We should park on a back street and run through the yards . . . and do what we gotta do and get out and run through the yards again. No streets, no parking lots, no nothing. Fuckin' lob it into his fuckin' shit from the trees."

I sat in stunned silence, praying that my recorder was on. We finished up the meeting and went our separate ways. I rode my bike back to the shitty motel where I was staying. I met the cover team and turned over my recorder to see what I had.

It was on the whole time. I had them on tape for two hours talking about possessing bombs and using them in attacks on the Hells Angels. The recording was chilling, and it was the cornerstone of our case.

I wasn't back in the gang yet, but I was heading that way, and now I had hard evidence to start building a racketeering case against the Pagans. I called Kotchian and let him know we were onto something big.

CHAPTER 23

There are a lot of rules to being in a gang, but perhaps none is more important than getting a gun.

It was time for Ken Pallis to get one. Ken Croke had his service weapon, but Ken Pallis didn't carry. That became a problem for Roadblock.

"Hey, man, do you have a piece?" he asked me one day.

I had thought about what to do if I was asked this question, so I was ready for it.

"Nah, Massachusetts, man. It's a pain in the ass. I borrow them when I need them," I lied.

"All right," he said, expressionless.

He said nothing more about it. In typical Roadblock fashion, he kept me guessing.

ATF has a pretty firm rule that undercover agents cannot carry illegal firearms. I'd need a loophole.

I brushed off the conversation with Roadblock, but then a couple days later, J.R. came up to me at the clubhouse.

"Hey, my boy's got something for you if you need it," he said.

"What's that?" I asked.

"A piece," he said.

He and Roadblock had apparently discussed my not having a gun. It may have been another test, but more likely, they wanted me to have one so that I would be armed when I was on guard duty. The more guns the better was their motto, especially given the war brewing with the Angels.

"Okay, yeah, I need one, with everything going on down here," I said.

A few nights later, I was on watch outside the shop when J.R.'s nephew, Justin, stopped by. J.R. came outside to talk to me.

"Hey, jump in the car with Justin. He's got that piece for you," he said. "You guys figure it out, do what you have to do."

I hopped in Justin's car, and we drove a few blocks away and pulled behind a building. He pulled out a .22 semi-automatic handgun. He worked the action on it and showed me the magazines. The whole time I was just watching and worrying that it would go off and I'd be accidentally shot.

"That's cool. That works," I said, and paid him $200.

That sale gave me a gun trafficking case on J.R. and his nephew and a conspiracy charge on Roadblock.

Justin drove me back to the shop and dropped me off. I went inside, and J.R. came over.

"You all set?" he asked.

"Yeah," I replied.

I started to say something more about the gun, but he cut me off.

"Yeah, that's good. I don't need to know anything more," he said.

They wanted me carrying on guard duty. The problem was, even with my Tier 1 and Tier 2 approvals, I was prohibited from carrying an illegal firearm. The .22 was operational but it wasn't a quality gun. ATF only lets agents carry their service weapons, which wasn't an option, or guns certified through ATF's Firearms Technology Branch, which that piece of junk definitely was not.

Normally, when a gun is purchased undercover, it is put directly into evidence. The tech folks run it through ballistics to see if it was used in any crimes, swab it for fingerprints and DNA, and trace the serial number.

A supervisor in Boston said I had to turn the weapon in to ATF.

"Tell them you sold it," he told me.

Some of my colleagues had no clue what my life was like out there. If I turned the gun in and told Roadblock and J.R. that I sold a gun they had arranged for me to buy, I might as well just show them my ATF ID. It would have been way too suspicious.

Kotchian had a conversation with an assistant U.S. attorney in Mike Sullivan's office. We needed them to find a way to let me carry that gun while I worked the case. If we were to prosecute J.R., his nephew, and Roadblock for the gun, we'd need to document everything. A good lawyer would raise doubt in a trial as to where the gun came from, what I did with it while it was in my possession, and whether it was even the gun that they sold me.

I explained to the prosecutor the importance that keeping this gun in my possession had to the bigger picture of the case. If I was to stay in the inner circle, become a prospect again, and perhaps get patched in to the Pagans, I simply had to be permitted to carry the .22 they sold me.

Sullivan's office recognized the importance of the gun to the case and signed off to let me keep it. But first we had to take time-stamped photos of it and send it to Washington to have it tested, modified for safety, and documented. We had to wait to send it Washington, though, because it would have also looked suspicious to Roadblock and J.R. if I disappeared from town right after they sold me a gun.

After several days, I said I had to go back to Boston for work for a couple days. I left town and got the weapon to George Karelas on the cover team, and it was sent overnight to the Firearms Technology Branch in Washington, D.C. In addition to running ballistics on it, they did some modifications so it would meet bureau regulations, or at least come as close to them as possible.

When I got it back, at least it worked properly. It was important to have that piece on me, because Roadblock, J.R., and others asked me about it regularly and wanted me to carry it. There was no way I could say I didn't have it.

A few days later, I was told to pack up my stuff—including the gun—because we were headed to a mandatory in Wildwood, New

Jersey. I called Steph and told her to get packed, because I'd need my old lady for this trip. I also told my cover team to get ready for a long weekend.

A beachfront town with a legendary boardwalk on the Jersey Shore, Wildwood was biker nirvana. It has always been a popular place with outlaw motorcycle gangs, and since 1996 it's been home to the annual Roar to the Shore biker rally. The event caused mayhem in the small seaside town, which has a year-round population of just five thousand people. In the summer, it's a popular tourist spot, and when the bikers come to town, it morphs into a carnival of debauchery.

The Pagans had an entire motel rented out and a thirst for revenge against the Hells Angels. After the ordeal I went through in Ohio, I was laser focused on getting my own brand of revenge.

CHAPTER 24

I hopped on my bike alongside Hogman, J.R., Izzo, Tracy, and a few other members and started the 235-mile ride from Rocky Point to Wildwood. Roadblock was banged up, so he rode in the chase car with the guns, drugs, and assorted contraband.

We were headed to the infamous Roar to the Shore, a legendary Pagan event that annually drew more than five thousand bikers for a weekend of drunken chaos. It's a mandatory, so all thirteen-hundred-plus Pagans and prospects were required to attend. I was no longer a prospect but had to go if I was to have a chance at getting back in. I figured in the worst-case scenario, I'd get more charges and keep building the case. Best case, I'd be back on my way to being a prospect.

Normally the ride from Rocky Point to Wildwood took about five hours. We made a lot of stops—more than on a normal ride—and the riding was especially slow because of driving rain. Bikes don't handle well in the rain, and hydroplaning is a big concern. In a car, you may crash if you hydroplane, but you're at least protected inside the vehicle. On a bike, if you hydroplane, there's a good chance of getting killed.

It was a chilly September night, and there was a monsoon. We rode in torrential rains. I was wearing my Vance leather biker jacket and jeans—not my colors, since I was no longer a prospect. The jacket was made of heavy leather designed to protect riders from the elements, but more important, it limited nasty road rash in a fall or a slide on the pavement. It repelled water a bit, but was worthless in that kind of downpour. I was soaked from head to toe.

It was dark as hell, and my riding glasses were being pelted with water, making visibility almost zero. I remember riding down a narrow two-lane highway behind J.R. and I couldn't see a thing except for his taillight. I focused on his light and followed him blindly, just a few feet off his back tire. If he had stomped the brakes, there would have been a horrible wreck. If he'd run off the road or driven off a cliff into the ocean, I would have been right behind him, plunging into the darkness.

Neither of those things happened, luckily. I white-knuckled it the whole way down to Wildwood, hanging on for dear life with every turn. The ride took us nearly eight agonizing hours.

We pulled into the parking lot of the Binns Motor Inn, a run-down old motel that the Pagans took over for the weekend. They rented out every room and turned the motel into a fortress of degeneracy and vice. The front of the gray stucco building was draped with a massive banner of the Pagans logo, sending a loud and clear message to everyone who was in charge. The horseshoe-shaped motel had a pool in the middle and was abutted at the open end by another cheap motel, making it virtually impossible for anyone to come in or out of the compound except patched members.

Armed Pagans stood watch on the roof, patrolling like soldiers. Old ladies and prostitutes came and went. Lines of chromed-out bikes were parked out front, and the sound of roaring Harleys filled the air. When the Pagans went on a run around Wildwood that weekend, there were hundreds, if not a thousand or more bikers. It was an awesome yet unsettling show of force, and the sound was deafening.

Only patched members could stay at the Binns, so I checked into a low-budget motel a few blocks away. I was exhausted, cold, and soaking wet. I parked my bike, wiped it down, and unloaded my bag of clothes from the side compartments, both of which were filled with water. I had wrapped my bags in plastic, so thankfully everything was dry. I went into my room, peeled off my leathers and jeans, and changed into dry clothes. The motel was a rat's nest, but it was still better than sleeping on the ground in a tent, like I did in Ohio.

I flopped onto the bed, but there was no rest for the weary. I got a text and was summoned to the Binns by J.R. and Roadblock, who were already politicking with other chapter presidents on my behalf. They were on a mission to get me back in and needed support from other chapter presidents if they were to convince White Bear and the rest of the Mother Club to let me rejoin as a prospect.

Biker rallies like Roar to the Shore draw civilians, wannabe bikers, biker enthusiasts, and others who love the culture, and are generally affiliated with only one outlaw motorcycle gang. Sturgis, in South Dakota, for example, is a Hells Angels event. The Roar to the Shore was a Pagan event. That meant that any biker club there needed to be one-percenter club on friendly terms with the Pagans, like the Mongols, or a support club sanctioned by the Pagans, like the Tribe or the Bandanas. It also meant that if the Hells Angels or another rival club showed up, there would be a bloodbath.

There was another rule: no biker could wear a three-piece patch on his cut unless he was in a Pagan-approved club. The three-piece patch includes three pieces on the back of an outlaw motorcycle gang member's colors: a banner on the top, a logo in the middle, and a rocker or insignia on the bottom. For the Pagans, the three pieces are the word "Pagans" at the top, the Surtr logo in the middle, and the letters "M.C." for "motorcycle club" at the bottom. Anyone wearing a three-piece patch better be sanctioned by the Pagans at Roar To The Shore.

Members of Pagan-approved support clubs also had to wear a Pagan-issued patch with the number sixteen—representing the letter "P," which is the sixteenth letter of the alphabet—or a Pagan "P" patch. They were on the lookout all weekend for any outlaw motorcycle gang member violating the rules. It's a funny thing with real outlaw bikers: they spot patches and know what they mean from a mile away. They were always looking at other bikers' colors and patches, the same way cops, firefighters, and soldiers take note of uniforms, stripes, pins, and medals.

Checking patches on bikers became second nature to me. Part of it was habit, but it was also a survival skill. Checking colors made sure I didn't miss a rival coming. To this day, I find myself checking out patches and colors whenever I see bikers.

One day, we were hanging out in front of the Binns when a guy blew past the motel wearing a three-piece patch but no Pagan support badge. He stuck out like a sore thumb and a group of a dozen or so Pagans, led by Pita, hopped on their bikes and chased the guy.

They pursued him for a few blocks, cut him off, and forced him into a parking lot. They surrounded him, jumped him, gave him a good beating, and stripped off his colors. I watched in horror, hoping the guy wouldn't fight back and I wouldn't have to intervene. Fortunately, he took his beating, and the guys let him go with some cuts and bruises.

In a situation like that, I had to walk a fine line between maintaining my cover and making sure no one was seriously injured or killed. If one of them went up and started stomping his head, I would have had to jump in before he was killed. In this incident, they were fairly merciful and no one was seriously hurt.

They had burning trash barrels outside the Binns, which gave the scene an apocalyptic feel. They left the guy laying on the ground, rode back to the hotel, and tossed his colors into one of the flaming barrels, eliciting wild cheers.

That sort of thing happened all weekend. It was chaos. I had to play it extra cool. I wasn't a patched member, nor was I even a prospect, so members who didn't know who I was could have turned on me in a second. When they went on benders like that for days on end, many got all strung out and some simply went crazy. Many just looked for someone to fuck up. All it took was a wrong look. If any Pagans had a problem with me, none of them—not Roadblock, J.R., Hogman, or anyone else—would have defended me. The brotherhood comes first, and I wasn't yet a brother.

CHAPTER 25

Later that night I went back to my motel, hoping to get some rest. I wasn't back long when I got another text. They told me to meet them at J.R.'s room at a motel next to the Binns where the Pagan chapter presidents were staying.

It was around one a.m. and my cover team was long gone. Steph was with me, but other than her, I was on my own. I called Kotchian, the case agent.

"Hey, man, I have to go back to the motel," I told him.

"Fuck, everyone's gone," he said.

For operational security purposes, the cover team needed to stay at least thirty miles away from the Wildwood area. It would have been hard to explain why a bunch of ATF agents were staying at local motels. Word would have gotten out quickly if there were feds in town, and that would have only increased the paranoia the Pagans always felt.

"Let me call you right back," Kotchian said.

He called the supervisor and told him the situation. Meanwhile, I got my shit together and told Steph we had to get over there. You have to understand, it wasn't an option. I couldn't question anything and had to do what I was told. I couldn't ignore the call or tell them I was tired. They said jump and I had to jump. Period.

Kotchian called me back.

"Tell them you can't go. Tell them you're busy," he said. "Just say you can't make it over there. That's what I'm getting on my end."

"I can't do that," I told him. "I have to go, and I'm telling you right now, I'm going."

"Ken, you can't do that. You can't go over there with no cover team," he said.

The discussion escalated, and soon we were screaming at each other. I was pissed. The ATF supervisor was sitting at home in his warm bed trying to tell me what to do and how to interact in an environment he did not understand.

I've said before that the case required luck and instinct. It got me where I was that night—inside the biggest outlaw biker rally on the East Coast—and I needed to continue to follow my gut.

"If you guys need me, you know where I'll be," I shouted, and hung up.

Kotchian called me back a few times and texted, but I ignored him. I had to.

Steph hopped on the back of my bike, and we rode over to the compound. When we got there, there were only a few members of the Mother Club and J.R. and Roadblock. They wanted me to meet the bigwigs and let them get to know me a bit.

We posted up in front of J.R.'s room where some of the old ladies were hanging out, drinking and smoking. The door was open. Steph went in and took a seat on one of the beds with the other women. We talked out front and soon a parade of Pagans began rolling in. There were a bunch of members from other chapters whom I had never seen before. They were all sizing me up.

The Mother Club and chapter presidents were paying tribute to the president of a support group called the Tribe, who had been killed in a bike crash. At one point a bunch of us went into another motel room. People were drinking and hanging out. A plate was being passed around with lines of what I thought was coke on it. It was dark, so I figured that if I had to, I could simulate using pretty easily. No one was paying much attention to me.

The plate came my way, I took my turn by simulating doing a

line, and passed it along. I didn't think much of it, but soon after, I felt like shit and got a raging headache. Turns out it wasn't coke at all. I found out the next morning it was meth.

I'm a certified drug expert and know all there is to know about cocaine, heroin, meth, or whatever. But it's almost impossible to tell the difference between meth and cocaine when it's cut up and laid out in lines, without tasting it. And if you taste meth, you might as well just take it. It's a porous drug, and if you get it on you or near you, you'll feel it.

That's exactly what happened. I didn't ingest it, but it got on my skin on my hand and near my face and that was enough. I had a raging headache. Had I known it was meth, I would have passed and no one would have questioned me. It's a mystery to me how people can live with that garbage in their system.

I left the room and went back to the area outside the door of J.R.'s room. Pita and his sergeant-at-arms, another beast of a man named R.B., came over. The door to the room was still open, and I could see Steph in there with the other old ladies and a couple Pagans.

"Hey, Ken," Pita said, peering into my eyes. "We want to talk to you. Let's take a walk."

R.B. was eye-fucking me. I had to go along. Usually, when Pagans asked me to "take a walk," it was to get out of earshot of someone for some reason, so I didn't question it and walked with them.

"Hey, Ken, that's bullshit what happened to you," Pita said, referring to me being kicked out. "They need you out on the island."

He talked about the Roadblock beating and how they needed me there to beef up the troops. As we walked aimlessly, I looked back at the motel and the door to the room where Steph was hanging out. It was still open. By then, there were between seventy-five and a hundred Pagans milling around the parking lot and outside. Guys were in and out of that room.

"Maybe you come down to Trenton with us," he said, out of nowhere.

It was a weird conversation that had no purpose. We just walked and talked, and the next thing I knew we were a half mile away from the motel. Had the guys lured me away from the motel? If so, why?

I had a sick feeling in my stomach.

"Shit, man, I need to call my old lady," I said, stepping away from them.

I dialed Steph's number. No answer. I realized she wasn't even aware that I'd left. I called again—no answer. I sent a text and then called again. No answer.

They started talking to me again, and I kept hitting redial. My mind raced.

Did they lure me away so they could gang-rape Steph? They were notorious for running trains on women—willing or otherwise. Steph was new and wasn't a member's old lady, so she was at great risk.

I was near panic. I felt like I'd abandoned my partner and left her in the worst of situations. She was on a bed in a shitty motel infested with drunk, meth-crazed bikers. The only security around were other Pagans. Those other old ladies there wouldn't do anything to help her.

"I gotta get back," I told Pita.

"No, hold on a minute," he said. "We're not done."

"Yeah, I know, let's talk in a minute. I need to get back," I said.

I was walking fast but trying not to run, because how would I explain breaking into a panicked sprint? I walked as fast as I could without raising suspicion, but I was going nowhere. I felt like I was walking in quicksand.

I rounded the block and saw the motel. The door was now shut. My heart sank.

I switched into survival mode and ran over to the door. It was unlocked, and I threw it open. I was sure I was entering a hellish scene.

There she was, still sitting on the bed, with a couple other old ladies, drinking and smoking. They all looked at me stunned. Now I had to pivot back away from Ken Croke the ATF agent, panicked for his partner, into Ken Pallis the asshole, controlling biker boyfriend. I slid right into character.

"Why the fuck didn't you answer your fucking phone?" I screamed. She was scared and so were the other old ladies. "When I fucking call you, you fucking answer."

"It was on the bed, Ken . . ." she started explaining.

"Shut the fuck up," I bellowed.

She had the phone on the bed on vibrate and didn't hear it. Neither Ken Pallis nor Ken Croke wanted to hear her excuses. Either way, she'd fucked up, and I was going to let her know it.

I grabbed her by the arm and walked her out of that pit of despair. It wouldn't have been unusual for a Pagan to backhand her in that situation, but I wasn't going there. There are certain lines I would never cross, case or no case.

We walked over to the far side of the parking lot. I was yelling at her and dozens of Pagans were watching.

"I'm sorry, Ken," she said.

"Sorry doesn't fucking cut it," I said. "When I need you, you answer that fucking phone."

She wasn't fully understanding. I wasn't only yelling at her, though. I was yelling at myself. I screwed up and could have gotten her killed. I was furious with us both.

I calmed down, and she realized what was going on. She was sincerely apologetic. I leaned into her face and spoke in a hushed tone, so as not to be overheard.

"I could have been calling you because I was in trouble too," I said. "This is a two-way fucking street. Those are the kinds of mistakes that can get one of us killed."

She understood. I felt terrible that I'd left her in that position and I was feeling terrible about the whole night. I wished I was back home.

We hopped on my bike. I ripped out and headed back to the motel. When we got back, we talked some more, with no Pagans around.

"I thought the worst. You know these animals. This is what they do," I said. "How would I live with myself if what I thought was happening happened and I didn't stop it?"

She was quiet.

"And how about if I had one second to live and needed you to come save my ass and you're sitting on a bed with some old ladies with your phone on vibrate?" I said.

"I'm sorry," she said. "I realize it could have been the other way too."

"We cannot have this happen," I said. "We cannot make these kinds of mistakes. Every one of these decisions we make can be the end of the game or worse. Any mistakes, and one of us will have to live with what happens."

I thought back to the conversation with Pita and R.B. It made no sense. To this day, I'm not sure what they really wanted or what they were up to on that dark walk through the streets of Wildwood.

CHAPTER 26

It was the last day of the Wildwood mayhem, and I was ready to leave. I witnessed some assaults and widespread drug use, but it was mostly petty stuff and I didn't get much in the way of charges for the case.

As I packed up my stuff to head back to Long Island, I got a text from Roadblock.

Get over to J.R.'s room now, it read.

I stepped out of my crappy motel room, got on my bike, and rode over to the compound. J.R.'s room was the same one where I had left Steph behind the night before. It gave me a bad feeling just being back there.

I parked, walked over to the room, and knocked. J.R. opened the door and inside were just him and Roadblock. I could hear someone in the bathroom but had no idea who it was.

"Have a seat," Roadblock said.

J.R. was sitting on one of the beds and Roadblock was on the other. I sat in a wooden desk chair facing them. In those situations, I was always worried about what unexpected news was coming. It was stressful. But I wasn't too worried that day because I knew they were going to tell me whether I was back in or not.

If I was out, then the case was basically over, and part of me was okay with that. There were worse things in life. If I was in, it meant my work continued, and I was okay with that too.

We sat in silence for thirty seconds or so. They loved to build up drama. J.R. leaned toward me and started to speak.

"Listen, bro, bad news. We tried, but you're out," he said.

They both just stared at me in silence. I stared back, unsure how to react. Roadblock sat like a statue. I looked back and forth at them in bewilderment. It looked like my run with the Pagans was done. I wondered if something had happened at Wildwood. Maybe I said something during that conversation with Pita that blew it for me? Or maybe the Mother Club just wouldn't separate me from Jesse, the national vice president who vouched for me that they had kicked out.

Whatever it was, I was pissed. I broke the silence.

"What the fuck did you guys drag me back down here for?" I said. "I don't need this shit."

They looked at each other, and J.R. cracked a smile. They both burst out laughing.

"We're only kidding, man," J.R. said. "We got you back in! We talked to the national president and he said, 'If you guys want him, you got him. But he's your responsibility.'"

Rooster, the Pagans' national president, told J.R. and Roadblock that he was giving me a pass because I didn't even know Jesse. Rooster was deviating from the rules, but J.R. and Roadblock persuaded him that they needed me in Long Island.

"It's on you guys," Rooster told them. "He's all yours."

J.R. and Roadblock high-fived me and slapped me on the back. They were happy as pigs in shit, because they knew they had another soldier in their battle against the Angels. It was all very self-serving.

"You should have seen your face!" Roadblock laughed.

"There is some bad news, though," J.R. chimed in. "The bad news is, your days don't count."

My heart sank. I had to start my prospecting time all over again from day one. None of the days I had before would count. I would have to serve those bastards for another six months. I wanted to punch one of them. I bit my tongue and thought about the bigger game I was playing—unbeknownst to them. I took a deep breath.

"That's bullshit. There was nothing wrong with my time," I argued. "That thing with Jesse had nothing to do with me."

"I know, Ken, but you can only win so many fights," he said. "This is one we're not going to win."

He threw me my prospect colors. I was in again.

"Okay," I said. "You sure? I don't want to go through this shit again and get screwed."

"You're all set," Roadblock said. "You can start prospecting again today."

"And you have to move down to Long Island now," J.R. said. "This has to happen ASAP."

A few hours later we packed up and headed back to Long Island. I had to get back home to get things together to move down to Rocky Point.

I had a lot of work to do.

CHAPTER 27

The whole ordeal of getting kicked out and then coming back showed the Pagans I was resilient and committed. The fact that I came back down and went to Wildwood when they needed me showed them I was loyal. I was earning more trust from J.R. and Roadblock. Hogman, Tracy, and Izzo all seemed to be cool with me being back in as well.

We got back to Long Island, and Steph and I made plans to head back up to Massachusetts to get things in order for our move to Long Island. The truth is, we both had to get many things in order for our undercover lives as well as for our real lives.

We laid the groundwork early for her not being around a lot, telling the chapter that she would be back home running her cleaning business much of the time. She'd come down when I needed her.

We found a house to rent in nearby Shoreham, a beachfront town just five minutes from the clubhouse and a short walk to Shoreham Beach on the Long Island Sound. It was a big, five-bedroom, six-bathroom, two-story wood-shingled home with a two-car garage on an acre of land. It was set back on a corner lot with lots of trees.

I wanted to pick a big house, because I knew that if they liked where I lived, they'd be more likely to come hang out at. And I could wire it.

The place was fully furnished and had a finished basement where we could have meetings. I had to figure out a way to explain how we could afford such a big beach house, because as far as they knew, I was a part-time mechanic and a lobster poacher and Steph cleaned houses.

The place was a great fit, because it was a seasonal rental. The two lawyers who owned it were looking to have it occupied in the off-season, so we told the club we got a sweet deal on it. We moved in late September 2009, after the busy summer beach season, and told the guys the owners gave us a price break because they considered us not only tenants but caretakers.

Steph and I loaded my pickup truck with our clothes and belongings, as well as a bunch of props to furnish the place, and headed down to start our new fake life in Long Island. I started my prospecting duties immediately and started counting the days.

I had the .22 on me whenever the club allowed, but Roadblock wanted me to have something more powerful to be ready for the Angels should they come to town. He knew the .22 wasn't a great gun and told me to talk to Hogman.

"I've got a sawed-off shotgun I can sell you," Hogman told me.

"Yeah, I'll take it," he said.

He drove over to the house in his truck and brought a sawed-off shotgun with him, which I bought for $200. Besides the gun being illegal, Hogman was a convicted felon, so he was facing some serious charges just for having that gun, never mind selling it to me.

One night, we headed over to the Wellington, the Pagan dive bar in Middle Island, just a short ride from Rocky Point. J.R. was on edge that night. We got to the Wellington and started drinking, when J.R. got a phone call. He started arguing with the guy and told him that he needed to get over there right away.

J.R. was looking for trouble that night. It may have been a test for me and Hogman, but he was looking to rough the guy up for some reason. Roadblock came over to us and said: "If you're given the signal you take this guy outside and give him a beating. And it better not be a light beating."

The guy, a civilian, showed up and started kissing J.R.'s ass.

"I meant no disrespect, man," he said, begging for mercy.

It didn't matter. J.R. was in the mood for a thumping. He gestured to me and Hogman.

"These two guys are going to take you outside and teach you a lesson about how you talk to a Pagan president," J.R. told him.

"Come on, man . . ." he started.

He was panicking as Hogman grabbed him. We started walking him toward the back door. I was walking next to him and Hogman was holding his arm tight. He pleaded with us. My mind raced as I considered how I could protect the guy from injury while keeping up my facade as a hardened biker.

Just as we got to the back door, which led out to a small deck, he tried to bolt. I reached out and snatched him by the back of his collar. There were three small steps going out to the parking lot, and he was trying to get away.

I yanked him and slammed him to the ground with a loud thud. He was a big dude and he came down hard. Harder than I'd planned. Out of the corner of my eye, I spotted Izzo with a gun in his hand. Roadblock and J.R. told him to be out front in case the guy got the better of us or if we did not carry out J.R.'s wishes. The gun wasn't just for the guy getting beaten—it was for me too if needed. I knew Izzo would use it.

Hogman pounced on the guy. The guy did not fight back. His head was on the curb and his body was on the ground. As Hogman pounded him, I pretended to join in. I threw glancing blows off the side of his head and shoulder, but really I was punching the cement. My hand got bloodied up pretty good. As I rained fake punches down, grazing him and listening to him wince with each punch and kick from Hogman, I thought about my family back home. I thought about how I could ever explain to my girls what I was doing.

I had no choice, because if I didn't participate, it would have been me on the ground right next to him being beaten. I also knew that it was a prime opportunity for me to make some bones in the gang and move up the ladder.

I crouched down near the guy's head, throwing my punches off

Me at age twelve (front middle) with my youth hockey team in Massachusetts.

ATF agents John Ciccone, Eric Harden, and me early in our careers in L.A. Ciccone was the case agent for the "Black Rain" case in which four ATF agents infiltrated the Mongols in California. Harden was the supervisor on the legendary case.

Suiting up for an arms-smuggling raid with the Special Response Team in 1991 on the Arizona-Mexico border.

Examining a mock explosive during a raid on a militia compound in 1995 in California.

Agent John Carr (middle), Eric Harden, and I return on a C-130 military transport plane from an operation in New Mexico in 1995. Carr was my contact agent for the Pagan case because he was an experienced undercover. He was the one person in the bureau who was constantly looking out for my well-being throughout the case.

ATF Agent Ron Blake and I pose with a cache of dynamite and detonation cords, both of which are high explosives, following a 1995 weapons trafficking bust in California.

In disguise during an episode of the ABC News show *20/20* with David Muir about undercover officers posing as hitmen.

Roadblock, Hogman, and me shortly after I was patched into the Pagans, December 2009.

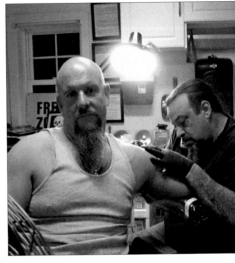

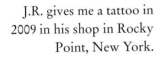

J.R. gives me a tattoo in 2009 in his shop in Rocky Point, New York.

In my colors on my Harley at a West Virginia run with the Pagans in 2010.

Mobo was a Pagan bar in Long Island, New York, where Billy Jacobson was brutally beaten by several Pagans in the bathroom.

Fender Bender and Cano several months prior to when Fender Bender was viciously beaten with axe handles by fellow Pagans in Ohio.

Pita and I hang at a biker event in Rahway, New Jersey.

On a run with the Pagans in West Virginia.

Mother Club members Cano, Hellboy, Bluto, Jersey Jim, Izzo, J.R., and numerous other Pagans outside the Binns Motel at the Pagan mandatory Roar to the Shore, September 2010.

Hogman and I meet in a mall parking lot in New York early in the investigation, where we were discussing the possibility of my prospecting for the Pagan Nation.

Customary greeting between bikers (kiss and embrace). Knowing that Hogman had a fetish for consuming products soaked in blood made this greeting ritual unbearable.

Left: White Bear in a rage, which was common, as his temper was notorious and unpredictable. The "13" on his colors represents Mother Club membership. Only Mother Club members can wear the #13. *Below:* I'm standing guard as sergeant-at-arms at a clubhouse in Youngstown, Ohio, where members of the Mother Club were meeting.

J.R. and I commiserate in front of J.R.'s tattoo shop in Rocky Point, New York, in 2010. The shop was the Long Island chapter's headquarters.

Bottom left: I'm carrying my axe handle just prior to heading to a major meeting of the Pagans, where Doc and several others were severely beaten with similar axe handles. *Bottom right:* I'm in Ohio in my Pagan "soft patch" T-shirt after the axe-handle beatings. I collected colors from several Pagans who were kicked out and delivered them to the Mother Club.

Numerous high-ranking Pagans and Mongols in New Jersey prior to meetings to form an alliance between the two OMG's. Photo taken September 2010.

Me (on right) with Roadblock (far left) and his half-brother, Trucker, in a Pagan bar in West Virginia.

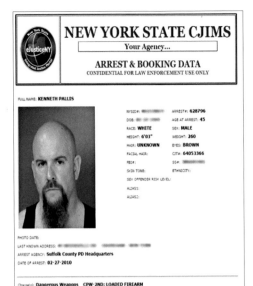

My booking sheet after I was arrested in Long Island while undercover. I spent a few days in jail posing as a Pagan so I wouldn't blow my cover and compromise the investigation.

Right: Trucker and me at his house in Maryland in 2010. I stayed there for a couple days. I had this photo taken so I would remember the address (number on the post to my immediate right). It became important to the case when we were serving warrants, including one for this house where we recovered weapons.
Below: Group photo taken at the Ohio mandatory.

I'm in a foul mood after three days in Wildwood, New Jersey, at the Roar to the Shore mandatory in 2010. My sergeant-at-arms patch is visible just below my extended finger.

Hellboy in an agitated state at a mandatory in New Jersey in 2010.

J.R., an unidentified Pagan, and me in New Jersey in 2010.

Pop Tart, Roadblock (middle), and I take a break while on a run to West Virginia.

Left: View from my bike with the Pagans on a run through a small town. *Below:* (left to right) Izzo, Pop Tart, J.R., Trucker, Roadblock, and me in J.R.'s yard in Long Island after "church." This was taken after Izzo and I traveled to deliver a message from J.R., who was the president of presidents, to the Mother Club in New Jersey. The POP is a position that precedes becoming a Mother Club member.

Izzo and me at a rally in Rahway, New Jersey, in 2010.

Right: A Cape May Pagan and me at the mandatory in Ohio, June 2010.

Below: (left to right) Me, Trenton, N.J., chapter president Pita, his sergeant-at-arms, Bluto, and J.R. in Ohio. It's worth noting this is a picture of two presidents and two sergeants-at-arms.

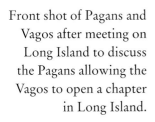

Front shot of Pagans and Vagos after meeting on Long Island to discuss the Pagans allowing the Vagos to open a chapter in Long Island.

Pop Tart and me at a mandatory in Wildwood, New Jersey, September 2010. This photo was taken immediately after a mother asked me to pose for a picture with her young son. This is when I whispered to the boy to promise not to grow up like me.

Group Pagan shot including several chapter presidents and sergeants-at-arms in the undercover house in Rocky Point, New York, in 2010.

In the undercover house, a loyal Pagan supporter being presented with a "P" diamond received for all his support to the chapter. (Left to right) Pagan supporter, J.R., Izzo, Hogman, me, and Roadblock.

J.R., not very happy after arrest.

All three photos display
guns seized or purchased
during the investigation.

This is the hole that I dug with Hogman and Tracy at Tracy's house in the Catskills and what was discovered by agents who searched the property at the conclusion of the case.

Within minutes after the case was taken down, and the first time I wore my badge around my neck in more than two years. Case agent Eric Kotchian, George Karelas, and other team members were at Tracy's residence for the execution of the search warrant.

the tar, while Hogman was down lower wailing away. Hogman moved up toward me and lifted up his massive leg to stomp on the guy's head.

Holy fuck, I thought to myself. *He's going to curb-stomp this guy and fucking kill him.*

It was the type of moment for which there isn't any training. I couldn't let it get any worse and had to intervene before they killed the poor slob.

As Hogman cocked his leg to stomp him, I swung my leg over the guy's head, a split second before Hogman's massive boot came crashing down. His boot smashed into my leg between my knee and thigh, sending excruciating pain shooting through my entire body. I continued to throw a few more grazing blows before J.R. stopped it.

"That's enough," he said. "Ken, get rid of this guy."

I picked him up roughly off the ground and led him over to his car. I didn't have to act mad, because I was fuming that I'd nearly had my leg broken.

"This is your lucky fucking night," I told him.

I opened his car door and threw him inside, slamming the door behind him.

"Get the fuck out of here," I yelled.

I meant it, both as Ken Pallis and Ken Croke. I wanted that guy out of there before I had to fake beat him some more or one of these guys changed his mind and decided to kill him.

I limped back toward the gang in stinging pain. I clearly took the worst of it. My hands were all swollen and bleeding, and my leg was all fucked up. I had the worst Charlie horse of my life and was pretty sure I'd damaged a ligament in my knee.

It was a mess, but I ended up saving that guy. If I hadn't thrown my leg under Hogman's boot, his neck would have been broken.

The guys were impressed by my theatrics.

"Bro, you fucking slammed that motherfucker," Roadblock said.

"Slam!!" added J.R., mimicking the thud the guy made when he hit the ground.

We went back inside and had some drinks to soothe the pain. I was careful not to drink too much, but I have to admit, those beers tasted good after that mayhem. We left the Wellington and went to another bar to continue our hijinks. The guy we beat called J.R. and apologized some more. He was afraid the beating was just the first of many, with good reason.

I went home and took a long, hot shower, cleaned the blood and dirt off my hands, and iced my leg. It was red, badly swollen, and starting to bruise. It hurt like hell too.

I had to heal quickly, though, because we were leaving for another mandatory. We were about to head to another carnival of chaos, this time in Lancaster, Pennsylvania.

CHAPTER 28

E very day living with those guys was a mindfuck, especially when I was a prospect. Every day I woke up, I wondered what sort of shit was going to happen. Would I have to jump into a barroom brawl? Would I be faced with a pile of coke and a choice? What sort of dumb shit would they ask me to do? I always had to expect the unexpected and could never let my guard down. It was a stressful way to live, and my brain was working overtime.

I was back in full prospect mode, and the case was progressing nicely in October 2009 when we headed to Lancaster, Pennsylvania, for a mandatory. The Lancaster event was in a remote field with a river running through the middle of the property, which was accessible only by a long, winding dirt road. The road was guarded by armed Pagans. No one was getting in. We were a mile from any main roads, which meant the cover team was nowhere near where they could be of any assistance. I was again on my own.

We rode our Harleys down the dusty road and set up camp. Me and the other prospects got to the usual: setting up grills, tents, lugging around coolers, chairs, tables, boxes of food.

I noticed the river and thought that it could be useful in an emergency.

If they try to kill me, I'll crawl into the river and float down it, I thought to myself, morbidly. *At least then someone will find my body.*

The Lancaster chapter's clubhouse was on the property. It was a two-story building with a full bar on the top floor. The first floor included meeting rooms, a few bedrooms, and a kitchen. There was a big grilling area out back.

The lower part of the property had a road that swung around to a massive field. There was a path through the woods marked by construction lighting strung through the trees. Pagans were camped and banners and flags were hoisted all over the place. Some Pagans openly carried guns. It was like *Lord of the Flies* for felons.

There were kegs, and music blared from speakers from tent to tent. It was always rock, blues, or country—Lynyrd Skynyrd, Motörhead, Waylon Jennings, .38 Special, Van Halen.

The Lancaster event was a joint event with the Sons of Satan support club. The Lancaster chapter's clubhouse was bombed by Hells Angels in 2002 in retaliation for the Hellraisers Ball attack in New York earlier that year. Lancaster chapter president Robert J. "Mailman" Rutherford, fifty-one, was killed in the melee. Rutherford, who was a postal worker for twenty-nine years, was honored every year at the Lancaster event. He was a martyr and a hero to the Pagans.

Hells Angel Raymond G. Dwyer, thirty-nine, was charged with Rutherford's murder, but he beat the rap after prosecutors said he fired in self-defense. The New York brawl touched off a spate of violence between the Angels and Pagans that included the firebombing of a Pagan tattoo shop in Philadelphia and a deadly shoot-out and knife fight inside a Nevada casino that left three Hells Angels and a Mongol dead.

The violent history and Rutherford's death made the Lancaster gathering a particularly serious and intense event. It was a reminder that the two gangs were always at war. The armed guards at the top of the dirt road were there for good reason.

The longer we were there, the more strung out guys got. Open drug use, prostitutes, guns, and debauchery were everywhere. One

night, I was walking through a darkened path that was only partially lit by plastic light bulbs strung along the trees. At the end of the
path it opened into a large, dark field, and I walked past a group of
Pagans—six of them. I didn't know what chapter they were from, but
I recognized two as guys I'd seen at another event.

One yelled to me: "Prospect, get over here."

Fuck, I thought to myself. *Here we go.*

One of them had a flashlight. My black T-shirt was soaked from
sweat and was hanging down low below my neck. My gold chain was
dangling.

He flashed the light on it.

"Hey, what's that?" he sneered.

"What?" I said.

"Around your neck."

"It's a chain," I said.

"Let me see it," he said.

I held it up and showed it to him.

"No, let me see it," he repeated.

He wanted me to take it off and give it to him. I knew he planned
to take it. But that chain was sacred to me. It was a crucifix given to
me by my mother twenty years earlier as her way of trying to keep
me safe throughout my career. There was no way I was giving it to
that bastard.

"No, not happening," I told him.

One of the other guys stepped forward toward me.

"Didn't you hear him?" he asked.

"Yeah, I heard him," I said. "But this thing means something to
me. I'm not giving it up."

"I want the chain," the first one demanded.

He grabbed at it and tried to pull it.

"What's that, from a girlfriend?" he asked.

"No, it's from my mother," I said. "You ain't getting it."

He got in my face and reached for it, but I blocked his arm away.

I knew it was about to be on, but I was taking that motherfucker with me, that was for sure.

He lunged at me, and I drove my shoulder into his chest, smashed my forearm across his head, and drove him into the ground. The exhale of air that came out of him was amazing. His boys jumped in and started cracking me with fists, and one had an axe handle. They pummeled me, smacking me in the ribs and the shoulder. *Crack! Crack! Crack!* Each wooden blow cracked into my body with unnatural force. It all happened so fast, but at the same time it felt like slow motion.

I was on top of the first guy wailing away on him until an axe handle caught me in the side of my ribs and knocked me off him. I looked into his eyes as I fell off him and hit the ground. He was livid but he was scared.

I was worried he'd get up and stab me. Those guys all carried blades, and if he killed a prospect he would claim it was self-defense and the others would back his play. There would have been no complaints had they gutted me and left me there for dead. I thought about that river. Where the fuck was it? Could I get up and run and get to it?

As soon as I fell off him and landed on the ground, one of them kicked me hard. I tried to grab his foot.

"You're not very fucking smart," he grunted.

They continued beating the shit out of me until I heard a voice. It was one of the chapter presidents.

"What the fuck is going on?" he yelled.

They stopped kicking my ass. No one said a word.

"I said, what the fuck is going on?" he repeated.

He looked at me. He was the president of one of the Southern New Jersey chapters. I recognized him and the diamond on his back. He was pissed.

"Prospect, what the fuck is going on?" he asked me.

"Nothing, just a misunderstanding," I answered.

I was hurt pretty bad, but I wasn't going to show them.

"I'm fine," I lied.

The chapter president lit into them and told them they were out of line. Pagan code prohibits stealing from prospects or members, although that rule is sometimes violated, especially when bikers are drunk and strung out for days on end. I think they were from Southern Jersey and Delaware, but I never found out who they were, unfortunately.

The Diamond, a common term used among the Pagans as a way of recognizing the chapter presidents, helped me up, and we walked away from the pack.

"You fuckin' guys be smarter," he shouted at them. "Ya fucks."

He turned to me.

"What happened?" he asked.

"Somebody wanted something from me I wasn't going to give him," I said. "It's over with and that's it."

I didn't say anything more. We walked back toward the tents, and he went on his way. I walked around the back of the field and sat on a stone wall to check myself out. I knew I had a cracked rib at least. I couldn't breathe. My arms, legs, and head were fine, but I knew I had bruises on my ribs and a nice welt on my head.

Pita heard about the fracas and was pissed. He started asking a bunch of questions. I provided very few details and was just hoping it would be the last beating for the weekend. He eventually let it go and decided not to make a bigger deal out of it.

I never really got a good look at the guys. It was pitch black and we were in the middle of nowhere. I never came across them again. I talked to a doctor a few days later, and he wanted me to get an X-ray, but I never did. I likely had some cracked ribs, but I knew there was nothing they could do for that anyway. Ibuprofen, ice, and a few beers took care of it.

I never wrote a report about it and never officially told ATF, although some of the guys knew unofficially but kept their mouths shut, not wanting to give the higher-ups another reason to shut down the case. All I know is that I took a beating in the dark in the woods of Pennsylvania from a bunch of Pagans and never gave up that cross.

My mother, God rest her soul, would have been furious with me for not giving up the chain, but I also think she would have been happy to know that I was still wearing the cross she had given me for protection. It worked that night.

CHAPTER 29

At the Lancaster event, I met some Mother Club members, among them Cano.

I had met Cano—real name Sergio Cuevas—once before and had heard plenty about him. The case agent had run background checks on lots of the guys and knew Cano was a killer. He carried a .380 caliber pistol and a knife engraved with the words "one percenter."

Born in Puerto Rico, Cano was one of the only non-white members in the Pagans. There were no Black members allowed, but they did allow some Latinos in, although it was rare. Strangely, Cano was one of the more racist members I met.

He was a real piece of work. He was short—just five feet four inches tall—and weighed a hundred and fifty pounds. He had a gray goatee, the requisite Surtr tattoos up and down his arms, and beady, hazel-colored eyes. In 1963, when he was twenty-four and living in Puerto Rico, he married his wife, who was just twelve.

He had a long rap sheet. In 1967, he got probation for a sexual assault in Elizabeth, New Jersey. His record also included drug and weapons trafficking, robberies, gambling violations, conspiracy, being a fugitive from justice, and several assaults.

But where he really made his bones was in 1974 in Richmond, Virginia, when he and several other Pagans went into a biker bar that was the clubhouse for the Confederate Angels, a support club of the Hells Angels. The Confederate Angels were said at the time to be merging with the Hells Angels. Cano was convicted in April 1975 of gunning down twenty-one-year-old Confederate Angel Billy Ray Greene and shooting two other men, one of whom was left paralyzed. A third man was pistol-whipped. Three other Pagans were convicted in the attack.

Cano was sentenced to twenty years for murder but was out of jail by 1982, when he was arrested in Philadelphia on gun and drug violations. The guy was dedicated to his craft. And he was intense.

One afternoon during the rally in Lancaster, I made my way down to the Lancaster chapter's clubhouse. J.R. and I made the ten-minute walk from the upper tier of the property through the woods and down to the lower section, where the Mother Club had its campers parked. I walked past a sea of grills, tents, and campers and was invited into the bar on the second floor.

Cano was there and walked by me without a glance. He had no interest in talking to me. I headed back outside. J.R. and I were standing near the grills behind the clubhouse, hanging out, when I heard someone call to me.

"Hey, prospect, come over here," the voice said.

It was Cano.

J.R. walked over with me, because I was his responsibility. Anything that I did reflected on him, so he made sure he stuck by my side.

"So, you're out on Long Island, right?" he asked me.

"Yes," I answered.

"You guys out there have to get your shit together," he said, looking up at me intensely. "That's no joke out there. You guys have to take care of business and make things right."

He was talking about retaliation against the Angels for beating Roadblock.

I knew he had killed at least one Angel, and the rumor was he had killed another one. I didn't say anything. He started again, looking at me with a grimace.

"You have to go out there and take care of fucking business," he said. "You go out and kill a Hells Angel, bring me back his colors, and you'll be a fully patched member. Your prospecting is over."

I couldn't believe my ears. J.R. stood stoically.

"But if you fuck up," he continued, "if you rat, or don't do your job, I'll fucking kill you."

"I'm loyal, man," I assured him. "I'll do my best. That's why I'm here."

I had to choose my words carefully. I couldn't commit to taking part in a murder. I had to be smart. If I told him, "Sure, I'll kill one," I'd be putting myself on the hook to commit a murder. What if Cano loved it and went back to the Mother Club and said, "Prospect Ken says he'll kill a Hell's Angel," and then they decided to go find one and take me with them?

I had to be vague yet appear committed to the cause. It takes a certain makeup to be a killer, and if they think you have it, they'll try to turn you into one. Cano clearly had that makeup. He was the real deal.

The day only got more intense. J.R. brought me into the clubhouse and sent me upstairs to the barroom. He told me to find a guy named Motheater. I walked in and made my way over to a tall, thin, old Pagan sitting at the end of the bar.

"You Motheater?" I asked.

"I am, prospect," he answered.

He started bullshitting with me about the weekend, prospecting, and just making small talk. It was a very unmemorable conversation that really went nowhere. As we talked, I couldn't for the life of me figure out why they sent me to talk to the guy. He had nothing of substance to say to me.

I later learned that he had a radio frequency detector, or an RF detector, in his pocket. It's a device that can detect if someone is wearing a wire. Had I been wearing one, as some in ATF wanted, it would have signaled his detector and vibrated silently in his pocket. If I set that thing off, I wouldn't be here to write this, I'm fairly certain.

Later, I found out there had been some chatter about me among members. They wondered who I was and where I came from. They wanted to know who knew what about me. They wondered if I was a cop or, perhaps worse, a rat.

CHAPTER 30

I was close to finishing my time as a prospect and becoming fully patched. My priority was building the case, but I'd be lying if I said the challenge of getting in wasn't part of what drove me. The buzz throughout ATF was strong, and my team in Boston was also getting antsy to see if I could get patched into the gang.

That's about the time when this case got flipped on its head. Andy Anderson, the head of the Boston office, was ordered to go to Washington to brief the top leaders in the agency on the case. My longtime colleague and friend Mike Sullivan was still serving as the acting director of ATF, so I had an ally in Washington, but there was a push by other higher-ups to shut the case down.

Assistant Director Mark Chait, who oversaw field operations in D.C., had grown tired of the risks associated with the case, which by that time had been dubbed Operation On The Road Again, for some unfortunate reason. Name aside, with me on the verge of being patched in, our work was coming to a head in Long Island, but in Washington, there was a movement to bring it to a screeching halt, and Chait was pushing to shut it down.

"Why don't you guys wrap up what you've got on this thing and call it a day?" Chait told Andy.

"No way, we're not even close," Andy argued. "We've got a guy inside for the first time ever. Why would we want to shut it down?"

Andy was told explicitly in Washington to pull me out and shut the case down. The truth was, some of the brass were more concerned about how the case would reflect on their own careers if I was killed or turned to the dark side. No one in ATF wanted me to break bad or get killed, but for some, their motivations weren't out of concern for the safety of me or my family. Having an agent get hurt or a potential public relations snafu would be damaging to their hopes of future promotions. It would stick to them, and they didn't have the stomach for it.

Deep undercover work is always dangerous, but the longer you're in, the more dangerous it becomes. If you get made on day one, they just ask you to leave. If you get made as a cop after you've been inside for any significant period of time, they'll kill you. Rule number one of organized crime: eliminate the witness. That applies to undercover cops too.

ATF also got more nervous the longer the case went on, because they knew the risk to my life only increased the longer I was in. Also, these cases can kind of be run quietly for a short period of time, but the longer they go, the more people in the agency learn about them. They eventually make their way to upper management, and as they do, they are subject to more intense scrutiny and micromanagement.

To his credit, Andy fought for the case and for me. He knew the sacrifices I and the cover team had made to get the case to that point. We were on the cusp of getting inside an organized crime operation like no other law enforcement agency before us. What we would learn about the inner workings of the Pagans would provide invaluable knowledge for generations of agents to come. We needed to play it out.

Mike Sullivan also had my back, and with support from the two of them, the case was kept open, on one condition: they had to transfer it out of Boston and put it under the New York Field Division, in the Long Island field office. It was unacceptable and a terrible move, but it was nonnegotiable.

For me, it meant I'd have to learn how to work with a whole new team based out of the Long Island office. The guys who started the case with me were a handpicked, trusted team who I knew would move mountains to save my ass. I had no idea who these guys were in the Long Island office, and for me, it was a huge risk to leave anything to chance at that point in the case. There was a reason why ATF had never transferred an undercover case out of a field division. I hated the idea.

Regardless, I was overruled. ATF Headquarters mandated the transfer to New York, but the U.S. Attorney's Office made it clear that the prosecution was still under the Boston office, although that too would soon change. It was the first time ATF moved a case from one field office to another, and it hasn't happened again since.

The Long Island field office was a bad place to move the case for many reasons. The office was in Melville, New York. There were a couple of solid agents there, but the office as a whole had a reputation of being a landing spot for burned out or retiring agents riding off into the sunset of their careers. That was a problem for me, because the cover team needed to work long hours around the clock. They needed to be fully engaged and ready to roll at the drop of a hat. I needed hard chargers, not guys watching the clock to get to the country club for a round of golf and some drinks.

I was comfortable with my handpicked team, who knew everything about the case. We were in a rhythm, and shaking things up at that critical moment was not only unnecessary, but also a huge, potentially deadly mistake, in my eyes.

ATF in Washington made the decision anyway, despite my protests and those in the Boston office, and the case was moved to the New York Field Division in late 2009. They argued, correctly, that ninety percent of the case was in Long Island at that point. What they didn't understand, though, was that the guys on my team were essential to my survival and the success of the case. Removing anyone from the team put me at risk. We were allowed to keep Karelas and Kotchian as a compromise.

There was another reason why it was moved to the Long Island office: there was a newly appointed Special Agent in Charge of the New York Field Division.

He was a yes-man, which is just what Washington wanted on

the case, given the potential risks. Most in ATF were all about doing what was needed to be done to put the most violent criminals behind bars, but some were more concerned with career trajectories. Cases imploded, I knew, when self-promoters or do-nothings in the wrong positions made it difficult to negotiate investigative hurdles. These types of cases hinge on smart decisions by experienced agents acting only in the interest of justice and public safety.

The New York SAC made it clear right from his first day working with us that we were to wrap the case up as soon as possible. He wanted it shut down yesterday.

As if having this SAC in charge at the top wasn't bad enough, the supervisor of the Long Island group was an agent named Paul Globe. He too was a yes-man and walked in lockstep with the SAC. Globe was not well liked by most of the agents under him.

I went from working with a group of trusted agents to an entirely new team that at times seemed more like a dysfunctional family—with Globe leading the way.

It concerned me that some making decisions didn't understand the necessary and calculated risks I needed to take to keep the case going. Nor did they grasp the delicate moment I was in as a long-term undercover on the brink of fully infiltrating one of history's most clandestine crime organizations.

The overwhelming majority of ATF agents and supervisors understood and supported proactive criminal investigations, and one in particular high up the supervisory food chain was instrumental in keeping the case moving forward: Steve Martin, the deputy assistant director. He was like a bull in a china shop. Not only was Steve a high-ranking official in ATF, he had also done long-term undercover cases himself and understood what it took to perfect those types of criminal cases.

Martin regularly called to check in on my well-being and ask what he could do to help. He pushed back hard against the New York SAC and others who posed obstacles, and ensured the case continued.

Martin had street cred, which was earned by doing the job and being in the trenches. His presence was refreshing and gave me security in a situation where I was constantly facing challenges.

Deputy Assistant Director Julie Torres was another supporter. She argued with the Washington ATF brass about the importance of continuing the case and had the clout to force them to listen, since she too had done some serious undercover work.

The move to New York did bring with it one major plus, and that was the addition of Special Agent Bryan DiGirolamo to the team. Bryan was a police officer in Washington, D.C., early in his career and worked in narcotics and the gang unit. He was recruited by ATF and assigned to a New York City field office. He worked on the Bronx gang squad and on arson investigations. He had a lot of experience with organized crime, drugs, and guns.

Bryan had just finished working a case involving the Bloods gang in New York and was looking for a break from the city. He lived on Long Island at the time and was named the new case agent, meaning he drove the investigation and prepared evidence for prosecution. He was a great criminal investigator and had a strong reputation with the U.S. Attorney's Office, which was very important. For all the tumult that would come from transferring the case to New York, Bryan was a silver lining.

CHAPTER 31

With the case under the New York office, I continued prospecting. One night we were at the Wellington bar entertaining some Pagans from out of town, including Pita. There was an off-duty cop there with his girlfriend, and she was drunk and flirting with J.R. One of the strictest rules of the Pagans is that no one can touch a president. No one.

The woman walked by J.R. and put her hand on his shoulder. Roadblock grabbed her arm and said emphatically: "Don't touch him."

A while later, she came back over and tried talking to J.R. His long, salt-and-pepper goatee was braided, and she grabbed it and tugged it playfully.

"Hey, do not touch him, I said," Roadblock insisted.

Roadblock had enough and went over to the woman's boyfriend.

"Hey, control your old lady or I will," he said.

"Oh yeah?" the guy said. "What happens if I tell you to go fuck yourself?"

The words barely got out of his mouth before he was being beaten bloody. The girlfriend jumped in, when Derek Dekker, a Pagan from the Elizabeth, N.J. chapter nicknamed Pop Up, pounced on her and cracked her skull with a billiard ball. Blood poured from her head while her boyfriend continued to get a beatdown. Blood streamed from his head too.

I was on guard duty in the back of the bar and heard the ruckus.

I ran inside and saw mayhem—fists and axe handles were flying. Pita ran toward me holding his side.

"I think I got stabbed," he said. "Let's go."

He and two other Pagans hopped in my truck, and we sped out of there. We met at the house of a Pagan supporter, and Pita checked out his wound. It was superficial, but he was bleeding. Someone gashed him with a knife during the melee. Roadblock listened to a police scanner to hear where cops were going. He listened to hear if anyone gave police information and wanted to find out if officers went to his or J.R.'s house.

The whole beatdown was caught on video. ATF agents retrieved the video, and it became another piece of evidence in the case. The woman and her boyfriend were badly injured but survived the attack. A year later, ATF agents went back to the bar and there was still blood on the wall from the fight.

I had already done two mandatories as a prospect, which fulfilled my requirements, but there was another mandatory coming up. I was stressed out that I was going to have to endure another hell weekend like I did in Youngstown and Lancaster. While I had to do a minimum of two mandatories while prospecting, there was no maximum. Some prospects ended up doing more than the required number. I did not want to join those ranks.

It was late 2009, and by that time, I was sometimes allowed to attend secret church meetings, which were usually held on Saturdays. Church was where they conducted chapter business. Sometimes they were short meetings, and sometimes they took hours, depending on the topic and what was going on with the chapter, the Mother Club, and individual members at the time.

They discussed all sorts of club activity, some of it as simple as going over who had paid dues and who hadn't. More often than not, there were detailed discussions about crimes—assaults, bomb and gun purchases, drug dealing, and even murder.

They were right to be as paranoid as they were. No one in law enforcement had ever attended church, but I was a regular attendee with a front seat to the inner workings of the most clandestine of the outlaw motorcycle gangs.

Church was usually at J.R.'s house, in his garage. Each time I arrived, I had to take the battery out of my cell phone and leave the phone and battery outside in the bed of J.R.'s truck. They had learned that cell phone batteries were used as bugs by the FBI. All weapons and any electronics had to be left outside. There were no exceptions and a violation of that rule was dealt with swiftly and severely.

The chapter had a briefcase, usually carried by Roadblock, which was used to store ledgers that documented the chapter's finances, including dues, expenses, money owed, and other detailed club information. Inside the briefcase was also a radio frequency detector to check for wires. On a few occasions, we had to literally strip naked and sit in meetings bare ass. Those were the worst sessions.

On December 10, 2009, I was summoned to J.R.'s house for church. I pulled up on my Harley, parked, and started walking toward the garage. No one was there. It was weird, because I noticed his wife's car was gone. His wife and three kids were always home, but no one was there that day.

I had a weird feeling right from the minute I pulled in. I walked up to the front door, and J.R. appeared in the doorway.

"We're doing it inside today. In here," he said, motioning me to come into his dining room.

We sat down, and the meeting started. They were talking about a scheme to drive up to the Native American reservation in northern New York to buy untaxed cigarettes. Cigarette trafficking is a lucrative racket for organized crime because the markup is better than dope. Crews can buy untaxed cigarettes on Native American land or cheaper and lower-taxed cartons out of state and resell them at a huge profit.

They were also talking about doing collections from the bars they were extorting, and there was some talk of selling guns they were planning to purchase from a store in Long Island. Each time, I memorized as much of the info I heard at church as possible and transcribed it into my case notebook when I was safely back at my house.

Notes were often taken in church as they figured out finances for various deals, wrote out lists, or went over other information. Financial details were logged in the ledger. After church, the ledger was locked in the briefcase and the notes were destroyed.

We wrapped up the session, and J.R. told me: "Prospect, go burn these out back."

He handed me the notes, and I walked outside. Izzo followed me. We walked into the back yard and over to J.R.'s grill. I opened the top, threw in the scraps of paper, doused them with lighter fluid, and lit them.

We stood there chatting as the papers burned, but I got the sense Izzo was there just to distract me. I looked over at the house, and J.R. and Roadblock were walking toward us.

"Prospect, get the fuck in here," Roadblock said harshly.

It was unusual for him to call me prospect when it was just a few of us around in Long Island. When we weren't at an event with other chapters, he usually called me Ken.

"You heard him," Izzo said, nudging me.

My heart started to race, but not as fast as my mind. I started thinking about all the possible scenarios. Had they learned something about me? Had I said something wrong? Did they find out who I really was? Every time something unexpected happened like this, those thoughts ran through my head.

I started walking toward the house. J.R. and Roadblock walked in front of me. Izzo walked behind us. We walked up a couple steps into the mudroom leading into the house and entered. I turned into the kitchen and moved into the dining room.

As we entered the house, J.R. stood on one side of me and Roadblock on the other. I looked inside the dining room and saw Hogman standing straight ahead of me with a shotgun pointing directly at my face. He wore an evil glare. He wasn't smiling.

Izzo crept up behind and bumped right up against me. I could feel his breath on the back of my head. I looked back and saw he was holding a chrome semi-automatic handgun. He stood there motionless. No one said a word.

On the wall, they had hung a Pagan banner. There were several items on the kitchen table, including a laminated piece of paper.

"Prospect, pick that up and read it!" Roadblock shouted.

My pulse raced. What the hell was going on?

I picked up the laminated paper and started reading it to myself. The first line was about being a rat. The whole page talked about what happened to rats—those who talk to cops about the gang. As I read it, I was sure that they had found out I was a cop.

This is it. They're going to kill me.

I thought I was dead. I ran through the situation in my head, and it started coming together. J.R.'s family wasn't there. They weren't acting normal. I wondered where I had gone wrong.

After I was done reading it aloud, Roadblock yelled: "That wasn't good enough! Read it again!"

As I read, I noticed a plate glass picture window on the front of the house. I thought about that being my escape route. I thought that whatever happened, whether they beat me, stabbed me, or shot me, I would get to that window and throw myself through it. That would be the only chance my cover team would have to find me.

Roadblock took out a huge knife. He held the blade in his beefy, filthy hands, looking at me. He lifted it and drove it downward, embedding it into the table just inches from me. It made a loud thud.

"This is what we do to rats," he sneered.

He took out a piece of paper and sliced it.

As this happened, J.R. walked out of the kitchen and down the hallway toward a bedroom. He disappeared from my view.

What the fuck is he doing?

I didn't know if he was going to get a baseball bat, a gun, an axe handle, or what. Nothing good was coming of this, I thought. Time had stopped. It felt like I had been standing there for hours, when in reality, it was a minute or two tops.

A few seconds later, J.R. emerged into the hallway and started walking toward me. He had an object in his hand. As he got to the end of the hallway, he wound up and threw something toward me.

I put my arms up to block it, and it hit me. It was soft. It was a rolled up T-shirt wrapped in a rubber band, kind of like the ones they shoot out of air cannons at sporting events.

I saw it was black. I unwrapped it and saw the Pagans logo on the breast.

The tone changed in the room from one of stress and deathly tension to one of relief. Hogman lowered the shotgun. Izzo backed off.

It was a soft patch. I was being patched into the Pagans.

"Holy shit," I said, trying to regain my composure.

"You're in, bro!" J.R. said. "You're one of us now."

I was overwhelmed with a rush of emotion. I went from thinking I was being executed to becoming a member of their gang. It was such a wild emotional swing it was impossible to process immediately, a weird mix of anger over the hell they had put me through and a sense of personal accomplishment for having survived their hazing and mental torture. After a few minutes, I realized the magnitude of what had happened. I'd done something no other law enforcement officer had ever accomplished: I'd become a fully patched member of the Pagans Motorcycle Club.

They all cracked celebratory beers and tossed me one. I half-ass drank it, but the truth was, after going from thinking I was being murdered to being inducted into a violent criminal organization, I wasn't really in a partying mood.

Izzo approached me. He looked me deep in the eyes.

"If you don't live up to this patch, we'll kill you," he said. "And it will be me that does it."

J.R. came over to me. He brought up the night at the Wellington when I grabbed the guy and slammed him to the ground, handing out a beatdown with Hogman on J.R.'s orders.

"Your club name is Slam," he said. "That was amazing that night.

We knew right then when you slammed that dude that you were going to be in and that your name was going to be Slam."

"Slam, huh?" I said. "Cool."

"We'll get your patches made up and get them to you next week," he told me.

Pagan patches can't just be made anywhere. It's not like you can go online, email some company the logos, and have patches made. Those little pieces of fabric art were handmade by a woman in Maryland. She was the only one allowed to make official Pagan patches.

"Thanks, man," I said, holding up the shirt. "You guys are my brothers. I'll live up to these colors."

I took off my prospect cut and pulled the soft patch T-shirt on. Roadblock and I left J.R.'s together and drove to grab a coffee. I needed to decompress.

We got a coffee at the 7-Eleven as we often did and stood in the parking lot. He knew I was going through a wide range of emotions.

"Listen, you did good," he said. "I hoped you'd make it. All that shit is part of it."

"I know," I said. "I get it, man. Doesn't mean it didn't suck."

He laughed.

"You're good with numbers, Ken," he said. "You're good with money. You're going to be our treasurer."

Bingo. They were letting me take over the books. I'd have the ledger in my possession every day. I knew that it had the potential to be a road map of evidence to charge them with everything from extortion to drug trafficking to buying and selling guns and explosives. If they were cooking the books, I'd catch it. All the payments in and out, I'd know where and to whom they were going. If they were extorting people, strong-arming, paying bribes, embezzling, I'd have it in my hands. It was a big break in the case, not only because it showed they trusted me, but also from an evidentiary standpoint. Financials are key toward bringing a RICO case, and now I had them in my possession.

"Cool," I said, downplaying it.

We talked some more about club business, and he talked about how he was still pissed off at J.R. for not coming out of the shop to help him when the Hells Angels attacked him. Their relationship was going from being strained to a deep hatred, and it wasn't going back.

That put me in a bad spot, because both of them were trying to pull me to their side. That dynamic posed a whole new set of problems, because choosing one over the other would put a target on my back. I had to play it smart.

Later that day, the cover team was doing surveillance outside the tattoo shop. Karelas spotted me outside wearing my soft patch. He got on his radio.

"Holy shit, you guys," he said. "Ken's wearing a soft patch. He's been patched in."

Kotchian called back to the Boston office and spread the word. News traveled quickly and the whole ATF knew before I talked to anyone, because it really was a shared accomplishment. I never would have gotten as far as I did without the hard work and sacrifices of Kotchian, Karelas, the rest of my cover team, and all the agents who worked on the case. It was a team effort, and my whole team deserved to feel good about what we'd done.

Word made its way to Ang back home. The next morning, I called her.

"Hey, you won't believe this—" I started to tell her.

She cut me off.

"I already know," she said. "You got patched in. Congrats."

"How did you know?" I asked.

"People talk," she joked.

She was happy and proud, but she was also upset because she knew it meant I was going to be undercover for the foreseeable future. Being patched in to the Pagans was unprecedented. I had landed in a situation that would provide generations of agents vital information that could never be obtained any other way. The only way to see the inner workings of the Pagans was to have someone all the way inside.

No informant, hidden camera, wire, microphone, subpoena, or surveillance operation could do what I could do as a trained federal agent with years of biker undercover experience living among them day in and day out. I was given full access to the club and all its activities. There was no way ATF was going to pull me out of there at that point. There were some brass who were as curious as I was to find out just how deep I could go and took the approach that we should milk it for all it was worth. There were plenty of detractors and those who thought we needed to shut the case down, but even the most vocal opponents were at least curious about what we could accomplish with me inside the Pagans.

"Ken, the life expectancy of a biker isn't good," Ang said. "The Hells Angels are coming at you. The cops are coming at you. You are one of them now."

She was right. I was one of them. There was no mistaking it. I walked a fine line between darkness and righteousness, and every day posed a new danger. I talked about the risk of breaking bad regularly with my superiors and other agents who had done long-term infiltrations. But no matter how much I talked about it or how conscious I was of that phenomenon, nothing truly prepared me for it. It was draining, terrifying, and exciting all at once.

Yes, I was still Ken Croke, father of three, husband, hockey coach, and ATF agent. But that identity was on the shelf. Now I was Ken Pallis. I was Slam. I was living that life. I was what they were. That was the whole point of being undercover. I ate their food. I slept among them. I talked like them, walked like them. I might not be killing and drugging like them, but I was living their scumbag life every day until the job was done.

CHAPTER 32

A week after getting my soft patch, we went to the mandatory in Pennsylvania. It was a much less stressful trip knowing that I was no longer going to be bossed around and treated like dirt for a weekend.

We set up camp, and J.R. went down to commiserate with the Mother Club and chapter presidents. He came back to our camp with a plastic bag in his hand. He handed me the bag.

"Here you go, bro, you deserve this," he said.

I opened it and saw inside that it was my patches. I have to admit, whatever I thought of those guys, it was quite an emotional moment. I had been through hell to get there, but there I was. I remember retired ATF agent Billy Queen telling me how he felt when he got his colors from the Mongols in the 1990s and what it meant, both in terms of his case and to him personally.

At that moment, I finally understood what Queen went through and what it meant.

I pulled the patches out of the bag, one by one. There was my Pagan cloud logo for the top, which included the word "PAGAN'S" in blue calligraphy letters in a white cloud with a red outline. I pulled out my bottom rocker patches, which consisted of the letters "M" and "C" in a white box with a red outline, signifying the words "motor-cycle club."

There was my large, yellow Surtr logo, outlined in red and accented with red flames. I was given a small Surtr logo for the front breast pocket and another patch for the other breast pocket with my club name, Slam, written in red in a white cloud. I also got a white diamond-shaped patch stitched with "1%" in red, signifying that I was now a "one percenter." That was a badge of honor among all outlaw motorcycle gangs that not only gave me street cred but also showed that I was one of them.

Finally, I pulled out a patch that read "property of Slam." That one was for Steph, my old lady, to wear on her jacket. J.R. and the guys watched me pull them out and look at them. They patted me on the back as I was officially welcomed into their world.

"We'll get these put on this week," J.R. said, nodding to the patches.

Just as there was only one woman allowed to make the patches, there was also only one woman allowed to sew them onto colors. For the Long Island chapter, that woman was J.R.'s old lady's sister. The next day, we brought them to her, and she sewed them onto my sleeveless denim jacket. My colors were complete.

Hogman was also patched in, though, because he was Roadblock's brother, he'd always been treated more like a patched member anyway, so for him, it was more of a simple formality.

With us both patched in, we started getting down to business. Part of my story was that I made money selling drugs to fishermen back on the docks in New Bedford. I was always talking about how those guys wanted crack and meth to help them work the long hours hauling in fishing nets, lugging crates, cleaning, and working in the processing plants.

New Bedford is the most lucrative fishing port in the United States. More scallops and fish come through that port than anywhere else in the country, and that's despite the weather being intolerably cold for four or five months a year. Those guys working the docks were tough, and they made good money. They were great drug customers, I convinced the guys.

"I can make a killing up there," I told Hogman. "The prices in Boston are high. I can buy shit down here, mark it up to make a nice profit, and it will still be cheaper than what they're used to paying."

"Cool," Hogman said. "I can hook that up."

In my first deal with Hogman, I bought an ounce of crack. He used a middle man, as he was still feeling me out. The dealer, a career criminal named Joe Williams, came over and dropped a baggie off. I set up regular buys. Each time they got easier as he trusted me more. My cover team was outside watching it all, getting the license plates of vehicles and keeping an eye on my backside.

Williams, a Black guy from New York, had a long rap sheet that included several prison stays for drug dealing. The Pagans didn't hide their disdain for African Americans, but Hogman had no problem using Williams to get drugs to make money. He would often spew his racist rhetoric, using every derogatory name you could think of when referring to African Americans. However, put some drugs on the table provided by an African American, and you would have thought he worked for the ACLU promoting racial sensitivity.

It was during those early deals with Hogman that I first got a sense that one supervisor could become a problem. Williams came into the house and dropped a package of crack on the table. Hogman had a gun on the dresser and paid Williams. Not only was Hogman now looking at a drug charge, but he was a felon in possession of a firearm during the commission of a felony. That was fifteen years right there.

I kept my poker face, but I was licking my chops. Of all the guys in the gang, Hogman was the one who disgusted me the most. I was told he had raped women, and I was getting more confident by the day that he was responsible for Bennett's death. I wanted to put him away for good. The world would be a better place without Hogman.

As Williams left the house and drove off, a cover team agent followed him. That was pretty normal, but the agent was in a Crown Victoria, the most obvious undercover cop vehicle that exists.

Hogman's cell phone rang.

"Yo, man, the cops are all over me," Williams said. "They're following me."

Hogman pulled the phone away from his face and whispered to me, "He's getting tailed."

I was stunned. This was bad. Either the cops were watching the house or me, Hogman, or Williams was a rat. I had to think quickly.

"Well, tell him to keep away from here or we'll bring the wrath of God down on him," I told him.

Hogman liked that answer.

"Keep that shit away from here. You obviously have heat on you and if you bring it here again nobody will ever see you again," Hogman told him.

I wrapped up with Hogman, took the drugs, and got out of there.

Later that night I had to meet one of the cover team members behind a remote strip mall to turn over the drugs. I asked who the genius was doing surveillance in the Crown Vic. The reply I got was a chuckle.

"Take it up with the supervisor," one responded.

I was furious that anyone on the case would be so reckless. I never did find out which member of the cover team it was.

"I'm in here living with these animals every day, and we have guys driving around in Crown Vics? We're just begging to help them figure out I'm a cop," I said, angrily. "Smarten up or we're going to have a serious problem."

I called Karelas and Kotchian and told them what happened. They told me they would do their best to ensure these types of mistakes wouldn't happen. I needed the guys I knew and trusted to make sure no one blew the case, or worse, made a mistake that would get me killed. It wouldn't be the last time my life would be put at risk because of someone else's actions.

After that screwup, I had to back off on buying crack from Hogman. It didn't matter, though. I already bought plenty from him, and he had a gun every time. I had enough evidence to put him away for a long time. And that was just fine with me.

CHAPTER 33

I was buying drugs from Hogman, Tracy, and other Pagans regularly. I bought and sold guns from them. I witnessed more beatdowns and sat in on planning sessions for revenge attacks against the Hells Angels. I was the treasurer and carried around the chapter's books, filled with documentation of corruption and financial malfeasance. The money trail is always key to a prosecution, especially in a RICO case, and that was certainly the situation for this one. We needed to prove that money was coming in and going out to further the criminal enterprise. With the books in my possession, and my eyewitness accounts of all the violence, drug dealing, and gunplay, we were in a strong position to get a lot of bad guys on a wide variety of charges.

While I was officially in the gang, there were still some Pagans who didn't fully trust me. The supervisor tailing Williams in a Crown Vic raised new questions about whether someone was a rat. It wasn't helpful to me.

Rocky Point was my home in those days, but I snuck back to see Ang and the girls when I could. Sadly for me, and Ang and the girls, once I got patched in, those trips were few and far between. There was always something going on in the gang, and even when I was home, I was often distracted and pulled myself away to deal with club business.

Almost every day, I was at J.R.'s house, the tattoo shop, Roadblock's house, on a run, or at one of the Pagan bars. I was tired of faking doing shots, faking doing coke, and fake swilling Buds. I wanted to be home and have a cookout with my friends—my real friends. Not those dirty scumbags.

The little downtime I had was spent writing reports and taking notes. I had a five-subject notebook, the kind you have in high school, where I wrote notes each day about what I witnessed. That notebook was my record that I'd use when it came time to write affidavits and testify.

I also had an ATF phone and an ATF laptop. I kept the phone, laptop, notebook, my badge, and gun in a huge safe at my undercover house. I made up a story that the safe belonged to the owners and that I had tried to open it but could not.

It was a real pain in the ass to remember which IDs were where, but it became second nature after more than a year of living with the Pagans. I set up an old computer table with a crappy old desktop PC hooked up to the Internet through a modem. It was mostly for show, but sometimes we used it for Pagan business.

I had a small filing cabinet stuffed with old bills and documents with Ken Pallis's name on them. Utility bills, store credit cards, rental agreements—anything to show that I was real and had a history, in case those guys went snooping, which they did.

When I could, I snuck back home in the undercover truck or on my bike. I usually took the ferry between New London, Connecticut, and Orient Point on Long Island. It was about an hour drive from Orient Point to Rocky Point.

One time I was driving back from Massachusetts in the truck and I had my ATF laptop and phone and my notebook in a duffel bag. I was always vague with the gang about when I was coming and going. The less they knew about my comings and goings, the better. It gave me more time to strategize, organize, and think.

"I have some business in New Bedford, and I'll be back sometime Wednesday," I'd say.

If they asked what time, I'd say, morning, or afternoon, or at night. Never a definitive time. I didn't need them knowing when I was leaving or arriving. I knew there was always a chance they were following me. I was still the new guy.

That day, Roadblock asked me specifically what time I was getting off the ferry. He put me on the spot and I had no good lie ready so I had to tell him which ferry I was on.

"We're coming to meet you," he told me.

I had all my ATF stuff in the truck, so I had to try to find a way to avoid seeing them before I could get home and get those materials back in the safe.

"I'm actually already on the road," I said. "Why don't you just meet me at the house?"

I pulled the truck over and hid the notebook, laptop, and other items underneath the seat of the truck's extended cab, shoving them underneath the jack. I was nervous. I knew that if they looked under there, they would find the laptop and know right away that I was a cop, since it had a sticker on it with a serial number that said "ATF." My phone, if they made me open it, which they would have if they'd found it, was loaded with ATF contacts. It would have taken them seconds to figure out I was a fed. There was nowhere I could stash them, so I just had to hope.

I pulled into Rocky Point and drove to the house. As I pulled into the driveway, Roadblock and J.R. were sitting outside, waiting for me. It was obvious they wanted to catch me before I went into the house.

It was another test. I was sweating bullets but had to appear totally normal.

"Hey, you guys beat me here," I said clumsily as I got out of the truck.

"Yeah," Roadblock said, eyeing me.

J.R. didn't say a word and walked right over to the truck. Roadblock made small talk while J.R. looked through the cab. I had my gun on me, so if I had to shoot my way out, I was ready.

"Hey, we'll help you carry your bags in," J.R. said.

He continued combing through the vehicle. I stood there watching him. They were always looking for anything unusual—a receipt, a note, a cop duffel bag. They were looking for a *mistake.*

If he told me to lift the seat, I was prepared to tell him no. I would have acted like I was protecting the money I'd just collected from drug sales back in Massachusetts.

I played it out in my head.

"Hey, you know I just did some collections. You guys aren't taking that money," I would have told him.

I'm not sure it would have worked. But it was my only shot. They either would have been offended that I suggested they might steal from me, or their radar would have gone up and they would have opened it and found my ATF stash.

Somehow, I got lucky again. J.R. stopped snooping. He lost interest and walked toward the house. I grabbed my bag and we walked inside. We talked about meeting up the next day, and they split. I exhaled and called my cover team.

"That was fuckin' close," I told them.

"Sit tight. We'll tail them," one of the agents told me.

I sweated it out until I received confirmation they were gone. Once I got the all clear, I went outside and got my ATF gear from under the seat and brought it in.

As if that wasn't enough stress, I was growing more concerned by the day about Globe and others in ATF not understanding the stakes. As the case expanded, I was less concerned about saying the wrong thing to Roadblock or Izzo and more worried that one of those agents would screw up and blow my cover. I started to feel that if anyone was going to get me killed, it would be someone in ATF. Second would be the Hells Angels, and third would be getting in a bike wreck. Getting killed by one of the Pagans was pretty far down my list.

It was a strange feeling, thinking that the felons surrounding me every day, selling guns, drugs, and bombs, were less of a threat than a couple ATF supervisors who had other motives and priorities not necessarily aligned with putting the Pagans in jail. Some higher-ups believed they always had all the right answers and knew what was best for the investigation, but it wasn't their ass out there trying to negotiate that twisted world. They loved telling war stories about cases they worked on. They got off on telling me how we should proceed, yet none of them had ever been in the position I was in. There were only a handful of agents who truly knew what I was going through. I was constantly battling to articulate why certain moves were necessary to build a stronger case, and had to defend against insinuations I was drifting toward the dark side.

Like all undercover agents, I was assigned a "contact agent"—a person with similar long-term undercover experience who understood what I was going through. My contact agent was John Carr. He had done a ton of undercover work throughout his career, including infiltrating the Mongols outlaw motorcycle gang as part of ATF's "Black Rain" case in Southern California in 2008. John knew the ropes. He listened, strategized with me, and worked to keep the wolves at bay so I could do my job. ATF had a system in place for that kind of case. If everyone followed the process, all would have been fine. But the Globes of the world thought they knew better, despite no real experience to rely on.

I'd always wanted to see how far we could go, to get to the top and tear the whole organization down. But goal posts moved, and no longer was it about tearing down the Mother Club. That strategic shift pissed me off. I said from day one that I wasn't going to sacrifice precious time out of my life to throw a few scumbags in jail. I wanted to take down the Mother Club. I wanted to expose the whole organization so that other cops up and down the East Coast could learn their tactics and take steps to stop their domestic terrorism.

As the philosophical gap grew, I detached from some in ATF. I got deeper into the role and felt more and more isolated. I felt betrayed by certain people in my own agency. I felt vulnerable. No one except the few who had lived a double life like I was living could understand the range of emotions I went through. I was exhausted from trying to explain why I couldn't contact the cover team on a daily basis. They simply didn't understand that the Pagans didn't keep schedules. I was called morning, noon, and night, at random, and ordered to go to meetings, to bars, or to show up somewhere to take part in drug and gun deals, never with any notice.

Most of the cover team members were supportive, but a few didn't grasp that plans changed by the minute. The Pagans weren't nine-to-fivers, that's for sure.

J.R., Roadblock, the Mother Club, and other gang leaders held their cards close to the vest until the last minute, when they were ready to abruptly launch their criminal plots. A few agents on the case simply didn't understand that when I was told to participate in those plans, I had to go immediately, without hesitation, and almost always without warning. It became exhausting to continually explain myself to a small group of obstructionists and malcontents.

I understood their frustration in some ways, as many put in long hours, but my life was on the line every minute of every day and I had to operate accordingly. Crime doesn't follow a calendar, and the case required patience, commitment, and flexibility. Not everyone is cut out for it.

The core members of my team had my back and were my lifeline, but those who weren't fully on board were becoming a major problem. As I got deeper into the gang, I became more conflicted about my relationship with the Pagans and my relationship with ATF. I never had illusions about my place with the Pagans or about the gang. I hated them and everything they stood for, but I began to feel a certain level of camaraderie with some of them. In that unpredictable environment, I felt some of the Pagans had my back more than a few of the agents who were clearly more worried about their careers than they were about me.

I spent more time with Roadblock, Hogman, J.R., and the rest of the gang than I did with my coworkers or my wife and kids. Still, I never developed any sympathy or compassion for any of them. They were rotten to the core. There were times when we were at events, drinking beers and laughing, that I had some fun, and I even found some of them entertaining. But I never got caught up in the lifestyle and never lost sight of my mission or the fact that the Pagans were a bunch of racist, misogynistic drug dealers, thugs, and killers.

The only guy I felt slightly bad about taking down was Doc. Doc, whose real name was Douglas Youmans, had a long criminal record for drugs, guns, assaults, and driving drunk, but he wasn't as much of a sick sociopath as the others.

When I spoke with Doc, there was a certain amount of sincerity in his words that I did not get from many others. He was a hard-core biker, but for him, it was less about crime and more about the brotherhood, the camaraderie, and having each other's back. Doc actually curbed some of the violence when he had the opportunity and wasn't always trying to get over on people, whether civilians or other bikers.

He loved to drink and drug, but overall, he wasn't out to hurt anyone. In my early days of prospecting, Doc looked out for me and helped keep me out of harm's way, including once hiding me out during witching hour in Ohio. I appreciated that and respected him for having a modicum of humanity, unlike many of the other Pagans. I'd soon repay his favor and then some.

Sitting with Doc, watching him innocently drink a beer and enjoy his little place in the Pagan hierarchy made me a bit sad, because I knew it would be me putting him behind the walls of a federal prison with the rest of them. That is, if all went well and I didn't get made or killed.

Another Pagan I started getting close to was Hellboy, a former mixed martial arts fighter and big meth tweaker who was sergeant-at-arms of the Elizabeth, New Jersey, chapter. Hellboy (real name: Robert Deronde) was five feet eleven inches and two hundred and fifty pounds of solid muscle and unharnessed chaos. He had strawberry-blond hair and blue eyes, and despite being more than fifty years old, he had a string of beautiful twenty-something girlfriends. He loved bragging about his sexual exploits. He told me he liked it rough and once squeezed a woman's fake breast so hard that he popped her implant. A real Romeo.

He damaged his shoulder in a fight and had surgery, during which he claimed doctors implanted a pig ligament. He was jittery, lifted weights constantly, and was a complete loose cannon. He sure earned his nickname as he was erratic and struck fear in most. He started selling me meth and seemed to trust me, but I was always on my toes when I dealt with Hellboy.

After all, this was a business with real risk. There were very few on either side I could trust.

If I was going to survive, rise up the ranks, and take down some serious players, I had to put aside the politics in the Pagans, as well as ATF, and be smart. I'd always have to watch out for the Hells Angels, who were like an ominous, threatening cloud that forever hovered over the club.

One wrong move in any of those worlds and things would come tumbling down.

CHAPTER 34

The distance between me and Ang was growing. I was caught up in doing my job and staying alive. It was hard for me to understand how much was changing at home, because I wasn't there and I wasn't emotionally available.

Ang noticed the distance and the changes in me a lot sooner than I did. When the case first started, when we would talk about plans and whether I could come home for some gathering or event, she got upset when I told her I couldn't make it. Once I was patched in, the case intensified greatly and I was less and less available, not only to go home but even just to talk or participate in our family in any meaningful way.

I was constantly canceling plans to go home. I was regularly calling her to tell her that I had been planning to be home for something—a holiday, a birthday, a family party—but wouldn't be able to make it. It became the norm, and as the case progressed, she learned to live without me. She wasn't mad and wasn't resentful; she was just dealing with the facts. She knew I wouldn't be there, so she pretty much stopped planning around me or expecting me at all.

Like all marriages, you rely on your spouse for advice, input, and support. She stopped doing that. Whatever the situation—a family argument, an issue at school for the girls, a relative's illness—she just kind of stopped bringing them up because she knew I didn't have the emotional bandwidth to deal with it. It was a matter of survival for her. She had to make decisions without my input. She couldn't wait.

Sometimes I'd get caught up on the situation at a later time, but often I didn't. She did what she had to do.

I realized that she and the girls were not as reliant on me as they once were. I thought it was fine, but it was becoming clear that we didn't have the connection we would normally feel.

They say distance makes the heart grow fonder, but that's bullshit. Time away never makes anything better. The time and distance apart, coupled with the stress, was not good for our relationship. I was trying to keep all the balls in the air, and the pressure was building.

The longer the case went on, the harder it got to get home or even call. We were constantly running here or there.

I was buying drugs, guns, writing reports, going to church, shaking down bar owners, and trying to keep my cover team in the loop to make sure we did everything we needed to do to stay safe and make ironclad cases.

On one occasion, I snuck home for a couple days to see the girls and drove to Bridgewater to check in with my old team. They were in the middle of a drug case and asked me to jump in and give them a hand, since I was home.

They needed me to do a gun and drug buy in Brockton from a known dealer. I didn't think much about it because it was the kind of case I had done a million times with those guys. I took the undercover Ford Expedition, which is covertly wired for video and sound so the cover team can see and hear what is happening. I drove to Brockton to meet the dealer, a scumbag nicknamed "B."

I knew who he was and wasn't too concerned. He showed up suddenly, popping out of a nearby alley, and he had another guy with him, which he had never done before. They both got into the car quickly, with the second guy sitting in the back seat.

Rule number one of undercover is, don't let a bad guy sit behind you, as it makes it impossible to see if he is going to try to rob or kill you.

"Who the fuck is this guy?" I asked B.

"He's cool. Don't sweat it, bro," B answered.

"How do I know he's not a cop?" I asked.

"Bro, he's cool," B assured me.

As B pulled the crack cocaine out of his sock, I was trying to keep a close eye on the dude in the back seat. B put the drugs on my scale and was showing me the weight when I saw the dude in the back pulling a handgun from his waist.

My gun was on my hip but was pinned between the seat and my belt. It was easier and quicker to go between the two front seats and try to grab the gun from this guy before he had a chance to pull it all the way out and point it at me.

I lunged, grabbed the barrel of his gun, and pushed it toward the floor of the truck, hoping that if he pulled the trigger the worst that would happen would be that he shot himself in the foot. As we wrestled with the gun, the cover team heard the commotion and started driving to the scene to help.

"What are you doing?" B yelled. "He is the dude with the gun you wanted to buy!"

"I have no fucking idea who he is!" I yelled. "He shouldn't be pulling that shit out in the back seat without letting me know."

I was relieved the guy wasn't trying to kill me, but the cover team was already racing our way. I gave them the wave-off signal, and the team sped by. The deal finished with me buying a gun and some crack.

It was a success, but had it gone awry, that case and the Pagan case would have gone up in flames. If I shot that guy—or worse, if I got shot—there would have been no way to continue with the Pagans, as my cover would have been blown. I would have been pulled off.

The guys from my group were glad for the help, but we all realized it was a mistake for me to have participated in that buy. Later, when I was home with Ang, I told her what I did. She hit the roof.

"Are you crazy?" she asked me. "You need to start saying no to some people, Ken. Let someone else do some of this stuff."

I was a bit stunned, but as we talked, it became clear that she was right. That was a short-term drug and gun case. I was in the middle of a long-term undercover infiltration case. Agents had invested a lot of time and the government had spent a lot of money for me to successfully build a criminal case to take some bad people off of the streets. It simply wasn't worth jeopardizing.

I never should have done that case. I should have said no. It could have been a catastrophic mistake, but again, luck was on my side.

Ang and I came to an agreement that I wouldn't do any other casework until the undercover operation was over. The problem was, neither of us knew when that would be.

I tried to get home and see the kids, but even when I could, I was so wiped out and distracted that I was mostly useless. I was becoming jaded and desensitized to the violence, the nomadic lifestyle, and the chaos.

Each time I rode back into our suburban enclave, I felt more and more like a stranger in a strange land. It was odd to feel myself drift away from the warm comforts of home and become more acclimated to a lifestyle as a loner bouncing between grubby drug dens, seedy motels, and shithole bars.

Ang and I love a good dive bar, but when you're living in them every day with your head on a swivel, it gets old. And depressing. I missed Ang's cooking, but I certainly wasn't missing any meals. It seemed every day I was at a barbecue with those guys, plowing through racks of massive beef ribs. It wasn't home, but, man, there were some good eats, I have to say.

I became more distant, and it was harder and harder for me to shed my role as Slam. The girls could see the changes in me. Gone was the clean-cut, in-shape, golf-shirt-wearing, smiling dad they knew. Now what they saw was an overweight, stressed-out, exhausted, gruff, and smelly biker. I wasn't smiling much in those days.

My brain was working on overdrive balancing the double- and triple-lives I was leading. I juggled lie after lie to Roadblock, J.R., Izzo, and the others. I ran through strategic scenarios in my head at all hours, concocting solutions to keep me safe, to appease ATF supervisors, and to nail down evidence to support criminal charges for the RICO case we were building.

Whenever I was home, my phone was like a time bomb. It would inevitably ring at the worst possible moments, and it would be Road-block or J.R. or Hogman. I had to answer it. There was no explaining to them that I was busy. Ever. I'd run outside to talk and make up a lie about where I was. If they'd ever heard kids or Ang in the background, it would have raised their suspicions. How would I explain a teenager's voice? To them, I didn't have any kids. How would I have explained Ang's voice, if they heard her in the background? I couldn't lie and tell them it was Steph, because they knew Steph's voice. If I told them it was Steph, they would have asked to talk to her and that would be that.

The daily mental exercises I went through to avoid land mines were mind-boggling.

Ang saw the stress and the changes in me, and it scared her. I was aloof. I was on edge. As much as she was worried about me crossing over to the dark side or getting killed, it was becoming clear the girls felt it too. They needed their dad. It was getting impossible for Ang to handle.

She was fighting a lot with our oldest daughter. Sometimes, the girls were picked on at school because their dad looked like a scum-bag biker. Rumors flew around town. Some parents wouldn't let their kids hang out with our girls.

Our youngest, Meaghan, was arguing with kids on her sports teams. Mostly just little girl stuff, but she needed her dad to talk to. And I wasn't there. That's probably the hardest part for me, as I look back. That I wasn't there. That I *couldn't* be there.

One day, Meaghan had a near-breakdown at the house. She was telling Ang about the girls on the team picking on her, and Ang was trying to calm her down. She lost it.

"I want Dad!" she screamed at the top of her lungs.

She collapsed in the corner of the living room in tears. Ang didn't know what to do. She couldn't even call me to let me know what was going on. God knows what I was even doing that day.

Ang went over and grabbed her by the arms. Meaghan was kicking and screaming, in a panic.

"Meaghan," Ang said, as gently as she could. "It's going to be okay. Dad is going to be home soon. You can tell him how you feel. I love you. He loves you. We both love you."

Meaghan continued to sob but stopped kicking and screaming. She collapsed into Ang's arms. It was a cathartic moment that had to happen.

In addition to the pressures of raising three girls without me at home, in the back of her mind was a very real fear that the Pagans would find out my true identity and we would all be at risk.

Despite her fears and the drama going on at home, Ang knew she could never call me. She always had to wait until I had a chance to call her. We'd go days without speaking. When we did, she filled me in on bits and pieces, but because of the distance, she knew she was mostly on her own to handle those crises. Besides the logistical issues that kept us from talking much, she also knew it would have been unfair to tell me about every crisis because there was nothing I could do about it as long as I was undercover.

It's not unlike when someone is in prison and doesn't want visitors. Often, inmates' visitors, while well intentioned, are nothing more than a reminder of a part of life the incarcerated person is unable to deal with anymore. It opens massive emotional wounds, fuels guilt, and often causes pain to everyone involved. That's kind of how my life was for a while.

Ang knew that telling me about the emotional pain she and the girls were experiencing would only heighten my stress and distract me. Any distraction, she knew, as my wife and as an agent, could cause me to make a potentially fatal mistake. I'm thankful she understood the pressures of the job and am forever grateful for all she did to carry our family through those difficult and often dark days.

She was also doing her best to be supportive of me, but it got harder as the case wore on. She was raising three girls without much help, and she worried more and more each day that perhaps she'd be doing it for good.

"None of this is worth it, Ken, if it's going to affect who you are," she pleaded with me. "I can't lose you to the other side."

She had some help from family members, but she put a great deal of pressure on herself to be everything for everyone—even at the risk of her own health. In fact, the heavy burden she carried had consequences, as she got sick in the middle of the case.

Ang got word to me that she drove herself to the hospital. She thought she was having a heart attack. My heart raced. I grabbed a bag, hopped in my truck, and took off, speeding toward home. At that moment, I didn't care about the Pagans or the case. I'd figure all that out later. My wife needed me. My girls needed me.

Ang called my sister Karin, who came and took the girls. Karin was often there to lend support and help Ang whenever needed. Ang was taken to a Boston hospital. We didn't know what was going on. The girls were terrified. Their dad wasn't around and now they were afraid they were going to lose their mom.

She was stabilized at the hospital and her heart was okay, but we found out she had a high white blood cell count. We were concerned she might have cancer. She underwent a battery of screenings, and thankfully, there was no cancer.

The doctor determined that the high stress Ang had been under for so long had caused the elevated white blood cell count. She literally worried herself sick. Prior to being discharged from the hospital the doctor met with us and recommended that she lower her stress levels. All I kept thinking was, if he only knew the whole story.

It was overwhelming, but Ang and I decided I had to continue. I had come too far and was getting closer to getting to the Mother Club.

I was now an officer in a Pagans chapter and was learning more every day about how the gang operated and just how violent they were. I felt good about where the case was headed and hoped I'd only have a few more months left.

I knew I'd have more tests, and Ang would have more challenges, but we agreed we'd give it our all to see the case through.

As much as we'd been through, nothing could have prepared us for the danger, deception, and darkness that lay ahead.

CHAPTER 35

Back in Long Island, it was business as usual with the Pagans. I was selling drugs and buying guns, and I had the trust of Roadblock and J.R. Or at least I thought.

There were still some who had questions about me, I learned. One day, Tracy came by my undercover house. I had some of the rooms wired, but I had to be careful because they could still sweep the place for bugs at any time.

I bought some coke from Tracy, as I was doing regularly. He left and went back to Roadblock's house where a bunch of the members were hanging out. They were talking about me and one of them mentioned that they were still checking some things out with me. Something had spooked them. Maybe it was a phone call they overheard. Maybe it was the Crown Vic that followed Williams.

Whatever it was, they still were wary of me, despite my status in the gang.

"We're checking some things out to make sure Slam's not an informant," Izzo said.

Tracy, who had moved up north to the Catskills, hit the roof.

"What are you talking about?" he said.

"We need to make sure," Roadblock said.

"Why didn't someone say something to me? I just sold him a bunch of coke," Tracy said. "You could have told me that before."

"Don't worry about it," Roadblock said. "We have a plan. We're going to find out for sure once and for all, and if he turns out to be a rat, we will take care of it."

The next day, I was with Hogman. I'd bought an ounce of crack off him when he dropped a bombshell on me.

"I have some work I need help with, but you have to keep it just between us," he told me.

"What's that?" I asked.

He told me about a cocaine dealer up in the Catskills that he and Tracy knew who burned them. It was a Black guy, he said. A guy I had met before. We had been in Woodstock some months before and bought some powder cocaine from a guy Tracy knew who lived nearby.

"We were up there, a deal went bad, and we ended up having to kill the guy," Hogman said. "We buried him in a plot of land. But the land has been sold and we have to move the body."

I was shocked but had to stay cool.

"No problem," I said. "Whatever you need."

It was a seismic moment in the case. I had a slew of charges, for guns, drugs, assault, conspiracy, extortion, and racketeering, but now we were talking about murder. We hadn't been able to make a case on Hogman or anyone else for the Bennett killing, but this was a new lead. I had my recording device on me and was praying I'd gotten the conversation recorded.

I finished up the meeting with Hogman and headed back toward my place, but first I had to meet my cover team and fill them in on what was going on. I often met whoever was on duty late at night in a dark parking lot, far away from the eyes of the gang.

Around one a.m., I met two agents from the New York office. I was exhausted and had been running around all day. I gave them the ounce of crack I bought from Hogman, signed off on it, and told them the story about the body.

"I'll believe it when I hear the recording," one of them said.

"Well, you tell me," I said, turning over the device.

They took it with them and downloaded it, but the thing never went on. I didn't have the conversation recorded. The device was a constant source of stress. Sometimes, it turned on inadvertently while I was out riding my bike and filled up with the sound of my roaring engine. By the time I got to wherever I was going, I assumed it was on, but it was already full and missed crucial conversations. At church, sometimes Roadblock and J.R. would put on huge blower fans during illicit conversations. You couldn't hear anything over those fans, and they used them specifically in case any place we met was bugged. The device had worked well many times during this case, but there were times it failed me. This was one of them.

I talked with Bryan DiGirolamo, and we decided to look deeper into the dead body mystery. Agents working the case with me started digging into unsolved murders and missing persons cases in the Catskills and surrounding areas.

I was given a couple more digital recorders. They held hours of data, but sometimes filled up with a whole lot of nothing, and I would never know it. We never really knew what we had until the recordings were downloaded and someone listened back. I was able to speak with Hogman and recreate the conversation in order to get the recordings we missed due to the previous malfunction.

Hogman mentioned the body several times. Each time, he'd give me a few more details.

"It was a drug deal that went bad," he told me once. "The guy started talking shit, so we smoked him."

Another time he told me they cut off his hands and fed them to pigs. The area where Tracy lived up in the Catskills was filled with slaughterhouses and pig farms. It wouldn't have taken much for them to dump body parts somewhere no one would find them.

He told me that he, Tracy, and I would be taking a trip up to the Catskills to move the body. The development set off alarms from Boston to Washington. There were some who wanted to shut the case down immediately, get indictments and warrants, sweep up as many of them as we could, and press Tracy and Hogman to take us to the body.

There were others who felt there was no urgency, despite news of the buried corpse. Those in that camp felt that the body had been buried for several months, so waiting a few more to develop more charges and more information about the murder would pay dividends.

I agreed with those in that camp.

As with everything else with the Pagans, there was no timeline, no schedule, and I was on a need-to-know basis. Hogman brought up the body when he wanted, and I just had to wait.

CHAPTER 36

With the drama surrounding the dead body dominating the case, there was another major concern that we had to address: the "Christmas presents."

Roadblock was still seething over his beating by the Hells Angels, and there was constant talk of retribution. We had Pagans from other chapters coming in and out of town, which raised tensions and caught the attention of local cops.

Every other day, it seemed, we had a false alarm where someone said the Angels were coming to town. Every time it happened, we called in backup. The local cops knew our chapter members, but when they saw chapters from outside our area roaring through town flying colors, they knew something was up and they stepped up patrols.

They were always discussing delivering Christmas presents—bombs—to Mario and the New York Hells Angels. After that church session that I was able to get on tape, where they discussed explicitly bombing the Angels, I had to come up with a plan to get one of the homemade bombs.

It was great to have them on tape discussing potential bombings, but it would be another thing completely to obtain explosives from one of the Pagans. Once again, I had to get creative.

I knew they had them stashed somewhere around Rocky Point and must have had someone local who made them. I needed to find out before we had a building bombed or one detonated in someone's truck or bike. I didn't want to wait until innocent bystanders were killed.

One night, several out-of-town Pagans were invited by Road-block to come to Rocky Point to go looking for some Hells Angels. The Pagans had a bunch of guns and a few bombs in one of the cars parked near the clubhouse.

Before we went hunting for Hells Angels, the local gang unit caught wind that there were a lot of out-of-town Pagans in the area, and cops came out in force to see what was going on. The area heated up and there were cruisers everywhere.

Roadblock decided it was too hot, so we called off the plan for the night. The problem was that they had all the guns and bombs in one of the vehicles and needed to get them out of the area without getting pulled over. I told J.R. there was too much heat on us, so I'd have Steph come by and drive the vehicle out of the area. The local cops would be watching us but not our old ladies, I told him.

"I'll get Steph to ride in here in her truck, grab the bags, and leave," I said.

J.R. liked the plan, so I called Steph.

"I need you to come over to the clubhouse," I said. "There's some shit here, guns and maybe bombs. I think I've got them convinced to let you drive this shit out of here."

We had a chance to confiscate a lot of artillery. J.R. was all for it, but as with everything else, he needed to talk to Roadblock. Road-block wasn't having any of it and was furious at the suggestion.

"Old ladies don't take care of problems. We take care of our own problems," he said.

It blew my plan out of the water. If I knew for sure they were driving around with a bomb, I could have had my guys pull them over. But I didn't know for sure if they had any. If I had them stopped and they had nothing, it would have been another red flag that someone in the club was an informant.

I spent a lot of time trying to figure out who the bomb maker was and how they were getting them. I was worried about how cavalier they were with their explosives. Did they have two or twenty-five? I had no idea, and it was frustrating.

I needed to find out what the bombs were, where they had them, and how many they had. I talked to another agent friend of mine who was an explosives expert, and we decided a good strategy would be to come up with a fake target to blow up.

It had to be something back in Massachusetts, though, where those guys didn't know anyone and didn't know the landscape, so I could control the entire scenario. If I came up with a plan, for example, to bomb a bar or clubhouse in Long Island, they could have taken it upon themselves and carried it out without my involvement.

I'd told them in the past about gunfights out on the water between lobstermen and fishermen. I told them stories about fishing boat owners who shot poachers.

So I came up with a story that a rival of mine back in New Bedford caught me poaching and poured sugar in the gas tank of my boat, ruining it.

"I want to get this guy," I told Izzo. "Piece of shit."

Izzo knew I always had money and that poaching and lobstering was my bread and butter. Money always talked with the Pagans, so Izzo was all ears.

"Yeah? I'll help you," he said. "What do you want to do?"

"I want to blow his boat up," I said.

Izzo thought for a second.

"I might be able to help," he said. "I can get one of the Christmas presents and you can use one to blow up the boat."

"Seriously?" I asked. "That would be perfect." .

"Yeah, man," Izzo said. "I think I can make that happen."

As always, things never happened according to plan. The bomb conversation waned and a few weeks passed.

Another part of my backstory was that I did collections for my boss, who I said was a loan shark. If people were late on payments, I was sent to make collections and remind them what happened when payments were missed.

I wanted Izzo to see me doing some collections because it would give me more credibility as a criminal, so I grabbed a couple of Bridgewater agents—B. J. White and Danny Meade—and we arranged some fake collections. It's called street theater, and it's a common practice during long-term undercover cases to bolster street cred.

I laid the ground rules with Izzo, because he was a bit of a wild card, especially if he was all strung out. If he showed up all wild-eyed and tweaking, with a gun, he could do something stupid and get one of the agents hurt or worse.

So I took complete control.

"Look, man, you're on my turf up here," I told him. "I'm in charge. The reason why the last guy I was doing collections with isn't doing it anymore was because he was too aggressive and did some stupid shit. I'm the one who decides what the right way is. You listen to me. That's it."

"Okay, cool," he said.

"If I give the nod, you do what you have to do. If I don't, you don't do shit," I said. "Got it?"

"Sure thing, man," he said.

I headed home for a couple days, and one day my phone rang. It was Izzo.

"Man, this Dunkin' Donuts coffee sucks," he said, laughing.

"Ha-ha," I said. "Yeah, I know. Where are you?"

"The Dunkin' Donuts on Route 14," he said. "Their coffee sucks."

My blood ran cold. There was no Route 14 in Long Island. He was in Massachusetts. He was in my town.

"Bro, where are you?" I asked.

"I'm here at your work, come on out," he said.

I was sitting at home in my civilian clothes. I wasn't expecting him for several hours and we were supposed to meet in southern Massachusetts, nowhere near where I lived.

"Aw, man, I'm out west in Springfield making a parts delivery," I said.

Springfield was about two hours west of where he was, so I figured that would buy me some time. He knew I did auto parts deliveries for my boss at the garage, so that added up too.

"Yeah, I know, I just went inside and they said you weren't there," he said.

My blood ran a bit colder. The guys at the garage had orders to tell anyone who ever came looking for me that I was out on a delivery. To have it actually happen was unsettling. I hoped none of them had said anything to raise Izzo's suspicions.

I had my undercover truck at my house. I felt confident he didn't know where I lived, but it was a small town, so I had to be careful. I called the cover team.

"Hey, fucking Izzo is in town," I said. "In my town. I need you guys to get eyes on him, track him, and don't lose him."

I ran into my bedroom and put on my grungy biker clothes. I sprinted outside, hopped in the truck, and drove out of my neighborhood as calmly as possible, looking around furiously to make sure neither Izzo nor anyone else was staking me out.

I called B. J. White and Danny Meade and told them we were doing the street theater earlier than planned today and gave them times and locations. I realized I didn't even say goodbye to my family. My head was spinning.

I had to get out of town and onto the highway without him seeing me. He'd know my truck immediately. There weren't many New York plates around that neighborhood and none on shitty pickup trucks. That vehicle stood out like a sore thumb to normal people, but to a Pagan looking for it, it might as well have a siren and lights on it.

My cover team found him and filled me in on his location. He was on the move. I had to get onto the major highway near my house, speed west, get off an exit, and head back east to meet him, pretending I was just getting back to the area from Springfield.

"Where the hell is he?" I asked one of my agents.

"He's getting on the on-ramp right now," the agent said. "He's right behind you."

"Shit," I said.

I was at the end of the ramp, merging onto a four-lane highway, and he was just a few hundred yards behind me pulling onto the on-ramp. I gunned it. It was a massive, open highway, and there wasn't much traffic on the road. I had to get out of sight as soon as possible, because if he saw the back of my truck, he'd try to catch me. It was a frenzied game of cat and mouse.

I hit the gas and sped up to 110 miles per hour. I called Izzo.

"Hey, man, meet me at the 99," I said, pointing him to a local 99 Restaurant.

"Sounds good, bro," he said.

My heart was racing again. I was speeding and thinking about what he might know. With Izzo, I was never sure if I was walking into an ambush. I pulled into the restaurant parking lot and rushed inside. I grabbed a table and ordered a beer. He pulled in just a few minutes later.

I sucked down the beer and thought about my strategy. I not only had to coordinate the fake collections, I worried about whether Izzo would snap and try to hurt one of my friends. He walked over to the table, expressionless.

"Hey, man," I said.

The waitress came by.

"Grab him one of these," I said, tapping my mug.

We sat and ate a quick meal, talking about the latest happenings going on within the chapter. After the meal I looked at him.

"Be right back, man. Gotta piss," I said. "Long ride."

What I really needed to do was turn on my recording device. I walked into the bathroom and went over to the urinal. I started going to the bathroom and was about to take out the device and turn it on when the door opened. It was Izzo.

He didn't go over to a stall or a urinal or the sink. He just stood behind me.

I craned my neck and looked over my shoulder at him. He had a shit-eating smirk on his face. He was wearing a long biker trench coat, one that went down past his knees. It was buttoned.

"What the hell are you doing?" I asked.

He grinned and unbuttoned his coat. He opened it like a flasher. In the inside pocket, I saw a cylinder and a fuse.

It was a bomb.

I was shocked.

"Bro, what's that?" I said, feigning ignorance.

"It's one of the Christmas presents," he said. "You want to blow up the boat, let's go blow up the boat."

"Jesus Christ," I said. "You brought that shit in here? You have it in your coat?"

He chuckled unsettlingly.

I had to get him and the bomb out of there. I also had to figure out how we were going to find a boat to blow up, or somehow get him to give me the bomb to go do it myself. Or pretend to anyway.

"Okay," I said. "Meet me out at the truck. I'll pay the tab, and I'll be right out."

He left the restaurant. I went back to the table and paid the tab. I still had to do the fake collections, but I couldn't do them driving around with a live bomb. I called Steph.

"Listen, I'm over at the 99. Izzo just showed up, and he's got one of the bombs," I told her. "I'm going to get him to leave it in his car. And we'll leave the car there. Tell the cover team to have the bomb squad on stand-by, and we'll roll them in to render the device safe after Izzo heads back to New York."

I hung up. I stood for a minute looking around the restaurant. There were other diners there. Our waitress came by and grabbed the check and the cash. I fake smiled at her.

If any of them knew what had just walked right past them . . .

I walked outside and met Izzo at his car.

"Hey, let's get rid of that thing," I told him. "We can't drive around with that. We don't need that kind of heat if we get pulled over or something goes wrong."

"Yeah, I guess not," he conceded.

"We'll come back and get it," I said.

He gave me the bomb. I had a large Dunkin' Donuts Styrofoam

cup in my truck, and the bomb fit inside it. I put it in the cup and carefully placed it into the trunk of Izzo's car.

"We'll leave this here and take my truck to do the collections," I said.

"Sure, whatever," he said.

I hopped behind the wheel of my truck, and he got in. I put the key in the ignition and looked back at his car, sitting there parked with a live explosive in the trunk.

I put the truck in drive and drove out of the parking lot.

CHAPTER 37

We drove the back roads to a sports bar a couple towns over. I pulled around back and parked next to a beat-up Toyota driven by Danny Meade, one of the agents from my team in Bridgewater.

To Izzo, Danny was a deadbeat gambler who owed my boss $1,000.

"Listen, I'm going to go talk to this guy, get the money, and I'll be right back," I told Izzo. "Wait here, but if I give you the sign, come on over."

I got out of the truck and walked over to Danny's car. He was sitting inside with the window down. I leaned in.

"Get out of the car," I said.

Danny stepped out of the vehicle. I grabbed him roughly.

"Hey, you're fucking late," I said.

I shoved him onto the hood.

"When I have to come down here, there are fucking problems," I said. "Give me the money."

Danny reached into his pocket and pulled out a wad of cash.

"Is it all here?" I asked.

"Yeah, man," he said.

"Good."

I shoved him onto the hood of the car again for good measure and walked away. Poor Danny had to put up with that. It's a wonder neither of us started laughing.

Izzo was impressed. I got back into the truck and drove to my next "collection."

We met B. J. White in the parking lot of a Home Depot. I had a bat in the car. I pointed to it and told Izzo: "I may walk back here and grab this. Sit tight."

Izzo liked my techniques, I could see. My big concern was that he would jump out to join in the fun and take it too far. He wasn't too strung out, so I felt confident he'd behave.

I shook down B.J. and walked back to the car. I opened the truck door, leaned in, and told Izzo I had to make a few calls about the boat so we could go take care of that business. I made a few fake calls while I walked around the parking lot.

"Hey, man, this ain't happening," I told Izzo. "The boat's not there. The guy's out to sea."

"That's okay, we can wait," he said.

"No, bro, you don't understand. He's a fisherman. He could be out for three or four days," I said.

"Shit," Izzo said.

"It's fine, man," I said. "Just leave it with me and I'll take care of it."

I thought for a minute. I knew the thing that motivated Izzo more than anything: money. He always responded to an opportunity to get paid.

"Listen, my boss wants this taken care of too," I said. "He'll give us three hundred dollars."

"All right," he said. "That's cool."

We drove back to the restaurant and got the bomb out of his car.

"Show me how to use this fucking thing," I said.

It had a fuse and a blasting cap with a low explosive. I felt a little better that it had a fuse because that meant it was more stable. It could still go off if I dropped it, but I would have been more concerned if it had an electric ignition. Who knows who was making these things?

He showed me how to set it off, and I put the bomb gently into the cab of my truck. My recorder was running.

"Okay, man," I said. "I'll hang out here for a couple days, take care of this, and be back."

I gave Izzo his $300, and he drove off. The cover team followed him to the Rhode Island border to make sure he was safely away. I stood outside the truck waiting. I had been around explosives my whole career. I wasn't too worried about the explosive self-detonating, but it wasn't exactly a comforting situation.

As soon as he was in Rhode Island, the bomb squad, which had been camped out nearby, came to the restaurant. I drove the truck around the back of the restaurant, safely away from any other vehicles or the building, and hidden from public view as much as possible.

The disposal team took the explosive out of the truck, examined it, and took photos. It turned out to be a high explosive in a tube. It had steel rods taped around the outside to increase the damage and death upon detonation. It was a pretty sophisticated bomb.

"Whoever made this knows what they're doing," one of the bomb squad members told me. "If this thing went off right here, it would kill all of us."

Now I knew for sure what the Christmas presents were. They were like homemade hand grenades that could take out a vehicle or kill a few people if tossed into a crowd. Dangerous stuff. Now I needed to find out how many they had, where they had them stashed, and where they were coming from.

A couple days later, I went back to Rocky Point. We had church. By that time, the dynamic in the gang was shifting. Roadblock was emerging as the leader. J.R. was afraid of him. Roadblock was always the alpha male of the two. While J.R. was the president, nothing happened in the chapter without Roadblock's knowledge. After Roadblock's beating, the tension between him and J.R. grew and permeated the chapter. It had been brewing for months, and as J.R. was being pulled more and more toward the Mother Club, Roadblock asserted his dominance in Rocky Point.

Certainly J.R. had questions to answer as to why he didn't help Roadblock during the Hells Angels beating and that only gave Roadblock more street cred as a silent power struggle developed. Often, Roadblock was the one members briefed as he was by that time handling most of the day-to-day business of the chapter.

Izzo told Roadblock about the plan to bomb the boat. He filled him in that the boat wasn't there, but that my boss paid him $300 for the bomb and was taking care of it.

A few days later when I walked into church, Roadblock was pissed. He glared at me and Izzo.

"You two guys," he started. "The Christmas present goes up there and it doesn't get used? You know who does that? Cops! Cops do that."

He was foaming at the mouth, livid. He ripped into us. As concerned as I was that he suspected I was a cop, it gave me some comfort that he was yelling at Izzo as well. That told me that whatever he thought, he still wasn't certain if one or both of us were rats.

"If I end up in a cell, you guys better pray you're not in the one next to me because I'll kill you both," he said.

He went on and on about how stupid we were to leave the bomb there. As he ranted, I figured out that he didn't think Izzo or I were rats. He was concerned that my boss was an informant or a cop.

"If this comes down, it's coming down on us," he said. "Give the money back to him and get the bomb back. I want the bomb back."

That bomb was long gone. It was evidence now. Even if I could get it back, there was no way, as an ATF agent, that I could give a live explosive back to a biker or anyone else for that matter. I had to once again think on my feet and come up with something quickly.

"I can't get the bomb back," I lied. "They used it."

Roadblock was incredulous.

"They used it, huh? On what?" he asked.

"They sunk the fucking boat," I said.

"That's something that a cop would say," he said. "Where? Where did they sink the boat?"

"Somewhere up around New Bedford," I said.

"I want to see it," he said. "I want to see the sunken boat. I want to see the damage to the boat from this bomb. I want proof that bomb was used."

His paranoia was in high gear. I needed to get this conversation over with and get out of there.

"I can get that," I said. "You know I dive. I can find out where they sunk it and go down there and get pictures of it."

"Yeah, I'm going to need you to go do that," he said. "I want pictures."

"Not a problem," I answered. "I'm on it."

CHAPTER 38

I spent some time working to prepare to stage a photo of a bombed-out boat at the bottom of the harbor in New Bedford, but we never ended up doing it. Roadblock asked a few more times but eventually he stopped asking for evidence of the sunken vessel.

He was on to far more devious pursuits, as was the rest of the crew.

Normally, in my line of work, if you successfully took a bomb off the streets and built a case, you were congratulated. There is constant covert talk of explosives being trafficked around the country, but it is actually very rare for an undercover agent to purchase an actual bomb. The Boston supervisors and agents were ecstatic about the purchase and removal of the dangerous device from the Pagans. There were high fives all around, but when word got back to New York management, you would have thought someone pissed on their Wheaties.

Globe accused me of purposely orchestrating the bomb sale to occur in Massachusetts in an attempt to keep the case in the Boston office. It was preposterous and deeply offensive, honestly.

It was all part of an egotistical power play to control the case. The New York guys wanted it all in their jurisdiction. I really didn't care. I just didn't want anyone to get killed by one of those devices. I wanted to identify who the bombmaker was so we could arrest him and stop him from making more bombs for the gang.

We met at a Dunkin' Donuts just outside of Boston. I walked in, grabbed a large iced coffee, and made my way over to a table where Globe sat with two supervisory ATF special agents.

"Hey," Globe said in a condescending tone. "How is that bomb case going?"

I thought a second.

"It's good," I replied.

"Oh yeah? 'Cause it's awfully convenient you did the bomb buy up here," he said. "You're just trying to keep the case in Boston."

"Excuse me?" I asked. "Look, if you have an idea on how I could have kept that bomb in New York and kept control of the situation, I'm all ears. The only way I knew how to handle that situation was to discuss using it up here. Plus, I didn't even know that he was bringing the device until he showed it to me in the restaurant. He was only supposed to be there for some street theater."

Globe smirked.

"Really, Ken?" he said, sarcastically.

"I'm doing my job, man," I said, getting angry. "We knew they had bombs. I got one of their bombs. It's in evidence now."

"And you just had to bring it up to Boston," he repeated.

I was fuming.

"You wanna play Joe Undercover? You think you know how this works?" I shouted.

People in the Dunks were staring. I was standing up and would have loved to grab him by the throat, but that's just what he wanted, for me to lose my cool and give management a reason to shut down the case.

"You want to walk in my shoes?" I shouted. "You think you can do it? Explain to me how I could buy a bomb down there and control it! If I told the Pagans that I wanted to blow up someone or something on Long Island, they would have just gone ahead and blown them up. The Pagans would have thought they were doing a brother a favor and were taking care of the problem," I said. "I would have had no control of who or when the explosive would be used. The public would have been in great danger."

Globe was blind to the facts. The exchange was more proof to me that it was a mistake having a supervisor with no long-term undercover experience overseeing the case. The only way to understand those types of cases is by actually working them when you are a street agent. You bring that experience with you when you become a supervisor.

People in the coffee shop were staring. I was expecting some kudos. I was expecting compliments from the supervisory agents for getting a bomb off the streets. Instead, I had some prick challenging me and accusing me of breaking rules.

I left the meeting, and they drove into Boston to the U.S. Attorney's Office. I headed back to Long Island, seething with anger over the argument with Globe. We were getting closer to taking down this whole chapter and moving toward the Mother Club. I was living the Pagan life every day and needed people I trusted. I didn't have time or the mental capacity to be bothered with accusations and unproductive debates. Every minute counted and every wasted conversation or phone call was one more step further away from me finishing the case and getting home to my family.

Back in Rocky Point, talk about moving the body continued. There were some in ATF lobbying hard to shut the case down rather than send me on a ride upstate to move a dead body. I had to go to Washington to go over the plan with top brass.

The area where we were headed was so remote that the cover team wouldn't be able to be anywhere close to me. If I was to go on that hell ride, it would be alone.

There were two camps in ATF on the issue. One group wanted to pull me out and shut the case down, because they believed it was unethical to participate in the exhumation and moving of a body. The other wanted me to go with them to move the body, but only after we installed remote cameras to keep an eye on the area. We'd recover the body when the case was over. The thought was that the guy was dead and would not be any less dead a few months later.

The body was buried on a piece of property that had recently been sold, near Swan Lake, New York, a mostly abandoned former resort community. If you've seen the movie *Dirty Dancing*, Swan

Lake was once like that. Located in a remote area of western New York, it's about four hours north of Rocky Point and a half hour from the Delaware River and the Pennsylvania border.

It's home to several Jewish summer camps, some of which are also abandoned. The plan was to dig up the body from where they originally buried it and move it to the woods behind Tracy's house, where he could keep an eye on it.

Tracy's place was on a large plot of land, surrounded by acres of woods. It had a long, dirt road leading up to the house that was often guarded by Pagans. It was a perfect place for criminals to hide and was a difficult place to stake out. A cop would stick out like a sore thumb up there.

Tracy's property was also protected by two highly trained Dobermans. We thought about whether we could sneak onto the property and install special motion-activated, battery-powered cameras. We ordered some from England and were planning to take them up to install them. Around that time, though, there was a massive volcanic eruption that filled the sky with debris and shut down flights from England, so we weren't able to get the cameras delivered.

Sometimes the breaks weren't lucky during the case. That was an unlucky one.

We also talked about sneaking onto Tracy's property with an ATF Special Response Team to dig up the body and replace it with a pig carcass so we could determine the identity of the deceased. We opted against that tactic because of Tracy's dogs. There was no way the team would have gotten past them without causing a ruckus.

I was able to convince supervisors in Washington that I needed to make the trip, despite the risks. We needed to find out for sure what was going on up there, including the identity of the deceased. We also considered whether it was another elaborate test by the Pagans. Had they discovered my real identity and were they preparing to eliminate the threat? If I was a cop, I had numerous felony charges on all of them, and they knew it. The potential it was a setup was very real.

CHAPTER 39

On February 18, 2010, I was summoned to Hogman's house. I grabbed my .44, which I'd bought a few weeks earlier from Hogman, my recorder, undercover phone and wallet, and drove my pickup over to Hogman's. He told me we were headed to Tracy's to move the body.

Hogman called Tracy.

"We're on our way," he said into the phone. "You better be ready on your end. We're taking care of this problem once and for all."

I was once again wading into an unpredictable and dangerous situation where one wrong move could be disastrous.

I knew there were still some in the club doubting me. I was pretty sure most of them believed I wasn't a cop, but the Pagans didn't get their reputation of never having been infiltrated by law enforcement by being sloppy. They were relentless.

Getting the call from Hogman to go, after the conversations we had about the body, was unsettling. I had been tested many times, but this was another level. I was being asked to go move a dead body in the dead of winter deep in the Catskills. Debate raged in ATF, as there were more than a few colleagues who thought they were planning to kill me.

I wasn't sure. Still, I made the call to go on the trip. In my mind, it was never an option.

We had a lot of gun and drug cases on them, and at least one bomb charge, but we needed more to build the type of RICO case I felt we had the opportunity to make.

It was time for a reckoning for the Pagans. I had an opportunity to damage the gang and take down some heavy hitters. Taking the trip to the Catskills was dangerous, but it was the only way forward. Not going would have ended the case, and we still had too many loose ends.

In order for headquarters to grant approval, I had to agree to wear a wire, for the first and only time in the case. It was a huge risk, but it was nonnegotiable.

The device was hidden in my clothing and used cell towers to transmit the conversation. I had to keep it with me at all times. It would broadcast to the cover team, which would be in the area but, as usual, not close enough to save me if necessary. I was on my own. I also had an audio/video recording device in the truck.

When I pulled into Hogman's driveway, he was waiting for me. He was wearing a walking boot, because he had shattered his foot in five places while kicking a former Pagan who was thrown out of the club. He tossed his bag in the back and climbed in. It was midday. We pulled onto Route 25A and headed west for the four-hour trip to Swan Lake.

Hogman was a behemoth of a man and took up a lot of space. He was stuffed into the front passenger seat of the cab. As he settled in, he pulled a gun out of his waistband and put it in the center console. It was not all that unusual for Hogman to carry a gun, so I initially did not think much about it.

As we drove northwest through the backwoods of New York toward the Pennsylvania border, we talked about club business. I got a little more information about the body. He told me it was a Black drug dealer who was going to rat. Hogman went on a white supremacist rant and degraded the dead drug dealer.

We were supposed to move the body from a piece of land about two miles from Tracy's house and re-bury it in a spot Tracy had cleared near his home. It was something right out of *Goodfellas*. I was just hoping I wouldn't end up like Billy Batts.

Hogman wasn't the brightest bulb, but when it came to criminal activity, he was strategic and smart. He always kept his facts straight and tested me all the time on information he'd given me. Fortunately for me, I'm also good at remembering details, especially when they involve crimes that play into cases I'm working on.

We had a good back-and-forth discussion in the truck. I could tell he was feeling me out, but just why, I still wasn't sure.

We exited off I-495 North and made our way onto Route 17, a meandering country road that winds past wildlife sanctuaries, small ski hills, shuttered resorts, and the occasional small town. It was February in the Catskills, and the roads were icy. There was snow on the ground.

We pulled into Swan Lake and passed a few abandoned Jewish summer camps, including the Pupa Boys Camp. It had the feel of a ghost town as we drove past run-down, boarded-up cottages, snack bars overgrown with weeds, and vacant lots strewn with debris and abandoned vehicles. Some were permanently abandoned, but others were just closed for the winter. All of it looked eerie and postapocalyptic, as though everyone just dropped everything and fled the area suddenly, never to return. We drove past rickety fences and acres of land without a living soul for miles.

"Good place to film a zombie movie," I joked.

We arrived at Tracy's, and he came out of the house. I saw that he too had a gun in his waistband. It was the first time I had ever seen Tracy with a gun when he was just around his brothers. I already had concerns that the trip would go badly. Seeing Tracy with a gun in his waistband significantly raised those concerns.

He had a couple of pickaxes and shovels. It was still daylight. Hogman grabbed his gun from the console and got out of the truck. We went inside the house, and they smoked a joint. When they were done, we grabbed the shovels and headed back outside.

"Let's go, man," Tracy said, handing me a shovel.

Hogman followed. He had his gun in his waistband. We walked a few hundred yards into the woods to a small clearing. Tracy had already treated the ground with rock salt to soften it up so we could dig. It actually worked.

I was running through scenarios in my head. Was I walking to my own grave? I did have a shovel in hand, so at least I had a fighting chance if they turned on me. Tracy started smacking the ground with a pickax, loosening up the dirt. I shoveled.

I was sure to keep them both in front of me. Each time Tracy took a swing and turned in a different direction, I turned with him. I wasn't going to turn my back to him to let him bury the pickax in the back of my skull. Although not funny at the time, as I look back, if anybody had had a bird's-eye view of us digging the grave, it would have looked comical, like a couple of guys dancing in an ever-deepening hole. We almost looked synchronized. He would move left and so would I. He moved right, so would I. The only difference with this dance was that I couldn't wait for it to be over.

None of us spoke, which only ratcheted up the tension.

Tracy swung. Dirt flew. I dug my shovel in and scooped it out. It was freezing, and you could see our breath each time one of us exhaled.

Over and over and around and around we went. The dirt piled up around the edges, and soon we were both inside a hole a few feet deep, digging away. I kept my eyes on Hogman, but he didn't move. He was like a statue.

We got down deeper and deeper. We kept digging until Hogman broke the silence.

"That's good," he said. "That'll do."

Tracy jumped out of the hole. I followed.

"We'll wait until dark," he said. "Come on, we gotta go kill some time."

They smoked some more weed.

"I went last night and dug up the body and hid it to save us time," Tracy told me.

"Jesus," I said. "So it's just sitting there?"

"It's cold out. But I'm not worried he'll get hyperthermia," Tracy said with a chuckle. "No worries, the body is well hidden."

We were in the middle of moving a body, and Tracy decided he needed to run some errands. We went to mail his tax return, of all things. I was surprised he even filed it.

I guess we had nothing else to do as we waited for nightfall. That's how those guys worked. They did have lives to manage, so sometimes they did the most mundane tasks in between crimes.

Tracy drove his truck with Hogman sitting shotgun. I was in the back.

We rumbled along a winding road when suddenly my wire started making a noise. The wire lost cell tower coverage because of the remoteness of the area and began making the sound a phone makes when it has been left off the hook for too long.

Hogman turned around and looked at me.

"What the fuck is that?" Hogman asked.

More than a year on the case without a wire and the one time I wore one, it went off—as I was helping move a corpse in the middle of nowhere, no less. I pulled the phone out of my pocket.

"I don't know what the fuck this phone is doing," I said, pushing random buttons.

It stopped, luckily. Maybe it was that they were stoned, but for whatever reason, they bought it and didn't ask anything more.

We finished Tracy's errands and headed back to his place. It was starting to get dark outside. They smoked more weed, and I texted my cover team.

"If this wire makes any more fucked-up noises, you'll find it in a snowbank," I told them.

The team was four miles away in the next town over. There was only one or two roads in and out of Swan Lake, and the population was only eighteen hundred people. Any outsiders were noticed quickly, so there was nowhere nearby that a group of cops could safely sit on a stakeout.

The clock ticked and darkness fell.

"All right," Hogman told us. "Let's go do this."

We took both trucks. Hogman drove mine, and I rode with Tracy. We made our way down a desolate road in the complete darkness to a wooded area. We pulled the vehicles off to the side of the road and parked.

The plan was for me and Tracy to go grab the body, carry it back to the trucks, throw it in the bed of my truck, and Hogman would drive away. We'd meet him back at the house.

As soon as we parked, Tracy jumped out and ran off into the woods.

It was nearly pitch-black out there. There was a full moon so there was some light, but not enough to see where he ran off to. I had no clue where I was going and was certain he had a gun. I didn't know if the transmitter was working and was sure the cover team had no idea where I was.

They're just going to off me in these woods and no one will have a clue where I am, I thought to myself as I crunched across the snowy ground in the darkness.

To make matters worse, I was recovering from minor knee surgery and had a slight limp. I had a damaged vein and ligament that I had to have cleaned up. I told the gang I slipped on the boat and screwed up my knee. The doctor told me to avoid a lot of moving, because it could rupture the stitches. Digging holes for dead bodies and running through the woods in the dark were probably against doctor's orders, yet there I was.

Throughout the case, I always tried to make sure that whatever was happening, I had control of the situation in some fashion. I tried not to let myself get into situations where one of the Pagans controlled my fate. Now I was in an uncontrollable situation.

Out there in those woods, they controlled everything.

"Yo!" Tracy yelled. "Over here."

He was running and moving in and out of the trees. I couldn't see him so I just followed his voice blindly.

I too tried to move from tree to tree. I tried to keep a tree in between us at all times, thinking I'd have some cover if he suddenly hopped out shooting.

"Over here!" he yelled.

It wasn't like anyone could hear us out there. I came through a small clearing and there was a big tree down, lying across the ground. Tracy was standing behind it. The light of the full moon shone on him, and I could see that his hands were empty. He didn't have a gun out.

My chances of making it out of there alive were improving, I thought.

"Over here, man. Here it is," he said.

On the other side of the log was a blue tarp, wrapped in rope. It was the body.

"Come on. Let's go," he said, grabbing one end.

I grabbed the other end, and we lifted it up. It was pretty light.

We started walking out of the woods carrying it. I felt liquid leaking onto my hands. A pungent, indescribably putrid stench hit me like a mallet to the face. It smelled like death with a side of shit.

I had to ignore it and act like it was no big deal. We got back to my truck. Hogman was sitting in the cab. We hoisted it into the bed as watery sludge seeped from the tarp all over us and the truck.

Tracy joked and called himself "the surgeon," saying he cut off the guy's head, hands, and feet. Hogman joked that he wished Tracy cut off his dick so he could have kept it for himself as a macabre souvenir.

Tracy tapped the side of the vehicle, and Hogman took off. I grabbed a towel and wiped the slime off my hands. I didn't want to think about what I was wiping off. We hopped into Tracy's truck and drove back to his house, careful to take a different route.

We pulled into his driveway, and Hogman was already there with the truck backed into the driveway all the way up to the house. We got out, dragged the tarp out of the back, carried it over to the hole, and threw it in. I was again covered in muck leaking from the tarp.

It was lighter than I expected, but he had been rotting in the ground for six months. I felt like I was holding a set of shoulders, but I wasn't sure.

I stood over the hole with the tarp inside. I turned back toward Izzo and Hogman, and they both were standing looking at me. They both had their guns in their waistbands. There was a shovel nearby, and I thought about lunging for it. I wasn't going to let them put a slug in me and throw me in the hole with that guy.

Tracy walked toward me and grabbed a bag of lime that was sitting nearby. He dumped it all over the tarp.

"Let's go, man," he said. "Cover it up."

We grabbed the shovels and covered the tarp, filling the hole back to the top with dirt. We packed it down tight, and Tracy threw some more lime on top.

We stood for a tense moment, and then Hogman turned and started walking back toward the house. Tracy followed. I exhaled a sigh of relief.

We walked into the house, and Hogman called Roadblock.

"It's done," he said into the phone.

He walked into a back bedroom alone. He got off the call with Roadblock and called me and Tracy back into the room.

"I just got off the phone with my brother. What we did here can never be talked about again," he said. "I don't wanna hear a word about that smart-mouthed nigger ever again. He got what he deserved. It's done. It's never to be brought up."

CHAPTER 40

Tracy and Hogman smoked another huge joint, and we left Tracy's to head back to Rocky Point. We went straight to the clubhouse, and Roadblock and J.R. were there.

I was still covered in grime and dirt from my journey in the woods. Roadblock looked me up and down when I walked in. I looked down at the dirt covering my boots.

"Oh yeah, I still got shit all on my boots from our trip to Tracy's . . ." I started to say.

He shot me a death stare.

"Oh yeah? What about your trip to Tracy's?" he said.

I didn't say anything more and neither did he. His warning was clear.

My ATF colleagues meanwhile were debating whether to go dig up the body. We didn't have a name and had no idea who the remains belonged to. We also didn't know how often Tracy walked by the grave or checked on it. If he noticed the body was gone, clearly it would have been found because I was a cop. Or Hogman. Either way, the case would have been done.

So we had to leave it there. It was an agonizing decision, because that could have been someone's brother, father, uncle, boyfriend, son, or friend. At the same time, we were building a RICO case, and murder was now possibly on the table again.

I went back to Tracy's over the next few months. Whenever I did,

I went outside and pretended to take a piss so I could check on the burial spot to make sure it was still there.

Hogman brought it up from time to time, despite Roadblock's warnings. He always referred to it as the "science experiment." He'd ask Tracy: "How's the science experiment?"

"It's fine," Tracy would respond. "It's fermenting like it's supposed to."

I didn't like the jokes.

"If someone discovers that, we're all going down for it," I told him.

The grave remained there undisturbed.

I earned more street cred from the burial. Everything was moving along, I was building solid cases, and while I missed home, I felt confident the end of the case was in sight. That's when I was thrown yet another curveball. A wild one.

One day I was hanging out on the sidewalk in front of the clubhouse in Rocky Point. I had a .25 caliber handgun in my waistband that belonged to J.R. He gave me the gun that day because there were rumors the "maggots" were going to make a move on the Pagan clubhouse. A bunch of out-of-state Pagans were also inside and around the clubhouse for support in case shit jumped off with the Hells Angels. Everyone was flying their colors. The cops had been harassing us, because they saw other chapters in town flying colors so they knew trouble was brewing.

Tensions were high, and it went on for several hours: cops watched the Pagans and Pagans watched the cops. Eventually things started to cool off. I was getting hungry. I planned to walk down a couple of blocks to grab a sandwich from a nearby Italian store. The problem was that I had J.R.'s gun in my waistband. I didn't want to leave it at the clubhouse in case the cops rolled in and a Pagan used it to shoot an officer.

I also didn't want to walk down the street with the gun in my waistband. I didn't see any cops around, so I walked across the street to my truck to hide the gun inside. I opened the rear door of my truck, slipped the gun out of my waistband, and put it into the map holder slot behind the front seat. I put a plastic poncho on top so nobody could see the firearm.

Just as I closed the door, the hairs on the back of my neck stood up. I sensed something bad was about to happen. Suddenly, an undercover cop car came to a screeching halt right next to my truck. Two cops jumped out and approached me. They asked for ID and wanted to know what I put in the back of the truck.

Roadblock, Hogman, and some of the others were standing there, so I had to go through this as Ken Pallis. I couldn't whip out my ATF badge, not that I had it on me anyway. I couldn't tell them I was undercover. I lied to the cops and told them that I didn't know what they were talking about.

They ran my plates and pulled my record. It was at that moment that I realized I'd made a big mistake in creating my backstory: I had included assaulting a cop on my record from L.A. Those guys didn't like that when they ran my information. They tossed my truck and found the gun.

They arrested me and threw me in the back of the cruiser. They busted my balls on the ride from the clubhouse to the station, referencing my conviction for beating up a police officer. It was a rough ride.

"Whoops," one of them said with a laugh. "Careful back there, buddy. It can get bumpy."

The Pagans immediately called their attorney to represent me. That created a problem, as the attorney would have access to everything about my background, as the courts would order the government to turn it over during the discovery phase of a trial. I prayed my cover story would hold up to scrutiny.

We got to the station, I was interviewed by a detective, and booked for being a felon in possession of an illegal firearm. I couldn't tell these guys I was an undercover cop. It was a small town. The Pagans had that town wired. If it got around the police department that I was an undercover agent inside the Pagans, it would have been only a matter of time before I'd be compromised.

So I had to ride the bust out, regardless of the stakes. I'd sort it out later. I used my one phone call to call J.R.

"We got you, bro," he said. "We'll get you bailed out. We got you a lawyer."

Ang got a call from ATF letting her know I had been arrested. She retreated to our bedroom, sat on the bed, and started sobbing. Our middle daughter, Shannon, heard her and went in and saw her crying.

"What's wrong, Mom?" she asked.

"Nothing," Ang told her. "It's fine."

Ang hugged her and walked her back to her bedroom, then sat on the edge of the bed with Shannon as she started crying.

"Please tell me what's wrong," she said. "Is Dad okay?"

"It's okay, Dad is fine. Something happened in his case tonight but it will all be fine," she said. "Don't worry about it."

Along with being concerned for my safety, Ang was pissed. No fourteen-year-old girl should see her mom crying and upset. There was no investigation worth causing that kind of stress to our family.

Ang waited for a few minutes until Shannon closed her eyes. She quietly got up off the bed and walked downstairs to the kitchen. She poured herself a shot of whiskey and downed it. Then she poured a second one.

The stress was getting to her. She was juggling doctor and dentist appointments, sports, homework, playdates, birthday parties, and keeping the house stocked with food. She felt like she was drowning.

Knowing that I was locked in the bowels of some county jail was too much for her to handle that night. The whiskey took the edge off, and she went to sleep.

Meanwhile, I was shuttled to the county jail, booked, and strip-searched. They did a retina scan on me to add to my file. To this day, Ken Pallis's retina profile is in the system at the New York Department of Corrections.

I was put into an individual cell. They took my Pagans shirt, and I had on only a tank top and my jeans. The cell had a metal bench and a filthy toilet. I used my jeans as a pillow. The toilet, two feet from my head, was covered in dried blood and pubic hair. I thought to myself: "What am I doing here? I live in a nice house. I have a family. Why am I doing this shit?"

If you've never been in jail, it's every bit as isolating and maddening as you might imagine. County holding cells are often especially isolating because unlike prisons where inmates stay for long periods of time, they are transient facilities, so they have minimal accommodations.

As I was trying to fall asleep, the guy in the next cell was yelling about some bullshit. I tried to ignore it but he wouldn't stop.

"Shut the fuck up!" I shouted.

"I'm going to rip your head off tomorrow morning, motherfucker, when we get out of this cell on our way to court!" he yelled back.

We couldn't see each other so neither of us knew what we were getting into. At that time, I was six feet three inches and pushing two hundred and sixty pounds, in a tank top, bald, and with a goatee. I wasn't exactly the guy you wanted to challenge in a prison fight.

He had no idea.

The next morning, a guard woke me up banging on the bars of my cell around five a.m. He handed me a cold egg-and-cheese sandwich from 7-Eleven and a cup of water. I scarfed it down, and the guards came back, opened my cell, and handcuffed me to a chain gang. The cell next to me opened up too, and I saw the guy who was talking shit.

He was a skinny little guy who couldn't have been one hundred and fifty pounds soaking wet.

"You got something to say now, motherfucker?" I said, glaring at him.

He was terrified.

"Sorry, man, I didn't mean any disrespect," he said.

"Next time wait and see what the person looks like before you run your mouth, motherfucker," I said.

We were led off the tier and into a garage, where we were herded into a van, chained together. They slammed the door shut, and the van pulled off for court. The van was split in half, one side for women and the other side for men. During transportation, there was only one woman, so one side was closed off for her to sit, which forced me to be crammed into the other side with six guys. We sat chained together in the dark, and I swear those guys drove like assholes on purpose. We were wedged up against the wall, on metal benches, shoved together like cattle, all of us smelling like shit and sweating our asses off. I'm not a claustrophobic person, but during that ride I felt trapped. It felt like the air around me was thinning. We sat in the van like that for more than two hours.

After that ride from hell, I was placed in a holding cell in the county jail. There were approximately twenty other guys in the unit. There was a two-tiered bench along the wall and I sat on the second tier, against the back wall, so I could keep my eyes on everyone. Just when I thought it could not get any more aggravating, a group of guys came up to me looking for trouble.

The leader of their little group walked up and barked, "I want to sit there. Get up."

There wasn't a chance in hell that was going to happen. One of the other guys chimed in, saying, "You heard what he said, get up."

"I'm not getting up," I said. "You want me to move, you're going to have to do it yourself. Good luck with that."

A moment went by, and he started to come toward me.

Oh shit, here we go, I thought.

I got ready to stand up to fight, but he sized me up and thought better of it. At the last second, he backed down and walked away.

Back in Rocky Point, J.R. called Steph and told her I was locked up. She called the cover, team and they headed over to the tattoo parlor just in time to see my truck being towed away.

An ATF supervisor called the county district attorney and informed him that I was undercover, but that no one else could know: not the judge, not the cops, not the prosecuting attorney. No one.

The DA told the supervisors that they could stall the case, but it was a felony and they couldn't by law pursue an indictment against me, knowing that it was a false arrest. They also couldn't dismiss the case, because that would tip off the Pagans that I had the case fixed, which would either mean I was a protected informant, a cop, or had agreed to a deal to become a rat.

I spent a couple of days in jail as my ATF partners scrambled to come up with the $50,000 in cash needed to bail me out. An undercover had never been arrested and gone through the system like that before, so there really wasn't a protocol for how to handle it. Ironically, it was the Pagans who secured the cash after my initial court appearance, and my new Pagan attorney posted my bail.

The case would linger in the court for a while, and the DA kept continuing it. The arrest was a problem, because the case had to be resolved at some point, one way or the other. What it really did was start the clock ticking on the case. It put pressure on us to speed up indictments and come up with a strategy to end the case and bring me home.

CHAPTER 41

I got out of jail, returned to Rocky Point, and got back to Pagan business.

We were leaving church one day at J.R.'s house when he approached me and said we had a job to do for White Bear, who was vice president of the Mother Club at the time.

"Listen, I got a call from White Bear," he said. "Black Betty has a guy that's been crashing over there. He's selling drugs, and she's been trying to kick him out. He's smacking her around, and he won't leave. He needs to go."

Black Betty was a protected old lady. Her late husband had been a member of the Mother Club, so she had protection for life. Anything she needed from the Pagans, she got.

"We need to go fuck him up," J.R. said. "We need to get rid of this guy, whatever it takes."

It was that last part that had me spooked. White Bear wanted him gone, even if we had to kill him.

I called Karelas and Kotchian and filled them in. I told them to stick close to us and have a marked police car near Black Betty's house to intervene if things got heated with the guy.

Tracy, Roadblock, J.R., and I got into my truck and drove over to Roadblock's house around the corner. We grabbed a few saps, which are small leather instruments filled with sand used to beat the tar out of someone, sap gloves, a sawed-off shotgun, and two handguns.

I needed another lucky break, or this could go badly. I drove to

Betty's house as slowly as I could, partly to give myself time to think and partly in hopes that the guy would listen to Black Betty, realize the stakes, and get the hell out of there.

"Let's go, Slam," Roadblock said. "Fuckin' step on it."

"I can't, man," I lied. "We got all this artillery. We get pulled over and we're all going down."

I rounded a corner and could see Betty's house far down toward the end of the street. A car was pulling out of the driveway—a black BMW. We pulled into her driveway and she came outside.

"You just missed him," she told us. "He'll be back. But you guys can go find him."

She gave us a few places he might be, including a couple of bars. We drove around looking for a while, but didn't find him. We didn't want to be out all night, because we needed to be up at four a.m. the next day to go to Richmond, Virginia, for the funeral of a Pagan killed during an ATF raid, of all things.

The Charleston, West Virginia, ATF field office had just wrapped up their case, which snared fifty bikers—mostly Pagans—in Kentucky, Virginia, Pennsylvania, New York, New Jersey, Delaware, and Florida. They had cases for kidnapping, robbery, extortion, illegal gambling, and drug and weapons violations. It was a big takedown that included charges on a couple Mother Club members.

While serving a warrant in Richmond, Virginia, ATF agents were confronted by a Pagan named James "Jimbo" Hicks. Jimbo, forty-five, grabbed a shotgun as the team entered the residence and was shot dead when he refused to drop it. He became a martyr in the club, and almost every Pagan in the country was going to Richmond for his funeral. Including me.

"We need to be up early to go to Richmond," J.R. said. "Let's regroup and we'll get the guy when we're back."

I headed back to my undercover house and got a message from the cover team to call Globe. I called him.

"We've got a problem," he said.

"Oh yeah, Globe, what's that?" I asked.

"We have to notify this guy that there's a threat against his life from the Pagans," he said.

As cops, we're obligated to protect the public, even a woman-abusing drug dealer like Black Betty's deadbeat boyfriend. There were two options: notify him he was a target or take steps to ensure his safety such as putting him under surveillance.

Telling him was not an option. That would out me as a cop or an informant. My plan was to control the situation. I'd take measures to ensure the Pagans didn't attack or kill him and have the cover team ready to intervene if things got out of my control.

"Paul, you can't do that," I told Globe. "It'll come back to me. I can handle this. I'm part of the muscle in the chapter. They're not going to touch the guy without me. I'll be with them."

"It doesn't matter. We have to notify him," he responded.

"No, we don't," I told him. "Don't do anything."

We argued on the phone for a few minutes. I was exhausted from arguing with Globe. It was a constant struggle with him.

"Look, it's my ass out here. Don't do a fucking thing," I yelled, and hung up.

I assumed he got the message. Wrong.

Globe took matters into his own hands. He went and picked up Kotchian and Karelas in his Crown Victoria and drove over to Black Betty's house. He parked across the street just as a female was walking up the stairs to enter the house.

"Hey, are you Betty?" Globe yelled to her.

"I'm not Betty," the woman answered. "Betty's in the house."

"Tell Betty the police are here and she needs to come out and talk with us," Globe told her.

The woman walked into the house. Betty was a hard-core biker chick. She knew the game and wasn't about to come outside to voluntarily talk to cops.

Globe thought it would be prudent to turn on his siren and used the vehicle's PA system.

"Betty, come outside. It's the police. We need to talk to you," he shouted over the loudspeaker.

Kotchian and Karelas pleaded with him to stop.

"You're going to get Ken killed," Kotchian yelled.

Globe's antics caused quite a scene on the street. As that was happening, the guy arrived back at her house in the black BMW.

"What the hell is going on?" he asked.

"ATF," Globe told him. "We have information that the Pagans are going to harm or kill you. Do you want our protection?"

"Go fuck yourselves," the guy said, and walked inside.

I was on my way back to the tattoo shop to work guard duty for a few hours before we closed up early for the night. On my way over, I called Karelas to let him know it would be a short night at the clubhouse because we were leaving at four a.m. for Richmond for the funeral.

"Okay, sounds good, Ken," Karelas said. "By the way, we should have let you kick the shit out of that guy. What a douchebag."

I had no clue what he meant.

"What are you talking about?" I asked.

"That guy you were supposed to go fuck up today at Black Betty's house. We ended up running into him," Karelas said.

"What? Holy shit. How the hell did you know?" I asked.

"Globe didn't tell you?" Karelas asked, as he laid out the story of what happened at Black Betty's house.

"Jesus," I said. "Hey, I gotta go. Call you back later. I'm almost at the clubhouse."

I was just a few feet from the tattoo shop. Roadblock's car was parked out front. I didn't want anyone seeing me on the phone as I rolled up. I was fuming that Globe did exactly what I'd asked him not to do. I was at serious risk.

Seeing Roadblock's car there didn't make me feel any better. He wasn't supposed to be at the clubhouse. That's why I was there to do guard duty. I had a bad feeling.

I walked inside the shop, and J.R. and Roadblock were in the back room—the only area without cameras. I knocked on the door and walked in.

They were both acting a little weird. I had no idea if they knew ATF agents had paid a visit to Black Betty's house. Did Betty call White Bear and tell him? How would I explain that?

Only four of us knew what White Bear told us to do: me, J.R., Roadblock, and Tracy. J.R. was president, Roadblock was sergeant-at-arms, Tracy was a nineteen-year member, and I was the new guy. It wouldn't take much for them to decide who was behind the cops showing up there.

Roadblock didn't say much and left. J.R. and I hung out for a bit before we locked up. Nothing was mentioned. I dodged a bullet at least for the night.

I headed back to the undercover house and called Globe.

"You motherfucker," I said. "You went over there anyway after what we talked about?"

"We had to, Ken," he said.

"I have to go to Richmond tomorrow and face White Bear," I said. "What if she calls him? What if he finds out the cops were there? How am I going to explain that?"

"Well, I guess we should just pull you out. It's too risky," he said.

"That was your whole plan all along, wasn't it?" I said. "You can't wait to shut this case down."

I ran through the possible scenarios in my head all night and didn't get much sleep. The next morning, I hopped on my Harley and made the seven-hour ride to Richmond with the chapter.

The whole trip I was sweating it out, wondering how the hell I would explain the cops showing up at Betty's house, if I was asked. The cover team followed us at a safe distance.

We pulled onto Laburnum Avenue in downtown Richmond and joined a procession for Jimbo. There were hundreds of bikes. The parade of Pagans stretched down the road as far as the eye could see.

There were also dozens of members of the local chapter of the Outlaws, an outlaw motorcycle gang allied with the Pagans. I was told there were three ATF undercover agents who infiltrated the Outlaws who would also be at the funeral. It marked the first time in ATF history that two sets of long-term undercover agents inside outlaw motorcycle gangs were at the same biker event at the same time. It posed some unique challenges as we had to come up with two separate operational plans and deploy two cover teams.

Our chapter rumbled into the parking lot and parked. There was country music playing and a light rain fell on the swarm of bikers taking in the outdoor service. Jimbo's sister gave the eulogy and described her brother as a family man who loved animals, hunting, fishing, and riding his Harley. She thanked all his Pagan brothers for being there.

J.R. got a call outside the funeral home. I didn't know who it was, but I heard him talking.

"Well, how do you know? Are you sure? How do you know it was them?" he said into the phone.

I was sure I was caught. My mind was playing tricks on me. I was filling in the blanks of his conversation and assuming the worst. My blood pressure rose as I looked around for a possible escape route.

There wasn't one, because I was surrounded by hundreds of Pagans, all of whom happened to be mourning a brother killed by the same agency that was at Black Betty's house and employed me.

I tried to remain calm. J.R. hung up the phone.

"The Hells Angels rolled by my house," he said. "And the shop."

I stifled a sigh of relief.

We went into the funeral home to pay respects to Jimbo's family. As I walked into the somber confines of the funeral parlor, I thought about the irony of the situation—being an undercover ATF agent at the funeral of a biker killed by an ATF agent.

Jimbo's mother came over and gave me a big bear hug.

"He loved you so much," she said through tears. "He loved everything you guys stood for."

I felt awful. Although totally justified, ATF had just killed her son and she was hugging me—unbeknownst to her, an undercover ATF agent. It was the one time in the case that I felt guilty. She was

a grieving mother. I felt bad for her, because she loved Jimbo uncon-
ditionally. I also knew that one day she might find out I was a cop,
and it would sicken her to know that she hugged an ATF agent at her
son's funeral.

Years later, while speaking at a law enforcement conference, I was
approached by a couple detectives who worked biker gang cases.

"We spent months trying to identify you," one of them told me.
"We saw this guy quickly rising through the Pagan ranks and couldn't
figure out who he was."

I laughed and said: "Well, now you know."

One of the detectives told me he had a great picture of me that he
wanted to share. I gave him my email address and he sent me a surveillance photo of the funeral parking lot. In the photo is me and the
other three undercover Outlaws, and I still have it to this day.

CHAPTER 42

White Bear didn't end up showing up at the funeral, and I never heard another word about the Black Betty situation from the Pagans. How they failed to put that together, I'll never know. Maybe Betty's boyfriend got the message and backed off or left.

It's also possible Betty might have thought her phone was tapped, so she never called White Bear to tell him. Whatever the reason, it just went away, luckily for me.

When we got back from Richmond, we all got funeral patches that said JIMBO in honor of Hicks. It was strange putting that on my colors, knowing he had been killed by one of my brother officers.

I went to several other Pagan funerals with the club, but the one that stands out the most is when I went to Pennsylvania for the funeral of a Mennonite Pagan who died in prison after serving forty years for a horrible rape and murder. It was March 2010, and Izzo and I left at four a.m. for the four-hour trek from Long Island to Gap, Pennsylvania, in the heart of Amish country, for the funeral for a notorious sixty-one-year-old Pagan named Leroy Stoltzfus. Every chapter was required to send two members, and Izzo and I were told to go.

Stoltzfus was the son of a Mennonite bishop, but he certainly didn't follow the sect's strict Christian traditions, which include a pledge to be pacifist and a prohibition on premarital sex. In 1969, Stoltzfus was part of a chapter that had a clubhouse near the Dreamland amusement park in Reading, Pennsylvania. He and three other

Pennsylvania Pagans came upon a parked car, inside of which were twenty-year-old Glenn Eckert and his eighteen-year-old girlfriend, Marilyn Sheckler.

They carjacked the couple and forced the young man to drive the car to a nearby train depot, where they forced them into a box truck. A Pagan drove the truck around town while in the back the bikers took turns raping the teenager in front of her boyfriend. When they were finished, they forced the couple into the woods next to the amusement park. Eckert was shot to death, and the young girl was choked and beaten to death with a rock.

Izzo and I went to a church in the middle of nowhere. A handmade wooden coffin containing Stoltzfus was slowly placed into a deep grave as each Pagan, including us, took turns lowering it into the ground. We each placed a shovelful of dirt on top of the box.

It was disgusting to me that the club turned out for services for a murdering rapist, who was the lowest of the low. I was happy to throw dirt on his coffin. Afterward, I told the cover team that if I could have taken a shit into the grave I would have. I wish I did.

Back in Rocky Point, I was still livid over Globe's decision to go to Black Betty's house. It was the last straw for me. I called the Assistant Special Agent in Charge of the New York Field Division.

"We need to talk," I told him.

I drove off Long Island and met him at a coffee shop in Queens.

"This is it. This guy is going to get me killed. Either he goes or I go," I said.

They couldn't remove me from the case right then because we were too close to getting all the indictments. Bryan DiGirolamo was working morning, noon, and night writing reports, logging evidence, writing affidavits, and building the staggering evidence file to present to the U.S. Attorney's Office. Bryan worked so hard on the case that his struggling marriage fell apart and he got divorced.

"Okay, Ken," the ASAC said. "Understood."

The ASAC took my concerns seriously and a short time later, Globe was reassigned to an operation in San Diego. I later got several calls from my ATF buddies in San Diego angry that we sent our problem supervisor to them.

The new supervisor brought into the Pagans case was Tom Kelly, who was Bryan's former boss back in New York. They worked together on the Bloods case that Bryan did before he transferred to Long Island to work on the Pagan case. Kelly was a good enough guy, but his arrival also spelled the beginning of the end for Kotchian. They butted heads right out of the gate, and Kotchian, who started the case with me back in Boston nearly two years earlier, was getting frustrated. Kotchian focused on the operational side of the case, while Bryan organized the evidence.

Bryan got word from ATF in Washington that he needed to hurry up and wrap the case up. Under the so-called rocket docket policy in New York, New York District Attorney's Office had to indict my case within ninety days or throw it out. There were several legal maneuvers to extend that period, but the fuse was burning. The case couldn't sit there forever. It looked too suspicious. If the case was dismissed, it would have made me look like a snitch. So our only option was to continually delay it, but that started looking suspicious too, even to my defense attorney, who was paid by the Pagans.

The RICO case was unfolding nicely, and I was rising up the ranks in the Pagans, but we had a timer on us. ATF ordered Bryan to get the case ready for prosecution and devise a plan to take down the club and pull me out. Bryan fought hard for more time and to keep me in as long as possible because he knew it was a one-time-only opportunity.

"Tom, if we're going to get him out of there and make these cases, I need some help," he told Kelly. "I'm buried in paperwork. It'll take me months to go through everything."

Kelly got Bryan help from other offices. Agents came in to help review audio, transcribe conversations, join the cover team, and write reports. ATF set up a home office for Bryan so he could work out of Long Island and eliminate his ninety-minute commute from Queens. He worked twelve-hour days, six days a week.

The shake-up within ATF ranks coincided with a power shift in the Long Island chapter of the Pagans. J.R. was promoted to POP (President of Presidents), which meant he oversaw all the other chapter presidents. It was one step below the Mother Club.

Roadblock was named "Diamond"—president of the Long Island chapter. With Roadblock being promoted, I too was promoted. I became sergeant-at-arms, which meant I was the top enforcer in the chapter. I had just done jail time and helped move a body, so I guess that was a reward for my loyalty.

Normally, members who got arrested were suspended until their case was resolved, as a way to keep informants out of the ranks. They made an exception for me, though, because they knew my value to the club.

The rift between Roadblock and J.R. was getting worse every day. Roadblock was starting to build an alliance with the Colombo crime family, a New York–based faction of La Cosa Nostra. He told me he once served prison time with Andy "Mushy" Russo, a Colombo family capo, and the crew wanted the Pagans to provide protection at Mob-controlled clubs in New York. Roadblock told J.R. about the arrangement and said only him and me would be involved.

J.R.'s promotion did little to ease the tension with Roadblock, so J.R. kept me close by his side. He brought me to meetings and events as his personal security guard and told me I was now the regional sergeant-at-arms, which meant I oversaw all the sergeants-at-arms in the New York and New Jersey chapters. It was J.R.'s way of keeping me on his side, as he could feel Roadblock's hatred toward him strengthening. Despite the split, the new arrangement with J.R. got me a step closer to the top of the Pagan ranks.

Around that time, we got information that the Vagos, an outlaw motorcycle gang from the West Coast, was planning to open a chapter on Long Island. The Vagos weren't a support club of the Pagans, but they had an amicable relationship. It was a potentially dangerous development for me because part of my backstory was that I used to ride with the Vagos when I was in Los Angeles.

The Pagans were planning to meet with the Vagos leaders to discuss their plans. I had to intervene, because if J.R. and Roadblock met with them, they would surely mention that I used to ride with the Vagos when I lived in L.A., but the Vagos would have no idea who I was. It would blow my backstory out of the water.

I needed to step in and take some control.

"I don't trust these motherfuckers," I told them. "There's no way they'd skip the whole middle of the country to open a chapter here. Let's meet with them, but keep quiet about my connections to the Vagos. I'll work my sources to find out what they're up to."

They thought it was a good plan. I started collecting intel from a Vagos informant I had in L.A. and kept J.R. and Roadblock in the loop. They liked getting the information, so they never brought up my connection to the Vagos. The plan worked and I was able to protect my cover story, even when the Vagos president came to J.R.'s house to meet with us. The Vagos opened a chapter in Long Island and built a relationship with the Pagans, but my cover was never blown.

It was yet another dodged bullet for me at a time when I was regularly putting out fires that threatened to end the case or put me in jeopardy. I had been living in Rocky Point for almost two years and spent almost all my time with bikers. I was largely desensitized to the violence and criminal lifestyle. When I did get to go home, Ang and I were distant. She was under a tremendous amount of stress. She was an accomplished agent herself, and was preparing for a federal trial in a big arson case she investigated. She was struggling to get her work done while running our home. It was exhausting for her to see that most of our family's energy was going into my case.

As much as Ang and ATF wanted to end my case, so did I. I just wanted to make sure that all the time I had already put in was worth it.

CHAPTER 43

The pressure of the double life I was leading was often overwhelming. ATF in-fighting, my court case, the frustration over Bennett's unsolved murder, and the mystery surrounding the body buried at Tracy's added pressure. As if that wasn't enough, another unexpected monkey wrench was thrown into the mix from an unlikely source: the media.

In 2005, I went undercover posing as a hitman for a man who wanted his wife killed and his daughter kidnapped and taken to Ecuador. Guillermo Vasco was serving prison time for stabbing and beating his wife in Worcester, Massachusetts, and asked another inmate at the Essex County House of Corrections if he could help him hire someone to kill her.

The inmate arranged for me to pay Vasco a visit in jail, posing as a contract killer. I had done similar undercover operations before, including in a 2003 case in New Bedford during which I posed as a hitman for a local crime family hired by a computer executive to kill his wife for $50,000 cash and a $20,000 engagement ring.

I had the look, knew the lingo, and had a knack for leading desperate men to provide enough detail to hang themselves. I worked on a few of those cases with U.S. Attorney Mike Sullivan's office, including the Vasco case.

That one was particularly complicated because he was incarcerated. I was able to get into the prison to see him by posing as his lawyer and got him on tape hiring me to kill his wife for $10,000 and kidnap his daughter for another $10,000. The cases were good public relations for ATF because we saved lives and took criminals off the streets, and there was always tremendous media interest.

Shortly before the Pagan case began, I was asked by ATF to do a segment for a ten-episode series on Discovery Channel called *Undercover: Double Life*. I was silhouetted out during the taping of the segment.

The show was to be the first of the ten episodes and was supposed to air in late 2009. ATF asked the producers to hold the episode, though, because I was in a long-term undercover case. They didn't tell them what the case was, but they made it clear that putting me on TV would compromise my identity and put me and my family at great risk.

The producers were livid. They had spent millions of dollars on the series and they needed to air the episodes. There was a nasty fight that went on for months between the producers and ATF brass over when they could air my episode. Discovery delayed it repeatedly, but in 2010, they said they couldn't wait any longer and told ATF they were planning to air it.

The producers argued that since I was silhouetted, no one would know who I was. Airing it as we were nearing the end of the case would have been a huge, potentially devastating mistake. ATF told them they couldn't broadcast it until I was safely extracted from my undercover role and the producers were warned point blank: If you air this, you can get him killed.

I knew the stakes more than anyone and was relieved ATF fought so hard. The Pagans were true-crime junkies and watched all those news shows: *60 Minutes*, *20/20*, *Dateline*. They picked up law enforcement tactics from the shows and gained intel on how to avoid making mistakes that would get them busted.

The Pagans were students of crime and biker culture. Many of them read biker undercover books, like Billy Queen's *Under and Alone* and Sonny Barger's famous book, *Hell's Angel*. And yes, they loved the biker TV series *Sons of Anarchy*. I watched many episodes with Hogman, Roadblock, J.R., and the rest of them. I can't think of a more surreal moment in my life than being an undercover fake biker watching a show about a fictitious biker gang with a bunch of real outlaw bikers.

Discovery, to their credit, held the episode, but it was yet another source of stress that I didn't need. I was busy trying not to get killed and not allowing the Pagans to kill anyone on my watch. That was getting harder by the day, and soon, their thirst for revenge against the Hells Angels would explode.

The stress of being away from my family was hitting me as well. On Easter 2010, I was stuck in Rocky Point. Ang and I are devout Catholics, and Easter is one of the most important holidays in our family. But in 2010, Ang held Easter dinner alone with the girls, without me.

Where was I? I was on a Pagans run in western Long Island with Roadblock, Hogman, J.R., and several other degenerates. We pulled into a nice family restaurant, on Easter Sunday, dressed in our dirty biker clothes.

The host came to the front desk.

"We are very full," he said. "Do you have a reservation?"

"Ha-ha . . . . Yes, it's under Roadblock," Roadblock answered. "Is that there on your list?"

The guys were getting unruly. Families were there with little kids, and we were getting scared looks. I felt awful. Everyone was staring at us.

The host looked around the restaurant. He saw the situation developing.

"I'll get you a table," he said nervously.

He put us at a big table hidden away in the back of the restaurant. I was completely embarrassed. It was a freak show. We weren't hidden away in the back for long, because it was a buffet. Roadblock, Hogman, and the rest of them stood up from their seats and attacked the buffet like wild gorillas, piling their plates high with food.

I took a walk outside to call Ang. Easter was always a special holiday for us and our daughters, and I felt terrible being away that day.

"Where are you?" she said.

"At some restaurant on Long Island," I said.

"You're out there with those animals having Easter Sunday dinner while your family is home without you?" she said.

"I'm sorry, Ang," I said. "I'm sorry."

It was another cruel blow to her, but she was strong and I knew she could weather the storm. With all the close calls and near misses I had, the decision was made at ATF that security would be provided for my family. They had security experts go to our house and meet with Ang to remove high shrubbery that could conceal people trying to break into the house. They installed heat-sensored lighting, an internal communications system, and reinforced doors and locks. Agents would be checking on her and the girls regularly. It was unsettling for her.

The girls didn't know a lot about what was going on, but they knew enough to know their dad was into some seriously dark shit—and that he wasn't home on Easter. The stress was escalating on all fronts.

It was time for me to finish the case once and for all and find my exit strategy before it was too late. I was working hard with Bryan, the U.S. Attorney's Office, and the rest of the team to get closer to taking down as many Pagans as we could, but there was so much going on in the club that the opportunities to stack up more charges was never-ending. I was inching closer to the Mother Club, and with my new status as sergeant-at-arms, I was in charge of weapons and discipline. Every day there was more talk of bombing or killing Hells Angels.

We were hoping to get the case finished by June 2010, but we needed more time. I was mentally and physically exhausted but determined to see it through. There were still some ATF brass in Washington trying to get the case shut down. There were secret meetings between the case agents, Kotchian and DiGirolamo, and the head of major crimes from the Eastern District U.S. Attorney's Office, who determined that the case would stay open until we had the goods on as many Pagans as possible. They too knew what a golden opportunity we had.

A date in mid-September was chosen to end the case so I could begin the process of getting back to my life. I was going to do everything in my power to make sure that takedown date stuck.

Ang grew increasingly frustrated as the date for me to leave the Pagans was delayed again and again. We had lost nearly two years of our life together, and she had raised our daughters for months without me around.

"No one wants this case over more than me, Ang," I told her. "I want to be back home as much as you want me back. I just have a few more things I need to wrap up, and it's going to take a little more time."

She understood. As my wife, she was frustrated, but as an agent, she understood it would be senseless—after all I'd gone through—to pull out early.

I was given a checklist of conversations and pieces of evidence I needed to nail down in order to make the case what we all knew it could be.

RICO cases are very complex and technical. We had to prove certain elements of each crime, which isn't easy, especially when you're dealing with the type of nomads and outlaws I was embedded with day in and day out. For example, we needed to prove that members paid dues which contributed to the criminal enterprise. We needed to show that the chapters paid tribute to the Mother Club, which also furthered the criminal enterprise. We needed to show that members were aware that Mother Club members were convicted felons in order to prove felony bodyguarding statute violations. We needed to show that they were all part of a corrupt organization involved in racketeering. The standards are high, and it took endless hours of work.

I said at the beginning that I wouldn't do it unless we were going to go all the way to the top, and we were almost there.

"Bear with me, Ang. I'll be home. I just have to finish," I told her.

"Okay, Ken," she said. "I've come this far. We can do this. But I do need you home soon. I need you home safe, and so do your daughters."

The next step was for me to go back to the scene of the crime in the Catskills.

CHAPTER 44

We had some solid evidence on Cano, the Mother Club member who oversaw the Long Island chapter, but we needed more to get him on the RICO case. He was going to Tracy's party in the Catskills, and as regional sergeant-at-arms, I was responsible for guarding him. It was a prime opportunity.

Going back up to that creepy, desolate zombieland was not a pleasant prospect, especially because I knew there was an unidentified drug dealer's body rotting in a hole just feet from Tracy's house. Hogman joked that we'd be able to check on our "science experiment."

Before I left, I stopped by the tattoo shop. J.R. was in the backroom and came out.

"Hey, bro," he said. "I have some good news. I got approval for you to get your Surtr sword."

A year after becoming a patched member, the Pagans allow members to get a Surtr sword tattoo on their neck. I was short of a year as a full member, but the club was once again making an exception for me.

He was ready to put me in the chair and tattoo me right then and there. Ang and I had enough issues to work through from the case without adding in a Pagan sword neck tattoo. I don't think my girls would have liked it much, and I definitely didn't want it. A neck tat would have also given more ammo to those connected to the case who feared I might have drifted to the dark side.

The club had already made a couple exceptions for me by making me an officer early and making me sergeant-at-arms, both of which rubbed some members the wrong way. It was the perfect excuse for me to slip out of the situation.

"Listen, we're taking heat already for me becoming sergeant-at-arms early," I told him. "I don't need to add to that drama. Let me do my time on this. Once I have my time in, I'll get it."

He bought it.

"I respect that," he said. "Cool. We can do it when you hit a year."

"Thanks, bro," I said.

Needle dodged.

We packed up and headed up to Tracy's place. Tracy was doing renovations. A blue tarp sealed off the section that was under construction.

Tracy had a beautiful wife and young daughter. His brother was a Pagan, and Tracy was a hang-around for many years when he was a teenager until he was patched in at age sixteen—the youngest Pagan ever.

He was a big drinker and a fighter. If we were out at the bars, he was always the one fighting. A lot of guys didn't trust him. He was sketchy, and if you got into business with him, you did so knowing that it would probably go badly and you'd get ripped off.

The Catskills chapter was based out of his Swan Lake house. It started with him, Doc, and a few others as an extension of the Long Island chapter. They moved up there and formed their own chapter, mainly because it was a secluded area where criminals could go largely undetected. It was a great stash spot for guns, drugs, and, apparently, dead bodies.

We headed up for a massive bonfire party. It was the usual mayhem—a bunch of drunk and tweaked-out bikers raging in the middle of nowhere, plotting disaster and chaos. Armed Pagans guarded the driveway.

The bonfire was the biggest I'd ever seen. You could have seen that thing from space. The image of all those bikers partying around that bonfire, just steps away from where I had helped bury a body weeks earlier, is burned in my brain forever.

The president of the Mongols, Comanche (aka Robert Santiago), arrived with another Mongol and two women. The Mongols, a heavily Latino biker gang with a chapter in New York, were bonded with the Pagans in their hatred for the Hells Angels and had a similarly violent reputation. Comanche was a career felon with a record a mile long for assaults, weapons, drugs, robbery, and even escaping from prison. He was carrying a sawed-off shotgun in a flannel shirt, which he brought inside.

According to Tracy, Cano was looking for a new cocaine connection and Doc introduced him to Comanche. They talked about building a cocaine partnership in which the Mother Club would allow Comanche to sell coke on Long Island as long as the Pagans got a cut.

Tracy was trying to make a quick buck off the party. He bought a bunch of food and beer and was planning to charge everyone who attended. He also wanted to take a cut from all the cocaine Comanche sold at the party.

Cano hit the roof.

"No one is fucking paying for the party. We don't charge our brothers" he told Tracy. "And you're not getting paid on the coke—I am."

Comanche and the women went into a back room with Doc and Tracy. After a few minutes, Tracy came out and told me I could get an 8-ball for $150 or a gram for $50. I gave him cash, which he gave to Comanche.

A little while later, Tracy and I walked into the back room. A softball-sized rock of cocaine was on the table. The two women were dividing it up and putting it into small plastic baggies. Tracy blasted a line and went over to the table to supervise. It would have been awkward if I didn't do any, so I went over to the dresser and simulated sniffing a line of my own. Just another night in paradise.

I was handed the drugs I bought and walked out of the room. Doc met me in the next room and asked me for a bump.

I had to keep what I bought for evidence, but I had to share with my fellow Pagan. You can't say no to a bro.

"Hey, here take this," I said, handing him $90 in cash. "Go get yourself something on me. You're the host. It's my gift to you."

He thanked me, went and grabbed himself a baggie, and did a couple lines. He showed me around the clubhouse, pointing out their arsenal, which included several guns. They kept a sawed-off shotgun hanging over the door.

We walked outside, where there was a bar set up and several grills, some of which were just a few steps away from the makeshift grave. It was eerie being back there, knowing what we had done a few weeks earlier.

Tracy went inside and grabbed a new semi-automatic rifle he'd recently purchased. He brought out his new toy and started showing it off. Cano walked over and took it out of his hands.

"Nice," he said. "Not bad."

A prospect worked one of the grills. Cano handed him a tree branch that looked like a set of antlers.

"Here, take these and put them up on your head like a deer," he said. "Go down there and I'm going to shoot them off your head."

The prospect looked like he had seen a ghost. He did what he was told and walked a few yards away from Cano. Roadblock howled with laughter and imitated the famous Al Pacino line from the end of *Scarface*.

"Say hello to my little friend," he shouted while using the Pacino accent.

Cano was laughing hysterically too. The prospect was terrified, standing there holding the antlers on his head, wondering if he was about to get shot. He looked like he might throw up. There were a few other Pagans who looked to be made uncomfortable by the whole scene.

I didn't think Cano was going to shoot him, or I would have had to intervene. It was a gamble, because you never knew what they were going to do, but I felt fairly certain they were just tormenting the prospect and weren't going to execute him right there in front of a bunch of Pagans.

Cano lowered the gun and told the prospect to get back on the grill. I, along with a lot of others, was relieved.

Cano's little stunt was bad news for him. He was a Mother Club member and a convicted felon, wielding a firearm next to a house filled with cocaine. I had him nailed. I also had Comanche on drug charges. I had more charges on Doc and Tracy.

And the body was still buried outside too.

CHAPTER 45

The first time I went to the mandatory in Youngstown, Ohio, in 2009, I was a prospect and it was sheer hell. In 2010, things were different. I was no longer a prospect, so I wasn't hazed and tormented, but I was a sergeant-at-arms, which gave me a whole new set of troubles.

We rolled into Youngstown and set up camp. It was rewarding to not have to lug around cases of beer, ice, food, tents, and grills and be bossed around like I was the last time. I got to relax much more than in 2009—well, relax as much as I could as an undercover cop surrounded by drunk and high felons.

On Saturday night, a bunch of strippers performed, and the partying was in high gear. Saturdays were always the worst at mandatories because guys got blind drunk and took every drug in sight. By nightfall Saturday, a lot of them were completely strung out.

I was at the clubhouse on guard duty for the Mother Club when I heard a loud argument. There were two guys screaming at each other and a bunch of Pagans were gathered around them. One of them was William Clerkin, a wiry, gray-haired Pagan from the Camden, New Jersey, chapter nicknamed Fender Bender. The other was Four Ply, a skinny New Jersey Pagan who always wore a floppy U.S. Army camouflage hat. He was berating Fender Bender, accusing him of being a rat.

Fender Bender had once before been falsely accused of being a rat in an infamous incident in which he was chained to a fence by Pagans.

He had his arms pushed the wrong way at the elbows until they both snapped. The Pagans later admitted they made a mistake, apologized to Fender Bender, and paid his medical bills. For some reason, the guy was still in the club. Slow learner, I guess.

Cano and a couple other Mother Club members intervened.

"In the future, if you want to accuse someone of being a rat, you better have proof," Cano told Four Ply.

The dust-up ended, or so I thought. That night was witching hour for the prospects. I heard a lot of hooting and hollering and was thankful I was not a prospect anymore. I finally climbed into my tent around five a.m. and fell asleep, only to be awoken at seven a.m. by J.R., Cano, and James Coles, aka Jersey Jim, a chapter president from Gloucester City, New Jersey.

"Hey, Slam, come out here. Bring your axe handle," J.R. said.

My paranoia was in full swing. I wondered if they'd found something out about me and were stripping me of my position and taking away my axe handle. I wondered if they were going to take it and use it on me.

"You heard what happened last night. We're having a meeting of all the northeast Pagans," J.R. said. "We're going to get to the bottom of this thing with Fender Bender and Four Ply. Bring your axe handle. If we motion to either of them, you beat them with your axe handle."

We went up to the corner of the massive field and all the New York, Pennsylvania, and New Jersey Pagans were up there—three hundred strong. Many of them hadn't slept all night and were drunk, high, or both.

Cano, J.R., and Jersey Jim were there, along with another Mother Club member, Will Grayson, aka Tung Foo. Tung Foo was White Bear's brother and was one of the seventy-three Pagans arrested during the infamous Hellraisers Ball melee with the Hells Angels in 2002 that left Pagan Robert J. "Mailman" Rutherford dead.

The bikers gathered in a horseshoe shape with Cano, J.R., Jersey Jim, and Tung Foo standing at the top opening. I stood by the mother club members, along with Doc, who was sergeant-at-arms of the Catskills chapter, and Ray Hamilton aka Bluto, who was sergeant-at-arms of the Trenton, New Jersey, chapter. The three of us sergeants-at-arms were armed with our axe handles. It was hot, the sun beating down upon us, and a trial was about to unfold.

"Fender Bender, Four Ply, step forward," Cano said.

The two emerged from the pack of sweaty Pagans and stood between the three sergeants-at-arms with their backs to us facing the Mother Club members. It must have been unsettling for Fender Bender and Four Ply, standing in front of Mother Club, knowing they had three sergeants-at-arms right behind them, waiting to pounce on command, and three hundred angry Pagans ready to join in if needed.

Cano had a thick Hispanic accent that was hard to understand, but when he got pissed, it was near impossible. He started ranting, nearly frothing at the mouth. He was sick of the in-fighting, and it was going to end right there.

"This is a brotherhood! You can't be falsely accusing people of shit," he shouted. "Our enemy is the maggots and all the people who support the maggots. We can't be turning on our own."

The maggots, of course, were the Hells Angels.

J.R., Jersey Jim, and Tung Foo stood silent. Cano started questioning Four Ply and Fender Bender, asking them what their argument was about. He grilled them both. Four Ply was being aggressive and defensive and annoyed Cano.

Suddenly, out of nowhere, Doc lunged forward. He was tweaking all weekend and was all strung out. He started swinging away on Fender Bender like Babe Ruth at batting practice. My recording device was in my pocket and caught the mayhem on audio.

Bluto leaped in and started wailing away on Fender Bender too. I didn't move. I couldn't jump in, but I was worried that I missed the signal from either J.R., Cano, Jersey Jim, or Tung Foo. Even if I saw a signal, I would not have been able to participate, but if I ignored it, I knew for sure I was next for an axe handle beating from Doc and Bluto.

They wailed away, and several other Pagans jumped in and laid the boots to Fender Bender, who fell to the ground. Mob mentality took over. It happened so fast, and before I could react, Cano intervened.

"Wait! Stop!" he screamed.

Everyone backed off. Fender Bender lay on the ground, half conscious and whimpering in pain. Cano looked at Doc.

"What the fuck are you doing?" he said.

"I was given the signal," Doc said.

"From who?" Cano fired back.

"From him," Doc replied, pointing to J.R.

Cano looked at J.R. J.R. shook his head.

"I never gave the signal," he said.

"What about you?" Cano said, turning to Bluto.

"I saw him and thought the signal was given, so I jumped in," Bluto said.

I was sweating bullets. I was afraid that I missed the signal and didn't do my job and would pay. In my head, I was preparing to take a brutal beatdown.

Then Cano and Jersey Jim stepped forward and snatched the axe handles from Bluto and Doc. They turned them on the two of them and started wailing away.

"Yeah, motherfucker!" Cano said, teeing off on Doc. "You like that, motherfucker?! How you like that?"

Cano and Jersey Jim rained blows down on Doc and Bluto, smashing them with reckless abandon in the head and torso. Both fell to the ground and were beaten mercilessly.

It went on for nearly a minute. I couldn't jump in because they were Mother Club. That would have been signing my own death warrant. I was praying they'd stop before they killed them.

Bluto was hurt badly, but Doc took the worst of it. He was near unconscious as vicious blows struck his rumpled body.

Finally, Cano and Jersey Jim stopped. You could hear a pin drop. Tung Foo stepped forward.

"This is what we're talking about. This shit has to stop," Tung Foo said.

"Take their fuckin' colors, Slam," Cano said to me.

He pointed to the six other Pagans who had jumped in and beat Fender Bender.

"Take theirs too," he said to me.

I stripped their colors off and stood there holding a stack of eight Pagan colors in my arms. I was still trying to wrap my head around what the fuck had just happened. Four Pagans were just beaten to within inches of their lives and the Mother Club was on the warpath.

"People need to be smart and understand," Tung Foo shouted, pointing at me. "Look at Slam right here. He's smart. He thinks for himself. He knew there was no signal. We need more people like him."

A wave of relief washed over me. I went from thinking I was going to be beaten to death with axe handles by a mob to being praised by the Mother Club for doing the right thing.

"Run their pockets," Cano said, pointing to Doc and Bluto.

A couple Pagans went through the pockets of Bluto and Doc and took their money. They had a bucket and passed it around.

"Put some money in there for Fender Bender," Cano said.

He looked at Bluto and Doc.

"You pieces of shit, you're out bad," he said, fuming. "We're seizing your bikes and selling them and giving the money to Fender Bender."

Two Pagans came over and helped Fender Bender up off the ground. They carried him over to a car, put him in the back, and drove him to the hospital. Doc wasn't so lucky.

"Get this piece of shit out of here," J.R. said, pointing to Doc.

J.R. was pissed, because Doc told Mother Club that it was him who gave the signal. That put J.R. at risk. Had Cano, Jersey Jim, and Tung Foo thought J.R. gave the signal without their approval, J.R. would have been the recipient of those axe handles too. He was livid and ready to kill Doc.

A couple Pagans picked Doc up off the ground and carried him across the field to an area where several New York chapters had tents set up. They plopped his limp body onto the field and left him there, cooking in the beating sun.

Bluto was taken over to the Trenton chapter and left there for his chapter to handle. Word came back from the hospital that Fender Bender was going to survive. I was relieved. That would have been some serious paperwork.

J.R. was on fire. He realized he dodged a bullet. We packed up our shit and headed to a small, run-down motel nearby to shower, before hitting the road for the ride from Youngstown back to Rocky Point. Doc was left in the truck with no keys and nowhere to go.

"I'm going to kill him. I'm going to kill him right here," J.R. told a group of us outside the motel. "Fucking leave his ass right here."

He was rallying the troops and preparing to kill him. I thought back to when Doc had my back and hid me during witching hour a year earlier at the same Ohio mandatory. I felt bad for him, and I also couldn't let a murder happen. I approached J.R. I needed to buy some time.

"Listen, man, if we're going to kill him, let's do it back home in our environment," I told him. "There are too many witnesses here. There's video at this motel and there's a bunch of people who will tell the cops they saw a bunch of Pagans here. It'll bring tons of heat. Let's get out of here and deal with it later."

He looked at me and nodded.

"Yeah, you're right, man. Fuck," he said. "But that piece of shit is out bad. We'll deal with it later."

He was pissed, frustrated, and exhausted and wanted some blood. Thankfully, he listened to me.

I went inside the room and talked to Doc. He was barely conscious. I shook him awake.

"Listen, man, you need to keep your mouth shut. J.R.'s hot. He wants to fucking kill you," I told him. "I don't know how this will play out. But don't argue. Just keep your mouth shut. We'll get you out of here."

He looked at me warily, dirt and blood caked on his face from cuts from the beating.

"Thanks, brother," he said, grabbing my arm. "You don't know how much I appreciate what you've done for me."

Doc was thrown into Tracy's truck and driven back upstate. We headed back to Rocky Point.

CHAPTER 46

By the time we got back to Rocky Point, J.R. had cooled off. Doc was brought up to the Catskills and disappeared. His days as a Pagan were over, but I'd soon be back in his life, not as a biker but as a cop.

I was buying a lot of meth from Hellboy, who told me he was getting it from a Mexican cartel. There was increased talk of delivering Christmas presents to the Hells Angels.

My head was spinning as I tried to balance my drug dealing and duties as sergeant-at-arms, while monitoring the internal politics of the Pagans and filing reports in a timely fashion. Bryan was my backbone and saved my ass. He was grinding day and night. He and the team had plenty of paperwork to do for the U.S. Attorney from Tracy's party and the Youngstown mayhem.

We had a church meeting to go over the chaos that unfolded in Youngstown. It was decided to hold it at my house. J.R., Roadblock, Hogman, Izzo, and the rest had become increasingly comfortable at my place. It was the nicest and largest house in the chapter, and it was secluded. It was a great call by ATF to pick that house, and it was about to pay off huge dividends.

Because of the violence in Ohio, that church meeting included Mother Club members and other chapter presidents. Cano, who was our chapter's Mother Club representative, Pita, who was president of the Trenton chapter, and a couple other Diamonds traveled to Rocky

Point for the debrief on the mayhem that led to Bluto, Doc, and six other Pagans being ousted from the club.

I had the house wired and the basement outfitted with cameras. I set up tables and chairs in the basement and got beers and food.

There had never been a Pagan church session caught on video. I was concerned the equipment wouldn't work or would malfunction, but was hopeful. Capturing an official Pagan church meeting would be historic, as it would be ironclad proof that the club was a criminal organization.

Outlaw motorcycle gangs like to claim they are simply clubs made up of like-minded blue-collar biker enthusiasts and that criminal activity is neither sanctioned nor condoned. Capturing church on recording would blow that claim out of the water, as almost every one I attended included blatant talk of criminal activity, from drugs to extortion to guns to assaults to murder.

A video of Pagan church would be a rare feat, not unlike the infamous Mafia induction ceremony caught on tape in 1989 in Medford, Massachusetts. That tape helped topple the New England Mafia as four mobsters pricked their trigger fingers and made a blood oath as they were initiated by mob boss Raymond Patriarca Jr. It cemented the reality that La Cosa Nostra existed. This would do the same for the Pagans.

The recording device held a couple hours of video, so I couldn't start it too early, but I needed to turn it on before anyone arrived. The guys started showing up and sat around upstairs drinking beers and eating.

We started late, and I was worried the device would fill up with dead air before anything worthwhile was recorded. We eventually made our way downstairs and got going.

Izzo had a radio frequency detector, looking for wires, and he used it on all of us as we walked into the basement. After he wanded us all, Hogman used it on Izzo. No one was to be trusted.

Cano took to the pulpit and went over the whole Youngstown

fiasco. Doc and Bluto were out bad, he told us. They were beaten out of the club. He pointed to me, and again I was praised for showing restraint. But he also talked about how Bluto was a sergeant-at-arms, despite not having more than a year in the club, just like me. We were both exceptions to rules that prohibited new members from holding officer positions.

"Slam is the exception," Cano said, pointing to me. "In the future, you can't be an officer until you've done your time."

I was also supposed to have been suspended while my criminal case was pending, another exception that was made for me because of my value to the Long Island chapter. Cano talked about how I was needed as we were on the brink of war with the Hells Angels.

What happened next had me praying that the recorder was functioning. Cano laid out an edict to take action against the Angels—immediately and forcefully.

"We have to get serious about Hells Angels in our area," he said. "Do whatever you have to do to get them out. It's time to get aggressive. Take care of your area and get them the fuck out of there however you have to do it."

We finished church, went upstairs, and the guys all left. I went downstairs after they were gone and heard a vibrating sound coming from the hidden device. The recorder was full and a vibrating alert was going off. Why the device had an alert, especially in that situation, I'll never understand. It was the latest technical glitch in the case that could have meant disaster.

I was stunned. Had that gone off while we were in the middle of church, I would have been screwed. There simply would not have been any way to explain it and I would have been in major trouble.

It was another lucky break. I didn't know how much I caught on video and wasn't sure what the angle would be and who would be visible, but I was confident we had at least part of the meeting recorded, including Cano's diatribe.

I called Bryan.

"Hey, man, I think we have church on video," I said.

I got him the device, and a couple days later, after downloading the file and reviewing it, he called me and confirmed that we had the whole thing. We had the Mother Club on recordings talking about members being beaten out and plotting revenge against the Hells Angels. We got them on video, in my undercover house, implicating themselves in a litany of federal crimes.

My sense of accomplishment was offset by being spooked by my dumb luck. I didn't know how much longer I could play with the house's money and didn't want to hang around to find out.

CHAPTER 47

We had an audio and video recording of church and were preparing RICO indictments and warrants when I went with the chapter to a Pagans tattoo convention in Asbury Park. As sergeant-at-arms of the Long Island chapter, the local chapter was happy to bring me along as they shook down bar owners along the boardwalk. We were like celebrities down there. People stopped and asked to take pictures with us, like we were pro athletes. It was bizarre.

We walked along the boardwalk and members of the Asbury Park chapter went into bar after bar. The owners or managers were expecting them. They handed the Pagans cash sometimes and other times handed them envelopes. The exchanges were friendly. Everyone understood the way it worked. It was some classic old-school extortion, and to be honest, I was rather surprised at how brazen they were. The payoffs only added to our RICO case.

Around that time, I was also doing regular security for J.R. and sometimes Mother Club members. I was called to a meeting one day with Hellboy. Not only was Hellboy the sergeant-at-arms for the Elizabeth, New Jersey, chapter, but he also handled security frequently for Cano, much like I did for J.R. Hellboy's status as an enforcer in the club was unquestioned.

He told me I'd been handpicked by Cano and Jersey Jim to be on the Hit Squad, an elite group of enforcers who answered only to the Mother Club.

"There's this secret group. We take care of the heavy shit. We take care of the serious business," he said. "Mother Club wants you to be a part of it."

It wasn't an option to accept.

"Sure, man. Cool. Whatever they need," I said.

I couldn't tell anyone else in the club about it. Roadblock was given a heads-up from Mother Club that they would need me for unspecified business from time to time and not to question it. He didn't know about the Hit Squad exactly, but he knew I was taking care of business for the Mother Club and that my status was increasing, which I don't think he liked.

The Hit Squad existed to handle the gang's dirtiest criminal work. Members were from all different chapters and were the first ones in when it was time to take out a Hells Angel. I found out just how serious it was when Hellboy and I were sent out on a mission one night to stake out a Hells Angel the Pagans wanted dead.

I met Hellboy in Northern New Jersey, and we drove together to a Home Depot where a Hells Angel worked. On the ride, he told me what was going on.

"There's a guy they want us to watch. They might make a move on him," Hellboy said. "We're going to take care of it."

I knew what he meant. He didn't have to spell it out. Our job was to watch the guy's routine, nail down his schedule and report back to Mother Club so they could plan when and how to kill him. Two other members of the Hit Squad were there as well. My fear was we would see the guy and they'd move to kill him before I had a chance to stop it.

Fortunately, the guy didn't show up for work that night. He'd live to fight another day.

The Hit Squad position only ramped up the pressure to end the case. With my unexpected recruitment to the Hit Squad, there simply too many variables. I was losing control. On Long Island, I would at least pick up chatter that something was brewing and have time to strategize to deescalate the situation or make a move to alter the course. In my role on the Hit Squad, Mother Club did all the planning in secret. We were just the soldiers called to execute the plan. By the time the Hit Squad was called, fates were already sealed. It was only a matter of time before I would have to identify myself as a cop and try to stop an attack.

It was good to know the Hit Squad existed. It gave another layer of insight into the inner workings of the gang, but it was an impossible situation for me as an undercover. It was too unpredictable and made it almost inevitable that the case would end badly.

My rising status in the gang earned me new respect. Pita, who was my nemesis when I was a prospect, grew to respect and trust me. He asked me if he could go on collections with me back in Massachusetts to make a few bucks, because he knew Izzo had helped me out.

We were at a party one time and were checking out each other's rings. I wore rings on all my fingers. One had the "one percenter" emblem, and there were skulls and other biker jewelry. Pita showed me a couple of his.

There was one he had with the Pagan logo and an emerald in the middle.

"Where did you get that, bro?" I asked.

"You can't get them," he told me. "The guy who made them is dead."

Pita had a long history of fucking with me. We once took a photo together and after the picture he looked at me and said: "Hey, Slam, is this going to end up on the ATF wall?"

I almost fell over, and to this day I don't know what he meant by it. A lot of the Pagans worried about ATF, so it was probably just a joke about us getting busted, but in the context of me being undercover, it was a chilling comment.

Another time, he asked to see my gun. He looked at it, worked the action, and then asked me: "Is this ATF issued?"

He walked away. Again, it was probably his way of mind-fucking me, but in the context, it stoked my paranoia.

A few weeks after the party where he showed me the emerald ring, we were at another event together. He approached me with the ring in his hand.

"Hey, bro, I know how much you like this ring," he said. "I'm going to give this to you."

"You're one of us," he said, handing me the ring.

While my status in the club earned me respect from guys like Pita and Hellboy, it caused tension with Hogman. He wasn't happy that his brother, Roadblock, president of the Long Island chapter, chose me over him to be sergeant-at-arms. He was competitive, and one time it backfired and almost killed him.

The whole chapter and members from other chapters and support clubs went on a run around Long Island. We were all flying colors and drove out west on the Island in a show of force to the Hells Angels and others. It was something we did regularly to mark our territory.

When we got back to J.R.'s house, he sent me and Hogman out to pick up some equipment we needed for our trailer. The Pagans, and all outlaw motorcycle gangs for that matter, were big on hierarchies and those translated into formations when we were riding.

The highest-ranking Pagan always rode on the front left. As Hogman and I pulled out of J.R.'s place on Swezey Lane, Hogman sped up and pulled around me to get out front on the left. I was surprised, because he knew I should be riding out there. I was hugging the center line and he crossed into the oncoming lane of traffic.

I veered right to get out of his way. I didn't give a shit. If he wanted to be petty, so be it.

We drove about a quarter mile and turned right onto Route 25A, a busy two-lane highway. Just as we turned onto the street, out of the corner of my eye I saw an object coming toward us fast. It was a minivan. I was ahead of Hogman by a few feet. I looked back and saw him get broadsided hard. He was launched off his bike fifteen feet into the air and went flying over me. I thought he was going to crash down on top of me. I watched in horror as his bike and body flew through the air, just missing me. He slammed to the ground just past me with a deafening thud.

I thought he was dead. It should have been me out there on the left getting clipped by that van, but his arrogance resulted in him being splattered on the ground like road kill. Karma is a bitch sometimes.

The driver of the vehicle was a Hispanic woman, and she had a child in the van with her. An ambulance arrived quickly. She was freaking out and yelling in Spanish.

I ran over to Hogman. He was barely moving and was moaning and groaning.

"Hey, bro, you all right? Can you move your arms and legs?" I said.

He didn't answer. His hands were bloody, and he had some serious road rash. I called Roadblock.

"Hey, man, Hogman's been in an accident. He's fucked up," I said. "I'm following the ambulance."

The EMTs worked on him in the ambulance, and Hogman coded out, meaning he was technically dead. They did CPR and brought him back, and the ambulance sped off, with me following. We arrived at the hospital, and he was wheeled inside on a gurney. I went into the waiting room where I was met by Roadblock and J.R.

"He's stable now, but he coded out a couple times," a doctor told them.

He had several broken ribs, a ruptured spleen, internal bleeding, a broken arm, a dislocated shoulder, and lots of cuts and bruises. He was lucky to be alive. His poor health was complicating his injuries.

For me, Hogman's crash was the last straw. Between being put on the Hit Squad and that wreck, it brought the realities of the operation too close to home. I was playing with fire. I loved to ride my Harley, but now every shift of the gear, every run was like putting a gun to my head in a game of Russian roulette. The bike was no longer fun for me. It was a symbol of chaos, treachery, danger, and mortality.

Too many things were going on. It was only a matter of time before I got in a bike wreck, was stabbed or shot by a Hells Angel, or had to blow my own cover to stop a murder. I almost felt like I was being slowly strangled.

CHAPTER 48

The clock was winding down on my criminal case, and my Pagan attorney was starting to wonder why it kept being continued. That usually happened when defendants flipped and became informants, so time was getting short before he told the gang I was a risk.

I was a phone call away from having to go out on an actual hit with the Hit Squad.

There were some in ATF who wanted to exhume the body from the grave at Tracy's in Swan Lake. They argued that we had a moral obligation to the victim's family to bring home the remains. We did, but we also had a duty to catch his killer. We needed to button up all the evidence and get all the warrants and indictments issued before we could dig up the grave and open a homicide investigation.

We were making no progress, unfortunately, on Bennett's murder. Local homicide detectives got nowhere with the case. No one in the gang talked about it around me, and there was simply no evidence. It was beyond frustrating.

Meanwhile, throughout that whole summer of 2010, the Pagans on Long Island were out actively looking for Hells Angels to shoot. One night, a bunch of us went out on the hunt in three cars, all of them loaded with guns. Thankfully, we didn't find any targets. Another night, a bunch of Pagans drove around to Hells Angels bars, ransacking them and sucker punching patrons. Local cops stepped up patrols, but the area was bordering on lawlessness. It was a powder keg and it was going to blow.

It all came to a head when J.R. and Roadblock went to visit Hogman at Stony Brook hospital while he recovered from the wreck. Mario, the president of the Hells Angels—the ringleader in the assault on Roadblock—also happened to be at the hospital, visiting his wife.

J.R. and Roadblock crossed paths with Mario in the lobby, and there was a stare down. As soon as they got out of the lobby, both presidents got on their phones. J.R. called me.

"Hey, bro, the maggots are here at the hospital," he told me. "Call Jersey, get some backup rolling this way, and come pick us up."

"Okay," I said.

"And, Ken," J.R. said.

"Yeah?"

"Go to the shop and grab the shotgun," he said.

I called for backup from chapters in Elizabeth and Ocean County. I sped to the shop and grabbed the shotgun and went to the hospital and picked up J.R. and Roadblock. For the next several hours, it was an intense, high-stakes game of cat and mouse with Mario and the Hells Angels.

J.R.'s motorcycle and Roadblock's car were in the parking garage. We needed to get their vehicles without them being jumped. The Pagans were ready for war. We had three carloads of Pagans, all of whom were armed.

Roadblock had a .380 handgun, J.R. had a .22-caliber pistol, and Trucker, who was Roadblock and Hogman's brother, had the shotgun. I had my .44.

In a second car was Pop Tart, who had a five-shot .38 revolver; Izzo, who had a .380; and a Pagan named Mad Max, who had a .357 Ruger handgun. In the third car were three other Pagans, one of whom was given a .357 Ruger by Roadblock.

They planned the whole thing like a law enforcement operation. They were doing surveillance on the Hells Angels and strategically placed the three vehicles around the hospital to protect J.R. and Roadblock, while ready to attack the Angels if they came into sight. There were also several marked police cars on the hospital grounds from the local Suffolk County Police Department, who were tipped off about a potential bloodbath.

One of the Jersey Pagans was dropped off to pick up J.R.'s bike while Izzo hopped into Roadblock's car. The Hells Angels had covered up a Pagans sticker on J.R.'s bike with a Hells Angels' "Support 81" sticker.

J.R. was livid. For the next several hours, we drove around to Hells Angels bars, Mario's house, Mario's business, and other Angels' hangouts looking for war. We even went by a location that was home to the Mortal Skulls, a Hells Angels support group.

I had no control over the situation and wasn't sure what I was going to do if we found Mario or any other Hells Angels. We drove around until four a.m., when, finally, J.R. and Roadblock called it off and we went back to Rocky Point.

I contacted the cover team and let them know the hunt was over.

"Thank fucking God," Bryan told me.

"I know," I said. "This is crazy, man. Enough. We need to wrap this up."

"I know, Ken," Bryan said. "We're close. Working twenty-four/seven to get the indictments done."

We needed to move fast, so I coordinated with Bryan and the cover team to tie up as many loose ends as we could so we had what we needed to secure search warrants. I had to "freshen up" some of our probable cause elements, which meant that I had to go back to several places to make sure the criminal activity we were alleging was still occurring at those locations.

Under the law, probable cause only lasts for ten days for drugs and a year for guns. For us to get search warrants from the federal judges for the locations where I witnessed criminal activity, we would have to make sure it fell within those parameters. I made rounds over the next couple of weeks to all of the locations–Hogman's house that he shared with Izzo, Roadblock's house, and a few others. I was at J.R.'s house and the tattoo shop daily, so those were covered too.

We planned for me to attend a few final events. I traveled down to

Elizabeth to meet up with Hellboy to buy some meth. Hellboy was a bad dude. When he was sober, he was fine. But when he was strung out, all bets were off. He was a steroid freak and a trained MMA fighter who would beat the shit out of anyone that got him mad—and he could do it too.

He was originally a member of the Tribe, but like me, he rose fast in the Pagans. He was one of the most feared guys in the gang and was Cano's right-hand man. Until one night in Elizabeth.

We were hanging at a Pagan bar called Jessie's Place, which also housed the Elizabeth clubhouse, located behind the bar. There was an apartment upstairs where Cano lived. Behind the building was a large courtyard and a couple garages covered by tarps and tents. The Elizabeth chapter held church in the garage and hosted cookouts and events in the courtyard.

Hellboy, who was tweaking on meth, and Cano got into a heated argument in the bar.

"Do what I said," Cano said, his voice rising.

"I don't give a fuck what you said, I'm not doing it," Hellboy shouted back.

He was raging and crossed a line. Mouthing off to a Mother Club member or disobeying an order got guys beaten out of the club or killed. Hellboy stormed off.

Cano grabbed me.

"Go outside and fuck him up," he told me. "Better yet, go get your .44 out of the truck and get rid of him."

I nodded and went outside. I was on the Hit Squad and had been given an order. I headed outside and ran into Hellboy. We had a strong relationship from all the drug deals we did together, as well as from our time on the Hit Squad, so I hoped he'd listen to reason. If not, it wouldn't have gone well.

"Hey, man, Cano just told me to kill you," I said. "I don't want to kill you, but I will. This is fucking serious."

"Fuck him," he said. "Fuckin' spic. I'm done with his shit."

I got closer to him and leaned in.

"Listen, man, do this for me. I need you around," I said, appealing to his ego. "These guys are clowns. There aren't many like us. You have to apologize."

He looked at me for a moment. We were standing out in front of the bar. Music and the sounds of drunken debauchery floated out from the open windows.

"Come on, man. Just tell him you didn't mean it," I pleaded.

He paused.

"Okay, Slam," he said. "I'll do it. But I'm doing it for you. Not for him, not for the club. But for you."

CHAPTER 49

On Labor Day Weekend 2010, we went back to Wildwood for the Roar to the Shore. It would be my final mandatory and the end of my life as a Pagan.

It was hard to believe that it was a year earlier when I went to Wildwood and was brought back into the club as a prospect. We went back to the Binns Motor Inn, but this time, I had a room there because I was not only a fully patched member, I was an officer.

One night that weekend, J.R., Pita, Pita's sergeant-at-arms, and I were hanging out at a party on a rooftop deck of a motel, when J.R. had words with the president of the Tribe, a Pagans support club. J.R. was fuming, because the Tribe president brushed him off during an argument. If there was one thing the Pagans wouldn't stand for it was disrespect from support club officers.

"We're going to call that guy out," J.R. said. "We're going to gut him like a pig and throw him off the roof so he lands between these two buildings. They won't find him for weeks."

Pita's sergeant-at-arms and I were the enforcers there, so it was on us to follow his orders. It was getting heated and J.R. was deadly serious.

I had a gun in my waistband with six rounds in it. I thought for a moment about how to get out of the situation. I looked around and there were scores of Tribe members around, not to mention a few hundred bikers hanging around the motel. I had to make a move.

I saw flashing blue lights from a police cruiser off in the distance.

I thought about ways to get the cops over to the motel. I couldn't let them kill him. I considered whether it was the right time to come out of the role, announce that I was an ATF agent, and call for backup. If I did that, they might listen and put down their weapons, or they could turn on me and shoot me or throw me off the roof. Most likely they would have thought I was kidding. I ran through the possibilities in my head. With hundreds of One Percenters surrounding me, six rounds of ammo, and no transmitter, the odds I could come out of the role to save the day were slim if not zero.

I came up with another stall tactic. I used their own rules against them.

"We need to get approval from Mother Club if we're going to do that," I said.

Pita agreed.

"Slam is right," he said. "Let's go talk to Mother Club."

We went back to our compound, and luckily, cooler heads prevailed.

I managed to avoid any more trouble that weekend, which was good because I was able to spend a lot of time observing and logging more pieces of the puzzle for the case.

A key element of the RICO case was proving the Pagans were a corrupt organization. I had a lot of evidence, between the Long Island chapter ledgers, the shakedowns in Asbury Park, and the endless beatings and drug and gun deals, as well as information I gleaned from all the high-level Pagan meetings I attended.

One thing I learned in my career, though, is that you can never have enough. Fortunately, we got some crucial evidence in Wildwood, where I witnessed chapter presidents paying tribute to the Mother Club in clandestine motel room exchanges throughout the weekend.

I could barely contain my glee as I saw chapter presidents, one after the other, walk into motel rooms and hand cash and envelopes to members of the Mother Club. I personally delivered an envelope of cash to the Mother Club from the Long Island chapter.

The payments, like the church video, were proof they weren't just a club of motorcycle enthusiasts. They had a systemic payment system, and that money was used to fund the gang's operations, including their criminal activity, which is the definition of a continuing criminal enterprise.

The RICO case was strong. Those payments I witnessed in Wildwood were the cherry on top of a messy sundae of violence, blood, drugs, and weapons that was two years in the making.

On the final night at Wildwood, Cano laid into Roadblock about the Long Island chapter's failure to get revenge on the Hells Angels. Cano wanted blood, and so too did Roadblock. He returned from his meeting with Cano and addressed a roomful of Pagans from our area. I stood in the room and listened as Roadblock issued a call-to-arms and laid out a detailed plan to find and kill Hells Angels. He had a list of targets that included bars, clubhouses, and the homes of Hells Angels members. He talked about delivering Christmas presents and said it was time to defend our turf, once and for all.

"I'm done with this bullshit. We're going after these motherfuckers. None of this fucking around," he said. "We're going to do the real deal. Be prepared to go to jail or die."

He whipped the guys up into a frenzy. The fuse was lit. They were ready for war.

We returned to Wildwood, and the Pagans made plans for Hells Angels attacks. We were out of time.

CHAPTER 50

On September 13, 2010, I snuck away from the club very early in the morning and drove to a cheap hotel just outside of Rocky Point. I met with Bryan DiGirolamo, prosecutors from the U.S. Attorney's Office, several ATF supervisors, and members of tactical teams. All of our work—mine, the cover team's, Steph's, Bryan's—was coming to a head. The RICO case we sought to make nearly two years earlier was now in our hands, literally. We had twenty-one arrest warrants and thirteen search warrants in four states.

I walked the team through each property, pointing out to the tactical commanders where weapons might be found, as well as where doors might be blocked by furniture. I showed them pictures I had taken over the past two years. I needed to give the officers who were going to kick in the doors of the houses as much information as possible to keep them safe.

I gave them descriptions of the neighborhoods, and we talked about which Pagans might not go down without a fight. Roadblock fell into that category. I was concerned he would try to go out in a blaze of glory.

I was also concerned about Hellboy, but we came up with a plan to handle him in the safest manner possible. He was a wild card, and if we caught him in the wrong moment, there would have been a dangerous situation.

We wrapped up the meeting, and I went back to the undercover house. I called Ang and filled her in on the plans.

"I'm coming home," I told her. "We have everything we need. I'm getting out."

On September 15, 2010, my life as a Pagan ended with one final crystal meth deal on a New Jersey highway.

I arranged for Hellboy to get me a pound of meth for $6,000. I told him I was heading to New Bedford and had fishermen and dock workers waiting for me to bring them their fix. We had negotiated the deal a day earlier and agreed to meet just off Route 495, about halfway between Elizabeth and Rocky Point.

We met in the parking lot of an industrial building, and he gave me the drugs. It was a routine exchange, like we had done many times before. The cover team was nearby and was waiting for my signal that the exchange had been made.

Hellboy gave me a bro hug, got in his car, and drove out of the parking lot and back toward the highway. We decided that a traditional drug "buy bust" with Hellboy was the safest way to arrest him. Doing a raid at his house in Elizabeth or trying to get him at the Elizabeth clubhouse would have been risky. He was unpredictable and extremely violent. The last thing I wanted was an agent trying to arrest him to come up on the losing end of a violent clash with a strung-out Hellboy.

A marked cruiser pulled him over around one a.m. as he drove back to Elizabeth, and he was arrested on drug charges, without incident.

At six a.m., teams of agents began fanning out across New York, New Jersey, Massachusetts, Pennsylvania, and Maryland, kicking in doors and putting Pagans in handcuffs. Back in Boston, a warrant was served at Boston Bob's house and he was arrested.

Hellboy was taken to the Suffolk County Police Department's 6th Precinct in Selden, near Rocky Point, where he was booked, put into an interview room, and grilled by Kotchian and DiGirolamo.

"You guys got nothing," Hellboy said.

"Not true. We have you selling a pound of meth," DiGirolamo told him. "And guess what? Slam is a cop."

Hellboy laughed in disbelief.

"No fucking way," he said.

"Yup. He's been a federal agent for twenty years," DiGirolamo said. Hellboy was stunned.

"No way. Not Slam. No way he's a cop," he said. "There are a lot of people I would believe that about. But not him. Not Slam."

Needless to say, Hellboy didn't get his one phone call right then. It was paramount that he had no contact with the Pagan Nation, to make sure nobody went on the run, destroyed evidence, or worse, barricaded themselves with the intent of shooting it out with agents. The plan was to extricate me from the Pagan world and move me to a safe location while the arrest and search warrant teams hit locations.

After Hellboy was in custody, I was whisked off to a hotel where I monitored radios and phones as warrants were served and Pagans were taken into custody.

Hogman was arrested at the hospital. Roadblock and J.R. were arrested at their homes. Cano was arrested at the Elizabeth clubhouse.

Izzo was arrested by armed agents as he was walking out of his house.

Agents searched the house for weapons and found a safe.

"Give us the combination," one agent said.

"Go fuck yourselves," Izzo replied.

Officers used crowbars and hammers to pry it open. We knew they had drugs and weapons, but weren't sure what we'd find inside. When they finally got it open, the agents stopped in their tracks and backed away. There was a bomb—another Christmas present. Everyone evacuated the house, and the bomb squad was brought in.

In Swan Lake, agents stormed Tracy's property and arrested him. They searched the house and recovered the Hi-Point 9mm semi-automatic rifle that Cano used when he threatened to shoot the antlers off the prospect's head at the party a few weeks earlier.

I was driven up to Tracy's house. Once he was in custody, I showed my fellow officers where we buried the body.

ATF agents and other cops watched me exit an unmarked car and walk past Tracy's house, toward the woods where we dug the grave.

I walked over and found the spot. It was clear where it was, because nothing had grown there because of the lime and rock salt that Tracy put down.

"There," I said, pointing to the makeshift grave. "Right there."

Two homicide detectives working with ATF agents grabbed shovels and started digging. They dug slowly so they wouldn't damage evidence. They didn't have to dig for long before they struck the blue tarp about one foot down.

They carefully dug around it, removing dirt shovel by shovel until the whole tarp was exposed. One agent took photos. Two agents wearing gloves reached down into the hole and lifted the tarp out and placed it on the ground.

The foul smell hit my nose and brought me back to that night when we put it there. An agent untied the rope and slowly started to open the tarp.

I saw two table legs, a pair of cowboy boots, a filthy old rug wrapped up, piles of moldy, damp clothing, and clumps of rotten garbage. It wasn't a body at all. They had made a phony corpse out of trash and soaking wet debris.

It was all a test. A twisted, sickening test.

They wanted to see if I would tell anyone about it or send cops to dig it up, which would prove to them I was either an informant or a cop. Hogman was an awful person, but he was a criminal mastermind. How he kept the story straight about the "science experiment" and everything that surrounded the whole ordeal was amazing to me.

We learned through post-arrest interviews that at some point over the winter of 2010, after I got patched in, some Pagans became concerned I was an informant, especially those who committed crimes around me. The first part of the plan was to use the fake dead body as a ruse to see if I would cave and show my hand. The second part was to eliminate the witness, if necessary, which was me.

I thought about how much time he and Tracy spent concocting the charade. Part of me was impressed they came up with such a devious plan. It was, after all, a good way to find out if someone was a rat or a cop. They just didn't bank on me being a step ahead of them.

They gambled and they lost, and I had the last laugh. Their Swan Lake mindfuck only motivated me and my colleagues in ATF to work harder and be more strategic to take them down.

I stood looking at the rotten debris and the stinky old carpet lying on the tarp and thought about the stress I went through believing that we had a murder to solve. The thought that it might have been someone's son or brother in that hole had haunted me throughout the case. I thought about the long hours officers spent combing through missing persons records and unsolved murders. I wondered if maybe they had real bodies buried on the property or perhaps somewhere else.

I drove back to the Suffolk County Police Department, where I had another loose end to tie up. Hogman's niece was in custody, and she was the only one who ever talked to me about Bennett's death.

One night she was drunk and made a comment that implied that she knew Hogman killed Bennett. She and Hogman were close. I got the sense that he told her what happened in the room the night that Bennett's life ended violently, with a knife slicing through his eye and brain stem.

I walked into the interview room and sat across from her. I was no longer dressed in my Pagan colors, as she was used to seeing me. I tried to play the role of a sympathetic friend in order to get her to talk.

"Hey, listen, I know you're surprised that I'm a cop," I said. "I realize you're not one of the bad guys here and your criminal involvement is minimal, but I was hoping you could help out on Bennett's murder and give some closure to his parents, who have suffered."

She was jittery. I sensed that she was close to opening up. I appealed to her on a personal level and tried to get her to talk by suggesting Bennett's death was perhaps an accident.

"Look, I'm one of you. I lived with those guys," I said. "I know we had that conversation. I know you know what Hogman did. I know he probably didn't do it on purpose. I know he didn't mean to do it."

She looked at me nervously.

"I know what you're talking about, but he never really told me about it," she said.

She was lying. She shifted in her seat and her demeanor turned. She shut down and turned on me, suggesting that I was a rat.

"This is all because of you," she said, referring to the arrests.

I got in her face.

"Look, don't mistake me for a Pagan," I said sternly. "I didn't turn on my brothers. I'm a cop. I've always been a cop. For twenty years. I'm not a Pagan."

"I don't want to talk about it," she said. "I want a lawyer."

It was a letdown that I couldn't break her. One of my main motivations in the whole undercover operation was solving Bennett's murder. From the beginning, I thought we could solve it. Hogman told Roadblock about it, and I suspected J.R. knew. I felt like if I got close enough to those guys that they'd talk about it, but they never did. They were smart. They knew that if nobody talked about it, they could never put a case on Hogman.

I felt bad for Bennett's family and wanted to get them some justice. His parents were good people. They pushed the Suffolk County Police Department for answers, but we never got a break in the case. I hope if they read this book they will have some answers.

When the dust settled, we had twenty Pagans in custody and seized forty, several pounds of methamphetamine, numerous ounces of crack and powder cocaine, other drugs and paraphernalia, thousands of rounds of ammunition and other weapons, tactical gear, and a bomb—one of the Christmas presents. The arrests and RICO indictments were announced in a joint press release on September 15, 2010, by Preet Bharara, the United States Attorney for the Southern District of New York; Loretta Lynch, the United States Attorney for the Eastern District of New York; and the ATF Special Agent-in-Charge of the New York Field Division.

The charges included racketeering, murder conspiracy, assault, extortion, drug distribution, witness tampering, and multiple fire-arms offenses.

"Violent and criminal motorcycle gangs are not quaint vestiges of the past," Bharara said. "Some of the defendants allegedly plied their criminal trade not in the inner city but in quiet communities like the Catskills."

Lynch added: "As this case demonstrates, violent street gangs do not limit their criminal activities to our inner cities and urban areas. Investigating and prosecuting those gangs is a priority program of this office, wherever they might be located."

The New York SAC, who I had butted heads with throughout the case, made it a point to thank me and Steph in comments about the indictments.

"Today's arrests affirm ATF's commitment to making our neighborhoods safer," the New York SAC said. "Targeting and arresting armed violent criminals remains one of our top priorities and we, along with our partners, will continue this fight. We have targeted several out-of-state firearms, explosives, and narcotics suppliers of this outlaw motorcycle gang and will continue to combat all of these illegal activities. I would also like to express my sincere appreciation to the ATF undercover special agents who gained access to the Pagans inner circles. By doing this, they put their lives on hold and at risk to ensure a complete and thorough investigation."

I was officially out of my role. I packed up my colors and my axe handle, got on my Harley, and rode off Long Island and headed north. I was a free man again. It felt good to be on the open road on my bike, without any obligations to the Pagans.

As the trees passed by and I rumbled along the highway, I tried to process what I'd been through. It was overwhelming. I was burned out and just wanted to get home. Then my undercover phone rang—the one I used to talk to the gang.

It was a number I didn't recognize. I picked up.

"Who's this?" I said.

"Nice job, Slam," the voice on the other end said. "You got them all."

The voice sounded familiar, but I couldn't place it.

"Who is this?" I repeated.

"When's your book coming out?" he said, laughing.

It was a Pagan.

"Pretty soon. I'll get you a signed copy. Tell me where to send it," I said.

"Yeah, we'll see," he said before hanging up.

I passed along the number to Bryan and he traced it to a Pagan we were familiar with. He was involved in our investigation but did not participate in enough criminal activities to meet our threshold for prosecution.

Bryan called the Pagan later that night. He wanted to know if he was going to be arrested, and offered to turn informant. He provided information that led to the arrest of Pagans in possession of automatic weapons in New Jersey and helped solve a bombing the Pagans committed in New Jersey. He also dropped a bombshell on Bryan.

"Cano has put a hit on Slam," he said. "Word is it's $25,000. Whoever shoots and kills him gets it."

We figured if Cano was trying to recruit someone to kill me he would probably be talking about the hit while incarcerated at the Westchester County correctional facility in Valhalla, New York. We had a jailhouse snitch and asked him to make contact with Cano, hoping to get Cano to admit a plot to kill me. Cano spilled his guts.

During the conversation Cano stated: "We have all his information. I want these guys out there doing surveillance to get him. If we get rid of him the whole case falls apart."

We tried to get the conversation recorded but the recording device failed, so we couldn't charge Cano with conspiracy to kill a federal officer. The hit on me was real, though, so ATF took steps to protect me and my family. Another Pagan source provided information a few months later that a second hit was put out on me for $50,000.

Surveillance cameras were installed at my house and agents were posted outside on guard duty around the clock. Ang and the girls hated having cops outside the house, but at the same time, it brought them a sense of safety.

The truth is, reports did not contain my real name but it was inevitable the Pagans would learn my identity. The law allows defendants to face their accuser and know their true identity. I knew that going into the case. I also knew ATF had my back and continues to have my back to this day. ATF regularly monitors my safety and the safety of my family.

I'm not going to pretend it wasn't unsettling to know that thirteen hundred bikers wanted to kill me. I was thankful that one Pagan stepped up and did the right thing, whatever his reasons. He has since fled the area and his whereabouts today are unknown.

CHAPTER 51

I got back to Massachusetts and rode my Harley into my bucolic town. I felt like an alien. The quiet, tree-lined streets, soccer fields, and our middle-class neighborhood of SUVs, backyard cookouts, and manicured lawns was a world I was once so comfortable in but now felt like I didn't understand.

When I got home, I was met at the door by Ang and my three daughters.

"I'm home," I said, choking back tears.

They were all crying.

"I love you guys," I said.

We had a big family hug.

"I'm so proud of you, Ken," Ang said. "And we're so glad you're home."

I walked into our living room, put down my bag, sat on my couch, and exhaled. A feeling of accomplishment washed over me.

I made it, I thought to myself. *I did it.*

The transition out of the biker life took quite a bit of time. The first thing I had to do was go see my doctor. Dr. Snider had been my family doctor for years. He met me at night and on weekends to monitor my health and protect my undercover identity. Early in the case, when I needed minor knee surgery, he helped coordinate the procedure to allow me to remain in my undercover role.

He was prepared to provide me with medical documents to maintain my identity if the club demanded them, although that never happened. He is a dedicated doctor. I am not sure there are many out there willing to get mixed up with a patient with my crazy background.

I was tested for a slew of diseases as a precaution: hepatitis C, HIV, and every socially transmitted disease imaginable. The gang included junkies and dirtbags who didn't take care of their health. A lot of them were infected with hepatitis C. Some shared needles. Many were whacked out on meth for weeks at a time and never bathed or brushed their teeth. I spent every day living among them, giving many of them loyalty kisses on the lips, sharing drinks, and sleeping in the same filthy rooms.

It was a nerve-racking few days waiting for the results of all the infectious-disease tests. Thankfully, they all came back negative.

Mentally, I was required by ATF to see a psychiatrist to make sure I had not gone to the "dark side" or became sympathetic to the Pagans' causes or actions. There had been a few cases where undercover agents succumbed to the lure of drugs and the outlaw lifestyle.

The therapist questioned me about my morals to make sure they were still intact and asked how I was feeling returning to civilized society. There were periodic therapist visits that ATF mandated for me, like all agents who do long-term undercover. They gauge changes in personality and priorities both during and after a long-term undercover assignment.

I was still acclimating to my previous life. As for my morals, I experienced a lot of horrible, disgusting, violent, and depraved events, and I rode right to the edge of sanity at times, but I never lost myself completely. I was confident that, in time, I'd get back to being myself and leave Ken Pallis in the rearview forever.

I did find it funny that they thought a shrink would be effective. I had just finished fooling one thousand Pagans for nearly two years. I think I could have fooled one shrink.

I wasn't afraid to delve into my psyche and explore what I'd just been through. I knew I would have some speed bumps as I reassimilated. I talked to my longtime friend, Darrin "Koz" Kozlowski, the agent who infiltrated the Mongols.

"Well, how do you feel?" he asked me.

"I feel fine," I said.

"Give it a couple months and you're going to see," he said.

He was right. As I got back into my life at home, one of the issues I dealt with was slowing down my brain. For two years, I had juggled two identities and my brain had worked overtime keeping stories straight and remembering crucial information that my life often depended upon.

Your mind is a muscle, and mine had been running a marathon. Suddenly, my brain was bored. It was no longer sprinting at top speed morning, noon, and night. I had down time. I had time to just be and think. Living without that constant adrenaline rush can be a difficult adjustment and has affected some agents in the past, contributing to depression, anxiety, substance abuse, and other problems.

Thankfully, I had Ang and the girls to keep me focused on what was important. The girls were just happy to have their dad home, but reconnecting to their world took some time. When I first came home, it just felt normal, like I was back where I belonged. But within a few days of being back home, I realized how much had changed. My life had gone on while in the Pagans, and my family knew little about it. What I didn't grasp at first was that their lives had all moved on too. I was always a hands-on dad and made it a point to keep on top of all the things going on in my daughters' lives. But now there was a bunch of stuff happening in my family that I didn't know about at all. There were new sports teams and teammates, parties I wasn't aware of, new friends, boyfriends, new teachers and classes, new hobbies, new clothes. The dynamics in the home were vastly different. Everyone had grown up and changed. I had to get up to speed.

The same was true with Ang. I had been out of the family loop for so long that she adjusted and was doing everything. I had no idea how much she had to change her life and adapt so that I could do what I had to do for the case.

She was like a single mother. We were distant in those early days. She didn't understand what was happening with me either. I was different. How could I not have been?

Fortunately, Ang and I recognized the distance and made a conscious decision to address it head on. We decided to basically start our relationship over. We started "dating" again.

We had regular date nights a couple times a week, with no kids. Sometimes we went out for dinner or for walks, and other times we would just go out on the back deck, tell the girls we were having private time, and have a happy hour.

We talked a lot about our lives. Sometimes we talked about the case, but much of the time, we did not. Everywhere we went, people wanted to know all about the Pagans and what it was like going undercover. I got sick of talking about it, and I think she got sick of hearing about it.

She was one of the few people in my life I could talk to without having to talk about the case. The individual cases were making their way through the courts, so I was still doing a lot of work with the prosecution team and remained focused on the job. Although I was out, the Pagans remained a part of my life for nearly four years, as the last of the cases wasn't adjudicated until 2014.

On our date nights, we mostly didn't talk about the case, but if there was something one of us wanted to talk about, the door was open. That time we spent reconnecting was so important and it worked. We got stronger and stronger, to the point where our relationship was stronger than it had been before. In a lot of marriages, a routine develops, and oftentimes spouses take each other for granted.

The case forced us to change our routine dramatically and upended our lives completely, leaving us with no choice but to start over and rebuild. I wouldn't recommend anyone go through what I went through, but in the end, Ang and I found a huge upside and that was that we have never taken our relationship for granted again.

I was in the kitchen one day and noticed the cactus we'd bought in

Lake Tahoe nearly thirty years earlier, when we got married. The pot was brimming with all sorts of new cactus plants that were growing off it. It had grown so much since the day we got it.

Over the years, it survived in storage during our many moves around the country. As I looked at it, it reminded me of all we had been through and survived. Like that cactus, we were all still together and growing. It's now been more than ten years since the case ended, and we still have the cactus. It's with us, healthy and thriving.

I got back to work with the team in Bridgewater but focused more on managing. I steered clear of the heavy work for a while. Meanwhile, the cases in New York made their way through the system. I traveled to the New York courthouses several times for hearings and depositions. It was always uncomfortable going back, and there was constant concern that I could be targeted for retribution, but I traveled with other agents. We were always armed and on alert.

I had a tense confrontation once at a federal courthouse in Long Island. I was having lunch in the cafeteria with another agent when across the room I saw Boston Bob's old lady and son. They knew me well, because I had stayed at their house several times in the beginning. Bob's case was scheduled for a hearing that day. He was facing ten years in federal prison for weapons violations.

I tried to ignore them and take the high road, but the son, who was a teenager, wouldn't stop glaring at me. I got up to throw out my trash, and he approached me aggressively. He was angry and ready to lash out.

I looked him dead in the eye and said: "Hey, you got something you want to say to me?"

He froze and two guards intervened. They scooped him up and dragged him away. He screamed, called me an asshole, and caused a ruckus. As he was being escorted out, he kicked out a glass window and was arrested for destroying federal property. He was put into the lockup at the courthouse with his father.

Due to the overwhelming evidence that we'd gathered during the investigation, all the defendants pleaded guilty prior to trial, so I never had to testify in open court. I didn't have any interactions with any of the Pagans I spent two years of my life living among, except for one time when I ran into Izzo and another Pagan named Pop Tart at the Suffolk County Police Department. I was there doing some paperwork when they were brought in for interviews.

"Fuck you," Pop Tart shouted.

I didn't respond. Izzo didn't say a word but gave me a long death stare. I remembered when he told me early in the case that if I turned out to be a rat or a cop, he'd be the one who would kill me. The menacing look he gave me that day in the police station was his way of reminding me of that conversation.

I never saw Roadblock, Hogman, J.R., Tracy, Cano, or any of the others again. I spent day after day and night after night alongside them for two years, and just like that, they were gone from my life. I didn't miss them, but it was a strange feeling to suddenly not have any of them around.

Their court cases progressed smoothly for the most part until the lead U.S. Attorney in the Southern District of New York went on maternity leave and was replaced by an Assistant U.S. Attorney who specialized in white-collar crime and asset forfeiture. He did not, however, have a firm grasp on violent crime cases, especially complex RICO investigations and gang prosecutions.

When he joined the case, he interviewed me, Bryan, and Steph. I walked him through the key moments in the investigation, including all the bar fights, assaults, and drug usage. When I gave him the background on the main players, he appeared disturbed. When I described Hogman and his blood fetish, he looked green, like he was going to throw up.

"You witnessed crimes and you didn't do anything to stop it?" he asked, incredulous.

"Yeah, every day. Otherwise it would have been a one-day case," I answered.

"And you participated in assaults?" he said.

"Yes, technically, but in most cases I took the worst of the beating by shielding the victim from the true assailant. I controlled the situation to ensure that the end result was not great bodily injury or death," I said, reciting ATF policy.

"Who gave you authority to do that?" he asked.

"The ATF director and the U.S. Attorney," I said.

"They don't have the authority to give you that authorization," he said.

"That is not true, and it's a little too late for this conversation. I have a signed memo from the ATF director and U.S. Attorney granting me the authorization," I replied.

My blood was boiling, and I walked out. It got worse.

Bryan later had conversations with the newly assigned AUSA , his supervisors in the Southern District US Attorney's office, the brass at ATF Headquarters and ATF Counsel. The new AUSA wanted me charged criminally and accused attorneys in his own office of unethical behavior. He clearly didn't understand the case and was in over his head.

He treated me like a perp. I had just given all I had for two years to stay alive, stop assaults and murders, and build a RICO case on an outlaw gang that had never before been infiltrated, and he wanted to trump up an assault case on me.

Bryan talked with ATF Counsel, and the nonsense was stopped. I was never charged, and the AUSA was removed from the case. He was replaced by Tim Sini, who was a pit bull and secured guilty pleas from all the defendants. Sini went on to become commissioner of the Suffolk County Police Department and later the Suffolk County District Attorney. We got guilty pleas on all the cases in the Eastern District as well.

J.R., Roadblock, Hogman, Izzo, Tracy, Doc, and Comanche, the head of the Mongols, all faced fifteen years to life in prison. Pita was facing up to fifty years. Hellboy and Bluto were facing forty years. They all pleaded out and received lesser sentences.

Under federal sentencing guidelines, defendants who plead guilty often get reduced sentences, as do those who agree to cooperate with the government. Sometimes the sentence reductions for those who co-operate are drastic.

Roadblock received the longest sentence at sixteen years. He got out in January 2021, winning an appeal for compassionate early release due to the COVID-19 pandemic and health issues.

Hogman got eleven years and was released in May 2020 due to health issues and the COVID-19 pandemic. He died two months after he was released.

Izzo received thirteen years and is still incarcerated as of this writing.

Pita got eight years and was released in January 2020. Cano, Comanche, and Tracy each got four years and were released in 2014. J.R. got five years and got out in January 2015. Doc got five years and was released in 2017. Bluto served five years and was reinstated into the Pagans in 2020. Boston Bob was sentenced to five years.

Hellboy only got two years and was released in 2012. In 2018, he was convicted of savagely beating a Hells Angel into a coma with a baseball bat at a gas station in Elizabeth, New Jersey with two other Pagans. He was sentenced to four years in prison and was released in 2021. All the other defendants pleaded guilty and were sentenced to prison terms ranging from three to ten years.

There have been numerous spin-off cases against Pagans all over the East Coast that came directly from our investigation. Some have resulted in successful prosecutions, and others are continuing to this day.

Did I stop the Pagans? Hell no. They have continued to wreak havoc up and down the East Coast. In fact, they have expanded into Rhode Island and Massachusetts.

We did dismantle the Long Island chapter, though, and managed to slow the Pagans' growth in New York, New Jersey, and Pennsylvania while taking an awful lot of bad guys off the streets. We put them in prison for a long time, which likely saved a lot of misery, kept drugs and guns out of the hands of criminals, and potentially saved people's lives.

When I think about this case, it's not about stats, like the number of guns or pounds of dope we confiscated, or how many years in prison were doled out. I wish we could have gotten charges for Bennett's murder and would have liked to have learned about other murders that may have been connected to the Pagans.

For me, it was about stopping the crimes we were able to stop and protecting people from violence and chaos. The work we did has led to countless other indictments of Pagans, while the intelligence we gathered from the inside has proven invaluable. There had never before been such an intimate and comprehensive dive into the inner workings of the Pagans. The work continues.

After the case ended, someone in ATF sent two anonymous letters to a couple United States senators, ATF internal affairs, the U.S. Department of Justice of the Inspector General, and the media, accusing me of a litany of violations, including misusing ATF funds, falsifying time sheets, and misusing government credit cards during the investigation. The letter writer also accused me of putting the public at risk and violating federal laws when I bought the bomb from Izzo at the restaurant in Massachusetts.

I was interviewed by DOJ investigators who conducted a fourteen-month probe into the allegations. I was cleared of all accusations in 2013. It struck me as a clear smear attempt by a disgruntled adversary. Whoever it was, they failed. I have no problem with anyone who wants to report wrongdoing, but put your name on it. If someone is trying to hide their identity, it suggests they are intending to hurt someone rather than right a wrong.

After the case, I was promoted to Assistant Special Agent in Charge of the Boston office and was the ATF on-scene commander at one of the bombing locations during the 2013 Boston Marathon terror attacks. I was later named Special Agent in Charge in Denver, where I oversaw field operations in Montana, Colorado, Wyoming, and Utah. I was promoted again to Deputy Assistant Director of Field Operations, East Coast, and worked out of ATF headquarters in Washington, D.C. In 2018, I was promoted to be one of eight assistant directors overseeing the agency's operations. I retired in 2019.

I speak regularly at law enforcement conferences about my journey into the Pagan abyss, and I'm often called in as a consultant or an advisor for other police departments and agencies working on biker cases. I still have my Pagan colors and my axe handle stored in a bank safe deposit box. I sometimes bring them out when I do presentations. I'm often asked to put the colors on for pictures, but I promised myself, when I left Long Island that day in 2010, that I would never wear them again. And I haven't.

A very proud day in my life occurred in 2021 when my daughter was sworn into ATF. Ang and I were there, and we presented her with my badge, and she took her oath. I know she'll be a great agent. Ang and I are simultaneously proud and nervous that she decided to follow in our footsteps. The badge is hers now, and she'll go on her own journey in pursuit of justice.

We are also very proud of our other two daughters, who are immersed in their own successful careers. Most children don't have to grow up with the stress our daughters had to deal with, and I often wondered during the case if it would negatively affect them in the long run. In fact, the opposite happened. They are all stronger because of it. I think our entire family emerged from the case stronger and more resilient.

For me, the case helped highlight what is truly important in life, which is family and friends who truly support you during difficult times.

Over the years, while speaking about this investigation, I was often asked two questions: Would I choose this career path again? And would I do another long-term undercover infiltration? The answer to the first question is absolutely. To me, it was the greatest job in the world. Ninety-nine percent of the men and women I worked with at ATF were amazing, dedicated law enforcement professionals. The answer to the second question is no. I am glad I did this case and proud of the fact that we took some violent people off the street. I will leave future infiltrations to others at ATF and in law enforcement. This type of investigative technique is one of the few ways to reach leadership of a criminal organization, but once was enough for me.

As I reflect on my life as a Pagan, I'm brought back to my love of motorcycles and riding. As a kid, riding bikes to me was adventurous and rebellious, to an extent, but also freeing. There were many times during this case that the bike was my only escape from the pressures of home, the job, and the Pagans.

But the bike was also a weapon. I lived in constant fear of crashing, and the bike came to symbolize danger and an outlaw lifestyle that kept me from those I loved most: Ang and my girls.

I had the Harley that I used throughout the case reassigned to another agent in my group. I just didn't have any use for it anymore. I sold my personal Harley Road King after the case wrapped up, and for a while I had no interest in bikes. In fact, I didn't ride for several years.

I'm slowly getting back to riding and am now in the market for a new bike. I'm reconnecting with the energy of the open road and the freedom you can only feel on a motorcycle. I'm no longer riding with criminals and killers. I'm retired from ATF and enjoying my life with Ang and watching my girls build their own lives and careers.

The bike now, for me, is freedom. No longer do I ride with evil.

Now, I ride on my terms.

ACKNOWLEDGMENTS

Writing a book is harder than I thought, and reliving some of these memories that I long ago buried has been trying. This book never happens without the encouragement and prodding of my wife, Angie, and three daughters, Kaitlyn, Shannon, and Meaghan. They pushed me to memorialize these events so that they are never forgotten. Although I initially disagreed, during the months of writing, I have come to believe that writing this book was the right thing to do. Thanks to my family for putting up with all the hardships this case brought to our lives. Angie always said, "What doesn't kill you will only make you stronger," and I think that is exactly what happened to our family.

To my mom and dad, although I know you would have wanted me to choose a different career path, you always supported me. You exhibited true parental love, which is putting the happiness of your child before your own happiness, even when you think the choices they make may not be the best. I only wish you were both still here to read this book, although fully understanding what I had done during those two years may have been more information than you needed or wanted.

My brother, Mike, thanks for all the advice you gave throughout the investigation. Thank you for making the times I was able to get away from the gang as normal as possible. My sister Karin, thanks for being such a fan of this case and for helping Angie with the kids, along with all the advice you gave her while helping to keep her sanity intact.

Rosa and Willie, the support you provided to Angie and the girls during this time was immeasurable. You were both there for Angie to lean on, and for that I am forever grateful.

Markus, my lifelong friend, thank you for being there during the tough times and constantly checking in on my well-being. Carr and Koz, thank you for being a sounding board and offering great advice. There are only a few of us who have done the long-term infiltrations, and your perspective carried a lot of weight in my decision making.

Andy Anderson, Steve Martin, and Julie Torres, I spoke often in the book about having "dumb luck" on my side. A great example of this fact is that you guys were all in upper management during this investigation and able to keep those few less competent senior managers at bay, allowing us to do our jobs. Without you, this would have been a one-week investigation.

Tim Sini, appreciate your skill and tenacity in the courtroom. Thanks for keeping the court proceedings and prosecutions on track.

Thanks to the Boston ATF crew—Jeff Kerr, B. J. White, Big Show, Tony Thurman, Brian Higgins, Joe Steele, Chris Arone, Danny Meade, Sheila O'Hara, Danny Campbell, Chris Scott, and John Mercer. I always knew you guys had my back and would be there if the shit went bad. Steph, this case never happens without your dedication and sacrifice. You also gave up two years of your life and entered this world where women are treated as second-class citizens, and you had to put up with a lot of shit due to the biker culture. Your commitment to the successful outcome was second to none.

Thanks to the New York crew: Howie Stern, Pete D'Antonio, and Rob Soukeras. This case was dropped in your laps, and you guys adopted me and the mission without a single complaint. You put my safety first, which was much appreciated.

George Karelas and Doug Brant, you both sacrificed two years of your lives traveling on the road with me and watching my back.

Never complained and had plenty of insight and advice that I followed throughout this time.

Greg Spiller, thanks for taking the risk and helping me make "Ken Pallis" come to life, and Dr. Snider for sneaking me into your office during the off hours and keeping me healthy enough to finish the case.

Dave Wedge, thanks for believing in the story and helping to get the thoughts on paper. Your storytelling skills are fantastic. My agent, Peter Steinberg, thanks for all the advice, and, Matt Harper, thanks for your patience, literary planning, and fine-tuning of the final version of this book.

Finally, I would like to thank the two case agents: Eric Kotchian, who sacrificed more than two years of his life starting and running the operational side of this investigation, and Bryan DiGirolamo, who was assigned as the case agent and pressed on despite constant pressure to shut the case down. Bryan, thanks for the countless hours you spent culling the mountains of evidence to ensure a successful prosecution.

—Ken Croke

Ken and I first met while playing pickup hockey in Bridgewater, Massachusetts. I was a reporter for the *Boston Herald* and played early mornings every Friday with a group of firefighters, police officers, corrections officers, and several ATF agents who worked at an office up the road from the rink. I didn't know Ken very well, but he was recognizable with his bald head, goatee, and six-feet-four-inch frame. I knew he was one of the ATF guys but never knew much about his work. I stopped playing with that group several years ago and lost touch with most of them, when out of the blue, in 2019, I got a call from Chris Arone, one of Ken's ATF colleagues. Chris told me he had a story for me and mentioned Ken. I couldn't quite place who Ken was at the time, but I agreed to meet up for a coffee.

I had just finished writing my last book, *Hunting Whitey: The Inside Story of the Capture and Killing of America's Most Wanted Crime Boss*, and was considering my next project. I'm often approached by people who say they have a story that would make a great book. I always try my best to find the time to listen, because I know that the one time I don't is the time I'll miss a great story. I'm certainly glad I took that coffee meeting with Ken. As he started telling me the details of his story in a Dunkin' Donuts in Middleborough, Massachusetts, my jaw dropped. It turned into a two-hour meeting, and when I left, I was sure I had my next book.

Books are journeys, and Ken and I certainly went on one with this book. We wrote this story together over the course of 2020 and 2021, throughout the COVID-19 pandemic. We spent endless hours on phone calls and texts, reviewing reports and discussing the details of Ken's life and the case, all while our world changed and became more uncertain than ever. While travel and quarantine restrictions were a challenge, we visited the many locations in Long Island and the Catskills where his story unfolded, and I got to spend some time with his wife, Angelina, and three daughters. I have the utmost respect for Ken and the sacrifices he made in the name of justice, as well as for his family, who went through a difficult and emotional ordeal while supporting his mission. Thank you all for sharing your stories and thanks, Ken, for the work you did on this case, as well as others throughout your storied career, and for your diligence on this book.

I'd also like to thank all the brave officers at the Bureau of Alcohol, Tobacco, Firearms and Explosives who spend their lives protecting others from harm; the United States Attorney's Office and all the other law enforcement agencies that worked on Ken's case; my agent, Peter Steinberg, at Fletcher & Co.; my esteemed business partner, frequent coauthor, and friend, Casey Sherman; all my police officer family members and friends—the job has never been tougher, or more important, so thanks for what you do every day; my dad, Roger, a tough old leatherneck, and his loving wife, Justine; my sisters, Nancy and Allyson; the whole Heslam family; my wife, Jessica, for being a great mom, partner, and friend; my two incredible children, Danielle and Jackson—I love you both more than words can express; our dear Grace—we love you and miss you every day; and last, to my late father-in-law, Mick Heslam, one of the toughest guys I ever knew. I know he would have loved this one. Cheers, mate.

—Dave Wedge

ABOUT THE AUTHORS

Ken Croke began his career as an ATF special agent in 1990 in the Los Angeles Field Division. As a special agent in Los Angeles, he worked on criminal cases focusing on violent crime, firearms trafficking, and gang cases both as an investigator and long-term undercover agent. In 1997, he moved to ATF Headquarters in Washington, D.C., where he was a project officer. He was promoted there in 1998 to chief of the International Programs Branch. Ken then transferred to the Boston Field Division in 2000, where he was a resident agent in charge and assistant special agent in charge. In September 2015, Ken was selected to serve as the special agent in charge of the Denver Field Division, where he oversaw all ATF operations and programs in Colorado, Utah, Wyoming, and Montana. In 2016, Ken was promoted to deputy assistant director (DAD) of the Office of Field Operations—East Region. As DAD, he was responsible for overseeing all law enforcement operations in ten ATF field divisions along the U.S. Eastern Seaboard and Caribbean. Ken's career with the ATF culminated in his appointment to assistant director (CHCO) for the agency.

Ken has extensive experience in gang enforcement and long-term undercover operations, including this two-year assignment, where Ken served full-time as the undercover agent infiltrating the Pagans, a violent national Outlaw Motorcycle Gang (OMG). He rose through the ranks to become an officer within the criminal organization, serving as the treasurer and as a sergeant-at-arms. Ken has served as an undercover agent in more than one thousand undercover operations.

Ken holds a bachelor's degree in accounting from the University of Massachusetts and is a member of the International Association Chiefs of Police, Police Executive Research Forum, International Outlaw Motorcycle Gang Investigators Association, and California Gang Investigator's Association.

Dave Wedge is a *New York Times* bestselling author, podcaster, and writer based in Boston. He has cowritten five books with acclaimed author Casey Sherman, including *Boston Strong: A City's Triumph over Tragedy*, a nonfiction drama about the 2013 Boston Marathon Bombing adapted for the 2017 movie *Patriots Day*; *The Ice Bucket Challenge: Pete Frates and the Fight against ALS*; *12: The Inside Story of Tom Brady's Fight for Redemption*; *Hunting Whitey: The Inside Story of the Capture and Killing of America's Most Wanted Crime Boss*; and *The Last Days of John Lennon*, written with James Patterson.

Dave and Casey host the true crime podcast *Saints, Sinners & Serial Killers* on the MuddhouseMedia network.

Dave has also written for *VICE, Esquire, Newsweek, DigBoston*, and *Boston* magazine and was an award-winning investigative journalist for the *Boston Herald* for fourteen years. He has also been a radio host on WRKO and has appeared on CNN, MSNBC, E!, Fox News Channel, *Good Morning America*, and many other local and national networks.